G000124502

PRAISE FOR

"In *Cruciform Christ*, my good friend Travis Bookout gives us an insightful and carefully exegeted series of reflections on the Gospel of Mark. Each reflection not only guides the reader into a deeper understanding of the life, teachings, and miracles of Jesus, but also excites the reader as to the unique, mysterious, and purposeful style of the Gospel's author. This book is a valuable resource for daily mediations, lesson development, or sermon preparation. Each easy-to-read reflection will inspire a moment of contemplative pause, producing a smile with an affirmative nod. *Cruciform Christ* is a must for every Bible student's library."

— TOM LANGLEY, PRESIDENT WORLD
ENGLISH INSTITUTE

"I like books that make me think. And I like books that take me on a deep dive into the Word. And I like books that inspire me and challenge me to be more devoted to Jesus. *Cruciform Christ* checks all those boxes. That's why I'm such a fan of it, and why I'm thrilled to recommend the book to anyone looking for the same thing."

— DAN CHAMBERS, D.MIN., PULPIT
MINISTER, CONCORD ROAD CHURCH OF
CHRIST AUTHOR

"Travis Bookout does a masterful job of dissecting *the Gospel of Mark* in short, bite-sized chunks, making it easy to digest while, at the same time, not sacrificing deep, reflective thought. Bookout appeals to history, culture, linguistics, and the whole of Scripture to illuminate profound truths and to inspire action on the part of the reader. I encourage everyone to make *Cruciform Christ* a part of their weekly routine for the year. I am confident you will be blessed and better for doing so."

— —CHRIS MCCURLEY, PREACHING MINISTER, OLDHAM LANE CHURCH OF CHRIST AUTHOR

"*Cruciform Christ* is a delightfully happy book. I had chills as my faith soared and my belief in the One who came to proclaim freedom was painted so clearly. Travis Bookout is meticulous in his presentation of his scholarship. He has quickly become one of our finest writers and we look forward to further treasures from his study. You'll find this book full of insightful observations from Mark's account of the son of man/son of God. Read it. It will make you love our Lord more!"

— DALE JENKINS, THE JENKINS INSTITUTE

"What happens when Christians who read through the Bible annually over 52 weeks (i.e., breadth) also commit to read through one book of the Bible annually over 52 weeks (i.e., depth)? I can only imagine the result would be incredible. I affectionately recommend *Cruciform Christ* as a way to enhance one's ability to read Scripture at a deeper level. Travis Bookout offers excellent and thoughtful analysis of many of the texts of Mark; or sometimes even just details in a specific story. He brings the stories to life allowing us to imagine walking the streets of Palestine with Jesus himself!"

— JEREMY BARRIER, PHD, PROFESSOR OF
BIBLICAL LITERATURE, HERITAGE
CHRISTIAN UNIVERSITY

CRUCIFORM CHRIST

52 REFLECTIONS ON THE GOSPEL OF MARK

TRAVIS J. BOOKOUT

CYPRESS

Copyright © 2022

Manufactured in the United States

Cataloging-in-Publication Data

Bookout, Travis J.

Cruciform Christ: 52 reflections on the gospel of Mark / by Travis J. Bookout

p. cm.

Includes Scripture index.

ISBN: 978-1-956811-00-1 (pbk.); 978-1-956811-01-8 (ebook)

1. Bible. Mark—Criticism, interpretation, etc. I. Author. II. Title.

226.306—dc20

Library of Congress Control Number: 2021919696

Cover design by Brad McKinnon and Brittany Vander Maas. Cover image "Christ in the Wilderness" (ca. 1515–1520) by Moretto da Brescia (Alessandro Bonvicino). Used by permission under Creative Commons Zero (CC0) license from The Metropolitan Museum of Art.

For information:

Cypress Publications
3625 Helton Drive
PO Box HCU
Florence, AL 35630

www.hcu.edu

For my parents, Steve and Karen Bookout,
with thanksgiving and appreciation for your steadfast faithfulness
and godly influence on my life.

FOREWORD

Mark's account of the gospel is powerful, action-packed, and all about Jesus. In the Gospel of Mark, we learn much about the authority of Jesus in our world and in our lives. We see His authority over the Law in 2:28 when He claimed to be "Lord, even of the Sabbath." He acts with the authority of God by appointing twelve men to serve as His apostles (3:13–19).

Perhaps the most impressive display of Jesus's authority is seen in His Divine control over the forces of nature. "He got up and rebuked the wind and said to the sea, 'Hush, be still'" (4:39). Astonishingly, "the wind died down and it became perfectly calm." When His disciples witnessed this amazing act of authority, they were not only in awe, but they were also terrified. The question they discussed among themselves was, "Who, then, is this, that even the wind and the sea obey Him?" (4:41).

This is the question that every human who wants to obey God must come face to face with in our lives. Who is this man? Who is this Jesus? In Mark, Jesus raises the question Himself. Jesus went out, along with His disciples, to the villages of Caesarea Philippi; and on the way He questioned His disciples, saying to them, "Who do people say that I am?" (8:27). He asks the question again to see how those closest to Him would respond. "But who do you say that I am?" Peter's answer is succinct, clear, and impactful. "You are the Christ" (8:29).

In *Cruciform Christ: 52 Reflections on the Gospel of Mark*, my friend and brother, Travis Bookout, shares deep insights from his personal study of Mark's Gospel that provide us with greater understanding as we individually seek to answer the question, "Who is this?"

One of the great blessings in my life is to have known Travis (and his sweet wife, Lauren) from the earliest days of his ministry for the Lord. It has been a tremendous joy to watch him grow from a young preacher with a great family heritage (thanks to his godly parents, Steve and Karen) to a man of God whose heart is filled with Jesus. Even though Travis is still a young preacher of God's Word, his reflections reveal that he has spent much time with the Savior.

In this volume, Travis helps us see the heart of Jesus. (You would also be blessed by reading his first book, *King of Glory: 52 Reflections on the Gospel of John*.) Travis invites us to join him on a journey he has already taken to learn more about the "most captivating figure in human history." It was a tremendous joy for me to follow Travis' journey.

In the process, I was challenged to grow closer to Christ. If you will read this book along with Mark's own reflections of Jesus, you will learn how we are loved by Jesus, challenged by Jesus to know the Father, and how our lives are forever transformed by Jesus. You will grow in your faith and you will fall more in love with the One who loved you so much that He sacrificed everything for you.

The selected passages found at the beginning of many of the reflections help us connect the Word of God with the reflections that follow. The questions at the end of each reflection are helpful and drive us deeper into the Gospel as well as deeper into the heart of our Lord.

I love how while reading *Cruciform Christ* we see the connection between the promises of God recorded throughout the Old Testament and the fulfillment of those promises in Jesus. For instance, in the fourth reflection we are taken back to the Psalms and reminded that "God loves and will protect His anointed. Even if all the earth turns against the anointed. God will grant victory to His Messiah." Praise God! This powerful statement was true when first mentioned in the Psalms, it was true when Mark alludes to it, it is true today, and it will be true forever.

The practicality in these reflections is most helpful, whether Travis is writing about "Kingdom Conflicts," "Hard Hearts," or "A Distraught Father." Through this journey we are constantly being pointed to Jesus as Son of God, Son of Man, and Savior of the world. There is nothing more important than pointing others to Jesus. And this can be done by anyone who communicates Scripture either through preaching, teaching, or writing.

It will be obvious, as you read each reflection, that Travis has accomplished one of the goals in writing this book. As he mentions in the introduction, this book "honors Christ as King," and "glorifies God."

We all owe a great debt of gratitude to Travis for helping us see Christ, honor Him as King, and better glorify God in everything that we do. My prayer is that this outstanding book will receive a wide reading among the people of God and that as you spend time in these reflections, your life will be as richly blessed as mine has been. I'm already looking forward to the next volume in Travis' "Reflections" series.

Jeff A. Jenkins
The Jenkins Institute
Lewisville, Texas
jeffajenkins@gmail.com

ACKNOWLEDGMENTS

This book could not have been completed without the help and encouragement of many along the way. Foremost, I want to thank Lauren Bookout, my wife and best friend, whose consistent encouragement and support was indispensable as I worked on this project. I also want to thank those who read my first book, *King of Glory: 52 Reflections on the Gospel of John*, and encouraged me to keep writing and taking on new projects.

I'm deeply appreciative of the Jackson Street Church of Christ in Monroe, Louisiana, and the Maryville Church of Christ, in Maryville, Tennessee, who supported me as I studied, wrote, taught, and preached much of this material. I was also helped by Garrett Bookout and the time we spent discussing the Gospel of Mark on our podcast: *The Open Book with Garrett and Travis*. Our conversations and his insights made an impact on my approach to numerous passages and reflections.

I want to offer a special thanks to those who read and offered thoughts, criticisms, and suggestions for this book (or specific passages): Chase Turner, Jered Hyatt, Troy Rogers, Garrett Bookout, Kyle Savage, Jeff Jenkins, Dale Jenkins, Dr. Jeremy Barrier, Dr. Dan Chambers, Chris McCurley, Tom Langley, and Dr. Ed Gallagher. Years ago, when I was taking Greek 4 under Dr. Jeremy Barrier, we translated the entire Gospel of Mark from Greek into English and discussed the text from beginning to end. I have no doubt that my experiences in that class play no small role in my reflections on Mark. I also want to thank Dr. Richard Hays whose influence can be seen on probably every page. His writings were regularly consulted and referenced as I worked on this book.

Finally, I want to thank the entire team at Cypress Publications: Bill Bagents, Brad McKinnon, Brittany Vander Maas, Jamie Cox, and everyone else whose tireless efforts and dedication made it possible for you to hold this book in your hands.

BIBLE ABBREVIATIONS

Old Testament

Gen	Genesis
Exod	Exodus
Lev	Leviticus
Num	Numbers
Deut	Deuteronomy
Josh	Joshua
Judg	Judges
Ruth	Ruth
1–2 Sam	1–2 Samuel
1–2 Kgs	1–2 Kings
1–2 Chr	1–2 Chronicles
Ezra	Ezra
Neh	Nehemiah
Esth	Esther
Job	Job
Ps	Psalms
Prov	Proverbs
Eccl	Ecclesiastes
Song	Song of Solomon
Isa	Isaiah

Jer	Jeremiah
Lam	Lamentations
Ezek	Ezekiel
Dan	Daniel
Hos	Hosea
Joel	Joel
Amos	Amos
Obad	Obadiah
Jonah	Jonah
Mic	Micah
Nah	Nahum
Hab	Habakkuk
Zeph	Zephaniah
Hag	Haggai
Zech	Zechariah
Mal	Malachi

New Testament

Matt	Matthew
Mark	Mark
Luke	Luke
John	John
Acts	Acts
Rom	Romans
1–2 Cor	1–2 Corinthians
Gal	Galatians
Eph	Ephesians
Phil	Philippians
Col	Colossians
1–2 Thess	1–2 Thessalonians
1–2 Tim	1–2 Timothy
Titus	Titus
Phlm	Philemon
Heb	Hebrews

Jas	James
1–2 Pet	1–2 Peter
1–2–3 John	1–2–3 John
Jude	Jude
Rev	Revelation

INTRODUCTION

The Cruciform Christ

The Gospel of Mark is short, fast, suspenseful, and puzzling. Jesus is announced in a cloud of mystery, bursting onto the scene in unexpected way, and meeting a dramatic and astonishing, but anticlimactic end. Jesus is presented as the Christ, the Son of God, and the Son of Man, bringing a gospel about the kingdom of God, but none of those words or ideas meet expectations. In fact, Jesus often demonstrates the reality of that presentation through the least likely means possible. Jesus is the opposite of what everyone thinks He should be.

His true identity is baffling, confusing, frightening, paradoxical, and seemingly ungraspable, being only hinted by Mark in hushed tones. The weight of His majesty is borne through suffering. The life of glory is conceived in rejection. His divine sonship is proclaimed at the foot of the cross. Jesus is the Cruciform Christ.

Tips for Reading

As you read through this book, I want to make a couple of suggestions to help you in your study. First, make sure you have the Gospel of Mark open with you. Before you begin it would be most helpful to read through the entire Gospel of Mark, preferably in one sitting. It is not too long; you can probably finish it in about an hour and a half. This will immerse you in the world of Mark's Gospel and train your mind to notice his unique contributions to the story of Jesus.

Second, most reflections have a selected passage for you to read before you begin. Read that passage. If the details of the text in Mark are not fresh on your mind, some of the reflections might be confusing.

Third, make sure you have an Old Testament handy also. I believe that one of Mark's primary teaching strategies is to echo Old Testament stories and passages throughout the story of Jesus. This is Mark's clearest way of revealing the surprising identity of Jesus. Matthew is much more likely to say, "This happened to fulfill what was spoken by the prophet. ..." Mark seems to rely on the Old Testament just as much as Matthew, if not more, but he doesn't always spell out exactly what passage is being fulfilled or paralleled. Mark leaves that to the reader. He is expecting you to read, reread, and dive deeply into his story of Jesus along with the story of Israel. We will point out many of these instances throughout this book.

Fourth, get comfortable with ambiguity. Mark often asks questions, or presents puzzles, that he does not answer or solve. Again, he invites the reader to be an active participant in joining the story of Jesus. One way to engage Mark is to note the unanswered questions and the details you wish you had and meditate and reflect on those omissions. I take stabs at explaining some of them, but I'm not an inspired interpreter and the ultimate authority does not rest with me. I invite you to reflect, mediate, and imagine your own solutions and explanations. I invite you to challenge the interpretations presented here and develop your own.

Fifth, as you read Mark and these reflections, search for areas of weakness within yourself. Try to place yourself within the story. An easy way to do that is to cast yourself as Jesus and try to find who in your life acts like the blind disciples, the dishonest Pharisees, the ruthless chief priests, or cowardly Pilate. Instead, search for times in your own life when you have become the blind disciple, dishonest Pharisee, ruthless chief priest, or cowardly Pilate. Read Mark with a desire for repentance.

Sixth, spend some time with the reflection questions at the end of each discussion. Some of them may be simple to you, some may be personal, and some may be challenging. I hope you'll dedicate some time to reflecting on these reflections. I hope you'll read this book, not only to learn, but to grow and to embody the challenging call of Christ.

My Goal and Purpose

This book is not strictly a commentary on Mark's Gospel. It is intended to be a reflective journey through Mark's Gospel. The first person to take this journey was me. There is no more captivating figure in human history than Jesus of Nazareth. I love studying the Bible, learning more about Jesus, and trying to grow closer to Him. This book was written with the goal of my personal spiritual growth in mind. I wanted to understand Jesus better and conform more closely to His image. I believe Mark is an inspired writer and interpreter of Jesus's life and I wanted him to lead me on this journey. In this book I write down what I saw along the way.

I also want this book to serve as a tool for your journey in the life of Jesus. I am praying for all who read this book to grow in their discipleship, to challenge preconceived notions about what it means to follow Jesus, to be more committed to the kingdom of God, to rethink politics, violence, wealth, and the reign of God, and to love Jesus more deeply than ever before. I want this book to challenge you to take up the cross of Jesus for yourself and follow wherever He leads.

Finally, I want this book to glorify God and Jesus Christ. I don't know that everything I write is correct. In fact, I'd be surprised if it is. But I hope everything I write honors Christ as my king. I hope God is exalted by all that follow.

CONTENTS

REFLECTION 1
THE GOSPEL

Mark 1:1—The Beginning of the Gospel

THE GOSPEL OF MARK is the surprising inauguration story of Jesus, the Son of God. With beautiful imagery and literary depth, Mark details how God's kingdom, through trials and suffering, overcame the powers of darkness and, through Jesus, took hold of the world. This story of God's invading kingdom is called the gospel.

What does gospel preaching sound like to you? Some describe the gospel as the five steps of salvation: 1. hear, 2. believe, 3. repent, 4. confess, 5. be baptized, or the "Roman's Road to Salvation," or the ABCs of becoming a Christian (Admit, Believe, Confess). Some say the gospel is about going to heaven when you die. Some use the term loosely to conveniently mean any sermon/idea they agree with: "that's gospel truth right there." The word gospel is sometimes used to describe the Bible, or the New Testament, or the first four books of the New Testament. Some say the gospel is the death, burial, and resurrection of Jesus because of 1 Corinthians 15:1–9.

There is a measure of truth in connecting the gospel to some of those topics above, but is that what Mark means when he writes: "The beginning of the gospel of Jesus Christ, the Son of God" (Mark 1:1)? When Jesus "came into Galilee, preaching the gospel of God" (Mark 1:14), what was He preaching? Was it one of those topics listed above?

Isn't it interesting that Jesus preached the gospel before He revealed His upcoming death and resurrection (Mark 1:14; 8:31)? He preached the gospel without listing the steps of salvation or a 1, 2, 3 plan of how to get to heaven. Jesus called for repentance and belief in the gospel, but He did not say repentance and belief (or baptism) were the gospel. Instead, those are things you do because of the gospel. Those are responses to the gospel, but they are not themselves the gospel.[1]

This is not to say that the plan of salvation and eternity are unimportant or that Jesus was unconcerned with them, but it might suggest that the word gospel, as Jesus used it, meant something different. The plan of salvation may be a response to the gospel and eternal life may be a benefit of the gospel, but the gospel appears to be something else. Jesus was "preaching the gospel of God, and saying, 'The time is fulfilled, and the kingdom of God is at hand; repent, and believe in the gospel" (Mark 1:14). To Jesus, the gospel of God is about the kingdom of God.

What is the Gospel?

The word "gospel" has multiple meanings. In the New Testament it's used about 162 times with a variety of shades of meaning and emphases. Today, we call the first four books of the New Testament "Gospels" because they are a genre of literature that tells the good news of Jesus as a story. Mark is surprisingly difficult to fit neatly into any preexisting ancient genre of literature.[2] Many scholars credit Mark with creating this new literary genre called "Gospel."

Throughout Mark, however, when the word "gospel" is

used, it's best not to think of a genre of literature. We should not think of a Bible book or the New Testament itself. We probably should not think of the plan of salvation or even going to heaven. The word "gospel" should instead make us think of God's victory. Mark is about to spend 16 chapters announcing the good news of the great victory and triumph of God's kingdom through Jesus; the good news of God is the coming kingdom of God.

Be cautious not to boil the gospel down to a handful of verses about salvation. The gospel is not presented as a collection of propositions or prooftexts which could never paint the whole picture. The gospel is not an argument. The gospel is the story of how Jesus brought about the long-anticipated inauguration of the kingdom of God. That is the good news Mark is presenting.

The church must emphasize the "gospel of the kingdom" that Jesus preached. Without understanding the kingdom, it will be impossible to understand the book of Mark. Worse, it will be impossible to understand the life, ministry, death, and resurrection of Jesus, which means it will also be impossible to understand the church's subsequent message about Jesus. Without understanding the kingdom, it will be impossible to believe Jesus's gospel or our role in the story and mission of God.

The Political Gospel

Jesus did not invent the word "gospel." He used a word that already had meaning and significance attached to it. To understand how Jesus used the word, we should think about what the word meant before Christianity existed. It's basic meaning is "good news." Sometimes it described joyous occasions in a person's life, like the good news of a healthy child being born or a loved one overcoming an illness, but it also functioned politically to describe victorious kings who destroyed their enemies, published peace, and established kingdoms. Gospel is a political word. It was used for the freedom of prisoners and exiles when their captors fell. It is gospel when they are allowed to return home. Each of these events could be described as "good news" or "gospel." It's not necessarily a word about spiritual or religious experiences or personal salvation.

In modern history, one could describe January 27, 1945, as a "gospel" day. That was the day of the Liberation of Auschwitz during the Vistula-Oder Offensive. Viktor Frankl, an Auschwitz survivor, describes that day of liberation saying, "we wanted to see the camp's surroundings for the first time with the eyes of free men. 'Freedom'—we repeated to ourselves, and yet we could not grasp it. We had said this word so often during all the years we dreamed about it, that it had lost all its meaning. Its reality did not penetrate into our consciousness; we could not grasp the fact that freedom was ours."[3]

For the prisoners, it was a day of bewilderment, solemn shock, and overwhelming emotion, the news was almost unbelievable, the freedom inspired awe. Others around the world celebrated, danced, kissed, and rejoiced that evil had been overthrown. Liberation, freedom, salvation, home, and peace are all "gospel" words. I believe this idea is getting close to what Jesus means when He uses the word gospel.

Two Helpful Gospel Texts

Two texts are quite helpful for understanding what the word "gospel" meant when Jesus announced it. The first is an inscription carved in stone for Rome's first emperor, Caesar Augustus. It is called the Priene Calendar Inscription (which you can google to find images and a full text). It was written in honor of Augustus' birthday, the day the "Savior" [σωτῆρα] arrived that he might end war and arrange all things, since he, Caesar, by his appearance (excelled even our anticipations), surpassing all previous benefactors ... Augustus was the beginning of the good tidings [εὐαγγελίων] for the world that came by reason of him.[4]

The word translated above as "good tidings," is the plural word "gospel" or *euangelion*. Augustus is described as the "savior" bringing the "gospel" because he ended war and made peace. The phrase "beginning of the good tidings" is extremely close to how Mark begins his Gospel. Some have wondered if Mark intentionally stole a phrase used to celebrate Augustus and applied it to Jesus. Words like "gospel" and "savior" were not unique Christian words about going to heaven. They were political words of imperial Rome. Jesus adopted them and transformed them so that their true meaning is found in Him and His kingdom.

The second text is perhaps even more significant for understanding the ministry of Jesus in Mark's Gospel. Imagine you were among the Jewish exiles during the years of Babylonian captivity. You live in a foreign land, your home lies in ruins, your temple is a rubbish heap, and your king has been deposed. Your children learn the culture and customs of your pagan oppressors. Daily they forget your heritage, your law, your prayers, and your God. Worst of all, it seems your God has forgotten you. He was (seemingly) powerless against the Babylonians, failed to protect His sanctuary, and ignored your pleas for help.

Despair has overwhelmed you and hope has become a cruel illusion. Then you see it. In the distance someone is running like mad. He is shouting at the top of his lungs, but you can barely hear. As he draws near a crowd gathers and you finally make out the words: "Babylon the Great has fallen! God has saved us from our enemies and rescued us again! God has taken His place as our king! Pack your bags! Captivity is over! We're going home!" With that moment in mind, the poem reads:

> How beautiful upon the mountains
> are the feet of him who brings good news
>   [gospel],
> who announces peace, who brings good news
>   [gospel] of happiness,
> who announces salvation,
> who says to Zion, "Your God reigns." (Isa 52:7).

Peace, salvation, happiness, and the reign of God as king are what the gospel is all about. In both of these texts, Roman and Jewish, the gospel is when war or exile is over, peace is proclaimed, and the true king begins his reign. The gospel is about the king and his kingdom. Rome's gospel was about the Roman kingdom and God's gospel is about God's kingdom.

When Jesus proclaims, "the kingdom of God is at hand; repent and believe the gospel" (Mark 1:15), He is proclaiming the joyful news that God's reign is imminent and people must change their loyalty (repent) and give their allegiance (faith) to it. God's kingdom is a real kingdom. It is a physical kingdom and it's on earth, but it is not "of" or "from" earth. God's kingdom rules differently than worldly kingdoms (Mark 10:42–45). It challenges, critiques, and condemns the way of the kingdoms of men. It is not limited by borders, defended through military, or bolstered by greed; the power of God's kingdom is seen in imitating the selfless, sacrificial, all-consuming love of Jesus.

In its historical setting, the Gospel of Mark is best understood as resistance literature. The Messiah challenges and critiques the oppressive kingdoms and regimes of the Roman Empire, and surprisingly, Jerusalem and the temple. A new gospel of a new kingdom is being offered as a legitimate option in a world that will struggle to find value in it, a world that will seek to destroy it.

Giving your loyalty to God's kingdom will require changing the way you have always thought about kingdoms, empires, powers, and authority. It will change your views on victory, violence, oppression, and force. Your perceptions of faithfulness, loyalty, nationalism, and allegiance must be transformed. Jesus, through demonstration, education, inauguration, and coronation, is bringing about the kingdom of God, in a way never seen before, and that is very good news. That is gospel.

Reflection Questions

1. What is the good news about Jesus? What is the difference between the gospel and the plan of salvation? How is the message of Jesus good news for eternity? How is the message of Jesus good news for the world right now?

2. Why is it significant that Jesus borrows language from the Roman Empire to describe God's kingdom? How is the gospel related to the kingdom? How is God's kingdom different from the kingdoms of this world?

Endnotes

1. Matthew W. Bates, *Gospel Allegiance: What Faith in Jesus Misses for Salvation in Christ* (Grand Rapids: Brazos Press, 2019), 26.

2. David Rhoads, Joanna Dewey, and Donald Michie, *Mark as Story: An Introduction to the Narrative of a Gospel,* 2nd ed. (Minneapolis: Fortress, 1999), 2–3.

3. Viktor E. Frankl, *Man's Search for Meaning*, translated by Ilse Lasch (Boston: Beacon Press, 2006), 87–88.

4. This translation is taken from Craig A Evans, "Mark's Incipit and the Priene Calendar Inscription: from Jewish Gospel to Greco-Roman Gospel" *JGRChJ* 1 (2000), 69.

REFLECTION 2
JESUS: SON OF GOD

Roman Son of God

THE PHRASE "SON OF GOD" probably makes you think of Jesus. Based on the last two thousand years of Christian tradition, we naturally, immediately identify Jesus as the "Son of God." Even non-Christians know who is meant by that moniker. Have you considered how odd it is that a crucified Jewish peasant two thousand years ago is known as the Son of God? This is especially surprising when you realize how many powerful, rich, important people were vying for that title.

Romans had a son of God (or a son of the gods). In fact, they had several. They had gods who had sons. Hercules was the son of Jupiter (the Roman equivalent of the Greek Heracles, son of Zeus). Hercules was a divine figure because his dad was a god, ergo, he was a son of god.

There were also humans, like emperors, who enjoyed wearing the title "son of god." During the lifetime of Jesus, Roman emperors were tinkering with the idea of being gods. Jesus was born during the reign of the first Roman emperor, Caesar Augustus, the adopted son of Julius Caesar (Julius came before Augustus, but was not technically an emperor). It's no doubt significant that Jesus was born during the reign of Rome's first true emperor. One may see that as a brewing competition for who the true ruler of this world will be.

Historian Daniel Schowalter describes how Augustus used his relationship to divinity for his political advantage:

> Since his adopted father, Julius Caesar, had been posthumously proclaimed to be a god by the senate (42 BCE), Augustus had used the title *son of god* (*divi filius*) as part of his official nomenclature on coins and inscriptions throughout the empire, announcing to all that the reign of Augustus enjoyed divine sanction.[1]

If your dad becomes a god, you get to be god's son, and people should probably listen to you.

To a Roman the phrase "son of god" referred to the emperor, whose father was a god and who enjoyed divine favor and status. The emperor was a cut above everyone else; he was no mere mortal. Tiberius, who was emperor when Jesus was crucified, was the son of god because his father was Augustus. Gaius (better known as Caligula) took it a step further and not only considered himself to be the son of a god, but was the first emperor to claim godhood for himself while living. He set up temples for himself to be honored and worshipped as a god.

Jewish Son of God

Interestingly, among Jews the title "son of God" was also used to describe their own kings. God is David's Father and David is God's firstborn in Psalm 89:26–27. When God promised David that "the throne of his kingdom" would endure forever, He said this of David's son: "I will be to him a father, and he shall be to me a son. When he commits iniquity, I will discipline him with the rod of men, with the stripes of the sons of men" (2 Sam 7:14).

It's hard to say this passage is explicitly predicting the future coming of Jesus because this "son" also "commits iniquity." This son is Solomon.

In a parallel passage in 1 Chronicles 28:6 God specifically named Solomon, saying: "It is Solomon your son who shall build My house and my courts, for I have chosen him to be My son, and I will be his Father." King Solomon is called God's son.

In Psalm 2 God anoints and establishes His king on Mount Zion, saying, "You are My Son, today I have begotten you" (Ps 2:7). God tends to use the familial designation "son" for His chosen king. The New Testament fittingly borrows many of these passages and connects them to Jesus, the ultimate coming of God's unique Son, His chosen king. This is why Nathanial says of Jesus: "Rabbi, You are the Son of God! You are the King of Israel!" (John 1:49). Kings of Israel are understood, in some sense, to be God's sons.

Israel itself is also called God's son. When God sent Moses to Pharaoh demanding Israel's freedom, he was instructed to say, "'Thus says the Lord, Israel is My son, My firstborn.' So I said to you, 'Let My son go that he may serve Me'; but you have refused to let him go" (Exod 4:22). Hosea borrows this language when he writes: "When Israel was a youth, I [God] loved him, and out of Egypt, I called My son" (Hosea 11:1).

Israel and her kings are called God's sons and Jesus is the ultimate embodiment of both Israel and the king. He takes the purpose, mission, and destiny of Israel upon Himself and becomes the "blessing to all the nations" (Gen 12:3; 18:18) that God promised to Abraham. Jesus fulfills the Law and, as an Israelite, does for Israel what they were unable to do for themselves. He is also the supreme king of Israel and ultimate son of David, who ushers in God's kingdom, bringing the gospel of God's kingdom. When Jesus is called the Son of God, both meanings should be remembered.

We should also remember the Roman association of "Son

of God" with divinity. Jesus was sometimes condemned for using "Son of God" in a divine sense. Jesus was uniquely God's Son like no other king of Israel (as can be seen in the virgin birth in Matthew and Luke). John 5:18 connects Jesus's claims of being God's Son to equality with God. This was considered blasphemy and they wanted to kill Him for it. In Mark 14:64 Jesus is also accused of blasphemy because He claimed to be "the Son of the Blessed" and the "Son of Man." He is then sentenced to death.

The Son of God in Mark

A lot of history and meaning lies behind the phrase "Son of God," and while we quickly associate it with Jesus, in Mark, Jesus interestingly doesn't explicitly use that title. Instead, He often calls Himself the "Son of Man." In Mark, the author (Mark 1:1), demons (Mark 3:11; 5:7), God (Mark 1:11; 9:7), and a centurion (Mark 15:39) call Jesus God's Son, but Jesus does not use those words.

Although, as referenced earlier, when asked in Mark 14:61–62 if He is "the Son of the Blessed," Jesus answered "I Am." This was His most clear claim to be the Son of God in Mark's Gospel and He was charged with blasphemy for it. He also vaguely refers to "the Son" in Mark 13:32, which we know is Jesus. Another time Jesus hints toward His identity as the "Son of God" is in Mark 12:6 where He tells a parable about the "beloved son" of a vineyard owner who is killed. This is the third and final "beloved Son" passage in Mark. The first two are declarations from God during Jesus's baptism (Mark 1:11) and transfiguration (Mark 9:7). When we read that the "beloved Son" is killed in that third passage we already know who He is.

The cross is central to understanding the "Son of God" in Mark. Jesus is introduced as "the Son of God" in Mark 1:1,[2] and the rest of the Gospel focuses on proving that point. The voice from the heavens at the baptism of Jesus is the first witness to His Sonship/Kingship. The record of demons, the voice from the clouds during the transfiguration, and Jesus's answer on trial all provide further testimony. Yet, it's essential to notice that not until the centurion at the cross, does a human character declare that Jesus is the Son of God. Ironically, the cross, with a crown of thorns on His head, is where Jesus is most clearly seen as God's Son.

Reflection Questions

1. What does it mean that Jesus is the Son of God? How is this related to divinity? How is this related to kingship? Did you confess that Jesus was the Son of God at baptism? Why did you say that? What did you mean? How has that impacted your life?
2. How is the phrase "Son of God" related to the Roman Empire? How would a Roman Emperor feel about someone claiming to be the Son of God? If Jesus is the Son of God, why wouldn't He say it more often?

Endnotes

1. Daniel N. Schowalter, "Churches in Context: The Jesus Movement in the Roman World" in *The Oxford History of the Biblical World*, ed. by Michael D. Coogan (Oxford: Oxford University Press, 1998), 391.

2. There are some early manuscripts that do not include the phrase "the Son of God" in Mark 1:1, and usually shorter readings are preferred. In this case, however, there is solid evidence that keeping the phrase is justified and that it plays an important role in developing and supporting Mark's theology.

REFLECTION 3

JESUS: SON OF MAN

Son of Man

A SECOND PHRASE that needs exploration is "Son of Man." This is a common phrase in the Old Testament (בֶּן־אָדָם); it's used about 107 times and generally means "human." It is regularly synonymously paralleled with the word "man" (Num 23:19; Job 25:6; 35:8; Ps 8:4; 80:17; 144:3; 146:3; Isa 51:12; 56:2; Jer 50:40, etc.) and implies human frailty and weakness. It is a way of saying, you are no God, you are merely human. For instance, Numbers 23:19 says, "God is not man, that He should lie, or a son of man, that He should change His mind." Interestingly, the Hebrew word for *man* in Hebrew is ādām (אָדָם), so it is literally "Son of Adam."

Ezekiel uses this phrase more than any other writer of the Old Testament. Ezekiel is called the "son of man" 93 times (this number will vary slightly based on translation, but it's close). Ezekiel was God's chosen, very human, prophet. In fact, the first time he is called "son of man" is after falling down in terror and awe before the throne of God (Ezek 2:1).

The most important usage for our study of Mark comes from Daniel, who gives us our best glimpse into the self-understanding of Jesus. Daniel uses the phrase twice: Daniel 7:13 and Daniel 8:17. Daniel 8:17 is similar to how Ezekiel uses it, to represent a human prophet. In that passage Daniel falls down in fear before the presence of the angel Gabriel. For grasping the identity of Jesus, Daniel 7:13 will be our interpretive key.

Daniel 7:13

Daniel 7:13 is the most important passage in the Old Testament for understanding Jesus's use of the phrase "Son of Man." It's possibly the most important passage in the Old Testament for understanding Jesus's identity and mission. We can be confident Daniel 7:13 is Jesus's key text because He actually quotes it several times.

Jesus uses this passage in His trial, where He finally and definitively answers that He is the Son of the Blessed: "I am; and you shall see *the Son of Man* sitting at the right hand of power, and *coming with the clouds of heaven*" (Mark 15:62). Compare that to Daniel 7:13, "And behold, *with the clouds of heaven* One like a *Son of Man* was *coming.*"

Jesus quotes Daniel 7:13 again when discussing the destruction of Jerusalem: "Then they will see *the Son of Man coming in clouds* with great power and authority" (Mark 13:26; Dan 7:13). Daniel 7 frames Jesus's use of the title "Son of Man."

Why would Jesus rely on Daniel 7 to describe His identity and mission? Let's take a quick look (you would do well to read all of Daniel 7 right now). Living as an exile in Babylon during the reign of Nebuchadnezzar, Daniel wakes up to see a vision of a seashore. As the winds and the sea rages, four dreadful and terrifying beasts emerge from the water. The first was a lion with the wings of an eagle, standing on two feet with the mind of a human. Second came a bear with one massive shoulder, chewing three ribs, ready to devour. Third, there was a swift leopard with four wings and four heads.

Each one of these animals should terrify you to meet out in the wild. I recently was hiking in Tennessee and stumbled upon a black bear. We saw each other, and I slowly passed as he watched me. It wasn't a huge bear, and it certainly wasn't aggressive, but my heart was pounding. The beasts that Daniel sees are huge, terrifying, ferocious, and any one of them could rip, shred, and devour human flesh in an instant. These animals are predators and carnivores and represent aggression, violence, and death.

The fourth beast isn't compared to any known animal; his power and might are unparalleled. He is unlike any known animal. This beast comes out of the sea, "terrifying, dreadful, and extremely strong" (Dan 7:7). He has iron teeth (see Dan 2:33, 40) and ten horns. Everyone who sees him should run and hide.

These four beasts (much like the statue in Daniel 2 and the goat and ram of chapter 8) represent kings and their kingdoms (Dan 2:36–43; 7:17; 8:20–21). Revelation 13 combines each of these images into one dreadful empire, empowered by the Devil himself, to wreak havoc on God's people and creation. Empires of this world wage war, kill, devour, and destroy as beasts do. They are predators.

Hope and salvation are found in none of these beasts, but only in the "Son of Man" who comes with the clouds to the Ancient of Days seated upon the celestial throne. Daniel 7:13 depicts the Son of Man in contrast to these beasts. His authority derives from the King who rules in the realms of men. The Son of Man was

> given dominion and glory and a kingdom, that all peoples, nations, and languages should serve him; his dominion is an everlasting dominion, which shall not pass away, and his kingdom one that shall never be destroyed (Dan 7:14).

Hope is restored, a new kingdom is established, the beasts and enemies lose their power when the Son of Man arrives. All peoples, nations, and languages that divide men are united together as one to honor and worship the Son of Man. This is a reversal of the division brought forth in the story of the Tower of Babylon. This is a picture of world wide unity. This is gospel. This is why it is a perfect description of Jesus's identity and mission.

The Son of Man in Mark

The phrase Son of Man is used frequently in Mark but only from Jesus's own lips. While Jesus never directly calls Himself the Son of God, He refers to Himself as the Son of Man more than anything else. The authority of the Son of Man is described in Daniel 7, but Jesus takes this authority to an unforeseen and shocking level when He says the Son of Man can "forgive sins" (Mark 2:10). Incredibly, Jesus also describes the Son of Man as "Lord even of the Sabbath" (Mark 2:28).

If you read the Old Testament and I asked you, "Who forgives sins?" How would you answer? Or if I asked you, "Who is the Lord of the Sabbath day?" How would you respond? The only possible answer to both of those questions is God Himself. According to Jesus, the Son of Man shares the authority of God. This is a new revelation. Forgiving sins and ruling Sabbath are not found in Daniel 7. In fact, later Jesus even states that the Son of Man will be "seated at the right hand of power" (Mark 14:62). Not just anyone can share the throne room with God, forgive sins, and rule Sabbath. The Son of Man is a divine identity.

I love the way Richard Hays asks this question:

> If Jesus is identified, through Mark's references to Daniel 7, as the eschatological Son of Man enthroned in heavenly glory,

the question inevitably arises of how to understand his relation to the 'Ancient One,' the God of Israel. If Israel's God is a jealous God who brooks no other gods before his face (Exod 20:1–3; Deut 5:6–7), who then is this figure who exercises everlasting dominion, with whom the heavenly throne room is to be shared?[1]

Clearly, the Son of Man is no mere mortal.

The Son of Man, in Mark's Gospel, is both a figure of divine unparalleled authority and of suffering, rejection, and sorrow: "The Son of Man must suffer many things and be rejected ..." (Mark 8:31). "Even the Son of Man did not come to be served but to serve, and to give His life a ransom for many" (Mark 10:45). Jesus uses the phrase "Son of Man" both to describe His glorious power and authority (Mark 2:10, 28; 8:38; 13:26; 14:62) and His destiny as the rejected Servant who gives His life for others (Mark 8:31; 9:9–13, 31; 10:33–34, 45). The Son of Man is destined for greatness, authority, and a kingdom, but only through rejection, suffering, and death.

There are many in Rome who will not appreciate someone else wearing the title "Son of God." To call Jesus the Son of God is a challenge to the Roman rulers and kings who claim that title for themselves. It is a way of saying there is a new king and even your cross can't defeat Him. To call Jesus the Son of Man is also a challenge to all world empires. It says that earthly kingdoms are beasts destined for destruction and ultimate authority rests with Jesus. It says that God has chosen someone else to rule this world and He is not in Babylon, Rome, D.C., or the Kremlin.

The kingdoms of the world will exercise their authority in putting Jesus on the cross, and Jesus will overcome them through the resurrection, demonstrating for all time that He is the ultimate Son of God and Son of Man and God's kingdom will not be overcome. The Son of Man will suffer before He reigns, but He will reign over all the world. His reign will not be limited by geographical borders, national pride, or native languages (Dan 7:14), but He will unite humanity from all the nations under His Lordship. By using the phrase Son of Man, Jesus reminds us that the beasts of this world are destined to destruction and He points toward the wider Gentile mission and the grand scheme of God to bless all the nations through Him (Gen 12:4; 26:4). He points to a new kingdom and a new king. He points to the Gospel.

Reflection Questions

1. What does it mean that Jesus is the Son of Man? How does Daniel 7 shape the mission of Jesus? Why are world empires often referred to as "beasts" in the Bible? How might we sometimes put our trust in the beast rather than the Son of Man? Who has true authority?

2. Why would Jesus so often refer to Himself as the Son of Man? Why is this more common than Son of God? Why is remembering the humanity of Jesus so important? Why "must" the Son of Man suffer? Why would God share His throne room and authority with a human?

Endnotes

1. Richard B. Hays, *Echoes of Scripture in the Gospels* (Waco: Baylor University, 2016), 62.

REFLECTION 4
JESUS: CHRIST AND MESSIAH

Jesus Christ

To CALL Jesus the "Son of God" is a challenge to the kings of the earth. To call Jesus the "Son of Man," especially against the backdrop of Daniel, is a challenge to the beasts, world empires. These are highly charged political titles. It is dangerous to talk this way. Rome does not crucify people for loving their neighbor, feeding the hungry, or helping the poor. If you start disturbing the peaceful status quo, drawing large crowds, flipping tables in the temple, claiming authority that surpasses Caesar, challenging the rulers of the world, and inaugurating a new and greater kingdom, then prepare for trouble. Of all the titles that Jesus wears, perhaps the most subversive and political is "Christ." Being a Christ will get you crucified.

Jesus is so profoundly recognized as the "Christ" that it has become part of His name: Jesus Christ. I think that's more than appropriate. Certainly He was not named "Jesus Christ" by His parents, but if you are going to use a description to distinguish Jesus from all others named Jesus, "Christ" is a pretty good way to do it. His identity is intimately wrapped up in His Messiahship.

We need to make sure we don't forget what it actually means though. Don't say "Jesus Christ" flippantly. That title is a proclamation of faith and loyalty. The word "Christ" (χριστός) is the Greek equivalent of the Hebrew "Messiah" (מָשִׁיחַ), meaning "anointed one." I will be using these words interchangeably throughout this book. Most translations of Psalm 2:2 say something like: "The kings of the earth take their stand and the rulers take counsel together, against the LORD and against His *Anointed*." The word translated "Anointed" is "Messiah" in Hebrew and Christ" in the Greek LXX. The Anointed/Messiah/Christ in Psalm 2 is also called the "King" and God's "Son" (Ps 2:6–7).

The word "Anointed" occurs many times in the Old Testament. It is used for those anointed as priests (Lev 4:2, 3, 16; 6:22). It is often used for Israel's kings (1 Sam 24:6, 10; 26:9, 11, 16, 23, etc.). It is even used for Cyrus, king of Persia in Isaiah 45:1. There is nothing divine about this word. It is not blasphemy to say that Cyrus or David were Christs (even though it makes me as a Christian uncomfortable to say). Being "Christ" does not necessarily mean one is moral or good, but it means they are chosen and anointed. That is how the word is used in the Bible.

A Tragic History

To say that Jesus was the Christ/Messiah comes with certain expectations which are really important for understanding the Gospel of Mark. In Psalm 2 the kings of the earth are conspiring and plotting to overthrow God's Son, the king, the anointed one. When God sees this, He chuckles at their foolish pride, and in fury declares, "I have set My king on Zion, My holy hill" (Ps 2:1–6). Then God turns to His anointed and says,

> You are my son, today I have begotten you. Ask of me and I will make the nations your heritage, and the ends of the earth

your possession. You shall break them with a rod of iron, and dash them in pieces like a potter's vessel. Now therefore, O kings, be wise; be warned, O rulers of the earth (Ps 2:7–10).

Those kings, like the beasts surrounding the Son of Man in Daniel 7, will not be able to stand.

God loves and will protect His anointed. Even if all the earth turns against the anointed, God will grant victory to His Messiah. The nations will fall before him. Remember the chants about Saul and David: "Saul has killed his thousands, David his tens of thousands" (1 Sam 18:7). Both of these kings were Christs; they were chosen and anointed to be kings. And God promised David that his kingdom would have no end: "And your house and your kingdom shall be made sure forever before Me; your throne shall be established forever" (2 Sam 7:16).

While that was a wonderful promise, by the 1st century, it was a hard one to believe. There had been no Davidic king for hundreds of years. Jerusalem and the temple were destroyed by the Babylonians in 586 BC. After exile and captivity the Jews were allowed to return home. They rebuilt the city, temple, and the walls around Jerusalem, but no Davidic king was established at that time. They were still under foreign domination. First by the Babylonians, then the Persians, and then the Greeks. After an unlikely successful uprising against Antiochus IV Epiphanes there was an attempt to reestablish a dynasty in Israel called the Hasmonean dynasty. For about 100 years there were kings in Judea again.

That all came to a halt in the Siege of Jerusalem in 37 BC when Herod the Great (with the authority of Rome) overthrew the Hasmoneans and claimed the throne of Judea for himself. Rome was now the ruling power of the world and the Jews were again in exile. They may have been living in their fatherland, but they were not a sovereign people. They were still ruled by pagan powers.

After Jerusalem was destroyed by the Babylonians things were never the same. There were brief flickering moments of hope like returning home, rebuilding the temple, overthrowing the Seleucids, and establishing the Hasmonean Dynasty. But they were all short lived. They never had a powerful king like David or Solomon again and there was no Messiah sitting on David's throne.

Trusting God's Promise

What happened to God's promise then? Where is David's kingdom? Those who continued to trust God hoped for a better future. They poured over the Hebrew Scriptures searching for clues about what that future might hold. There developed an expectation that one day a new Messiah, a Son of David would rise up, overthrow Israel's oppressors, and establish a great kingdom again. If David killed his tens of thousands, this Messiah would kill his hundreds of thousands. Even Rome would fall to this great king, because God laughs when the nations rage. Then God's promise would again be realized!

New Testament scholar Richard Hays succinctly puts it:

> In the first century context, the term 'Messiah' might well have evoked in the popular imagination the image of an anointed ruler who would overthrow Israel's enemies (particularly the Romans) and restore the royal throne of David.[1]

Evidence for this hope can be found within literature of the Inter-testamental period. Consider these lines in the 1st century Jewish prayer book, Psalms of Solomon:

See, Lord, and raise up for them a king, The son of David, to rule over your servant Israel in the time known to you, O God. *Undergird him with strength to destroy the unrighteous rulers, to purge Jerusalem from gentiles who trample her to destruction; in wisdom and in righteousness to drive out the sinners from the inheritance; to smash the arrogance of sinners like a potter's jar; to shatter all their substance with an iron rod; to destroy the unlawful nations with the word of his mouth* ... He will gather a holy people whom he will lead in righteousness; and he will judge the tribes of the people that have been made holy by the Lord their God ... And he will be a righteous king over them, taught by God. There will be no unrighteousness among them in his days, for all shall be holy, and their king shall be the Lord Messiah (Pss. of Sol. 17:21–24, 26, 32).

Or consider the words from 2 Esdras 12:31–33:

And as for the lion whom you saw rousing up out of the forest and roaring ... *this is the Messiah* ... who will rise *from the posterity of David*, and will come and speak to them; he will denounce them for their wicked ungodliness and for their wickedness ... first he will set them living before his judgment seat, and when he has reproved them, *then he will destroy them.*

If you are curious who will be judged and destroyed in this passage, it "is the fourth kingdom which appeared in a vision to your brother Daniel ... it shall be more terrifying than all the kingdoms that have been before it" (2 Esd 12:10–13). Oh, it's Daniel 7 again. It's the passage about the Son of Man that is so prominent throughout Mark's Gospel. 2 Esdras 12 specifically interprets the 4th beast of Daniel 7 as Rome, and declares that the Messiah will destroy them. This Messianic expectation leads to all sorts of confusion, bewilderment, and anger when Jesus the Messiah fails to live up to it.

Mass confusion

With that expectation in mind, the opening words of Mark's Gospel take on an entirely new meaning: "The beginning of the gospel of Jesus Christ, the Son of God" (Mark 1:1). Upon hearing these words, one might expect a story of a warrior king, chosen by God, rising up to destroy Israel's enemies (Rome) and establish a kingdom that would last forever. That would be good news, or "gospel" to most Jews. Instead of giving you that story, Mark presents a Christ, the Son of God, the Son of Man, who is arrested, beaten, and crucified by the 4th beast. Then Mark wants us to believe that this is actually the gospel.

In Mark 8:29 Peter identifies Jesus as the Christ. In Mark 14:61, on trial for His life, Jesus is asked if He is the Christ, and He answers "I Am." The Messiah has finally arrived. The hopes couldn't be higher, finally, Israel's enemies would suffer. Finally, the good news of victory would be proclaimed and foreign domination would end! This is wonderful, hopeful, and exciting news ... until Jesus opens His mouth.

When Jesus explains that He "must suffer many things ... and be killed" (Mark 8:31), can you see why "Peter took Him aside and began to rebuke Him (Mark 8:32)? When Jesus says He "is to be delivered into the hands of men, and they will kill Him" (Mark 9:31), can you see why "they did not understand this statement" (Mark 9:32)? Can you see why the disciples fled when Jesus was arrested, refusing to fight back? Can you see why they were so dejected, scared, and confused? Jesus was not what the Messiah should be! Can you see why Mark says they had a hard heart (Mark 6:52; 8:17) and could not understand (8:21)?

The big joke at the cross was that Jesus was Christ, the King of the Jews (Mark 15:26). The chief priests and scribes, who know well what the Messiah ought to be, saw Jesus and jeered and mocked, saying, "Let the Christ, the King of Israel, come down now from the cross that we may see and believe" (Mark 15:32). Notice that "the Christ" was equivalent to "the King of Israel."

It is utter foolishness to put your hope in a king who cannot defeat your enemies. Paul says,

> For Jews demand signs and Greeks seek wisdom, but we preach Christ crucified, a stumbling block to Jews and folly to Gentiles, but to those who are called, both Jews and Greeks, Christ the power of God and the wisdom of God (1 Cor 1:22–24).

Preaching the message of a crucified Christ is a hard sell. It's the opposite of everything known about crucifixion and expected of a Christ. This paradoxical and puzzling truth is the foundation upon which Christianity is built. The resurrection forces you to look again at the life of Jesus and to try to make sense of His death in light of His gospel.

Reflection Questions

1. What does it mean that Jesus was the Christ/Messiah? What was the common expectation of the Messiah? How did Jesus differ from those expectations? Why were the disciples so confused when Jesus taught about His death?
2. Did God keep His promise to David in 2 Samuel 7:12–16? How did God do this? Does God ever work

in your life in ways you never expected? How do we
know God keeps His promises?

Endnotes

1. Richard Hays, *The Moral Vision of the New Testament: Community, Cross, New Creation* (San Francisco: HarperSanFrancisco, 1996), 78.

REFLECTION 5
THE SECRET MESSIAH

Don't Tell Anyone

IF YOU WERE ORDERED to shut up about Jesus, would you? What if Jesus gave the order? One of the strangest motifs in Mark's Gospel is how often Jesus tells others to keep silent about Him. He seems oddly secretive throughout this Gospel. This has been noticed by many and countless theories have been proposed to explain it.

What do I mean by Jesus being secretive and private? Well, let's trace this motif throughout Mark's Gospel and see what we find.

First of all, in Mark 1:24–25 and 34, Jesus introduces His kingdom by casting out demons and unclean spirits. These unclean spirits, unlike the human characters, seem to know exactly who He is. The first unclean spirit shouts out, "I know who You are—the Holy One of God!" (Mark 1:24). Jesus immediately rebukes the spirit and says, "Be quiet, and come out of him!" (Mark 1:25).

When a spirit knows the identity of Jesus, Jesus orders him to "be quiet." Why would Jesus want him quiet? Verse 34 further elaborates, saying He "cast out many demons; and He was not permitting the demons to speak, because they knew who He was" (Mark 1:34). Jesus's identity is the key. Jesus did not let demons speak because they knew His identity. Again, in Mark 3:11–12 the spirits would say "You are the Son of God" and Jesus "earnestly warned them not to tell who He was."

We may think this is because they are demons and Jesus doesn't want demons revealing who He is, but we quickly find out that's not the whole story. Later in Mark 1, Jesus heals a man with leprosy and "He sternly warned him and immediately sent him away, and He said to him, 'See that you say nothing to anyone" (Mark 1:43–44). Jesus not only tells demons to keep quiet about Him, but He orders people also. Demons and humans are both supposed to be silent.

This theme does not end here. In Mark 5:42–43 Jesus raises to life a twelve year old girl, Jairus' daughter, and "gave them strict orders that no one should know about this" (Mark 5:43). In Mark 7:35–36 Jesus heals a deaf man, but first He takes him "aside from the crowd, by himself." After the healing, "He gave them orders not to tell anyone" (Mark 7:33–35). When Jesus later heals a blind man, He "sent him to his home, saying, 'Do not even enter the village'" (Mark 8:26). If the village saw that this blind man can now see, they would start asking the questions Jesus does not want answered. These miracles, raising the dead, healing the deaf, cleansing the leper, giving sight to the blind, all point to the mysterious identity of Jesus (see passages like Isa 35:5–6).

Not only does Jesus want people to be quiet about His miracles, He also attempts to move around and travel in secrecy. At one point, Jesus travels up north to Tyre and Sidon and when He entered a house, "He wanted no one to know of it" (Mark 7:24). After casting a demon out of a man's son, Jesus "went out and began to go through Galilee, and He did not want anyone to know about it" (Mark 9:30).

Jesus, what are You trying to hide?

Secret Teachings

Even in His teaching, Jesus seems to be hiding something. He wants some of His words to remain mysterious, cryptic, and private. Jesus tells His disciples,

> to you has been given the mystery of the kingdom of God, but those who are outside get everything in parables, so that while seeing, they may see but not perceive, and while hearing, they may hear and not understand, otherwise, they might return and be forgiven (Mark 4:11–12).

After teaching a series of parables, Mark writes that Jesus, "did not speak to them without a parable; but He was explaining everything privately to His own disciples" (Mark 4:33–34).

These passages are uncomfortable and don't fit with how we ordinarily think about parables and Jesus. Parables usually had the purpose of helping people understand, but Jesus uses them for the opposite reason. Jesus intentionally speaks in parables to keep people from understanding and only explains Himself privately.

When the disciples finally grasp a central aspect of Jesus's identity and Peter says, "You are the Christ" (Mark 8:29), Jesus rebukes Peter and orders all the disciples to "tell no one about Him" (Mark 8:30). Jesus then brings three of them "on a high mountain by themselves" (Mark 9:2) and is transfigured. After a booming voice declares Jesus as the Beloved Son (Mark 9:7), He stands alone with His disciples: "As they were coming down from the mountain, He gave them orders not to relate to anyone what they had seen …" (Mark 9:9).

This sketch of the secrecy of Jesus in Mark's Gospel does not cover everything, but it is sufficient to illustrate that Jesus seems to have a secret and He is extremely selective about who hears it. This motif has popularly been called "The Messianic Secret."

Time, Location, and Disobedience

Why would Jesus speak this way? When we examine this motif a little closer, several clues emerge that can help us understand Jesus's motives and secrecy. The first clue is the element of time. Several of these passages suggest a timeframe for the secrecy.

Discussing parables, Jesus says,

> A lamp is not brought to be put under a basket, is it, or under a bed? Is it not brought to be put on the lampstand? For nothing is hidden, except to be revealed; nor has anything been secret, but that it would come to light. If anyone has ears to hear, let him hear (Mark 4:21–23).

According to Jesus, keeping things secret would be like keeping a lamp under a bed. It would be pointless. At some point, Jesus plans to take the lamp out and put it on a lampstand. There is nothing "secret" or "hidden" that will not be "revealed" or "come to light." The Gospel of Mark should be read as an apocalypse, an unveiling of the mysteries concerning Jesus.

When does Jesus want His secrets to come to light? A hint is found in Jesus's words immediately following the transfiguration. Jesus tells His disciples "not to relate to anyone what they had seen, *until the Son of Man rose from the dead*" (Mark 9:9). This secret is not supposed to last forever, but only until the resurrection. Mark is able to reveal these secrets because they are not secrets anymore!

A second clue is found in Mark's geography. When Jesus is in public in Galilee, He generally tells people to keep quiet. When Jesus crosses the sea of Galilee to the east side, which is primarily dominated by Gentiles, Jesus is less private. For example, after healing the man called Legion, Jesus tells him, "Go home to your people and report to them what great things the Lord has done for you, and how He had mercy on you" (Mark 5:19). In Decapolis, a Gentile region, Jesus tells the man to make it public.[1] Jesus is also quite public in Judea during His final week (Mark 11:1–10, 15–17; 14:61–62, etc.).

A third clue is that Mark includes, along with this motif, the reality that most people disobey Jesus's orders. When Jesus orders someone to be quiet, they usually go and tell everyone they can find. When Jesus sternly warned the leper not to tell anyone, "he went out and began to proclaim it freely and to spread the news around" (Mark 1:45). When Jesus healed the deaf man and gave orders to tell no one, Mark writes, "the more He ordered them, the more widely they continued to proclaim it" (Mark 7:36). Even when Jesus tries to travel secretly, people usually find out about it: "He wanted no one to know of it; yet He could not escape notice" (Mark 7:24).

A Proposed Solution

Taking all this information together, what can we offer as a solution to this confusing secrecy? Some say that Jesus is simply trying to forestall the timing of His death. If word spreads too quickly, then the crucifixion will happen before He completes His ministry. I tend to think this idea is incomplete. Remember, people disobeyed Jesus's orders to be quiet. The crowds grew like wildfire. If He needed people to stay quiet to avoid early crucifixion, He would have been crucified too early because nobody stayed quiet. Everyone heard what Jesus was doing.

I believe the best solution is that Jesus didn't want people thinking He was the Christ or Son of God or divine until He revealed His true nature and destiny on the cross. Mark reveals the glorious identity of Jesus, paradoxically, through the cross (Mark 15:39). Among Jews there were diverse ideas about what the Christ was supposed to be, but none of them included the cross. We discussed in the previous reflection, many expected Him to be a military figure who would destroy Israel's enemies (Rome) and purge Jerusalem of Gentiles and establish a Davidic kingdom in Jerusalem that would never be destroyed. Jesus is not that kind of Christ. This Christ would rather die for His enemies than kill them.

In Gentile region (like Decapolis) where these Messianic expectations were not shared, Jesus could be less concerned with secrecy (Mark 5:19–20). Among the Jews, these expectations were widespread. The cross reveals the identity of Jesus better than false, preconceived, expectations. It is better to observe Jesus before developing a view of Him, than to force Him into a preconceived mold of what you think He ought to be. He won't fit.

Peter rebuked Jesus for saying the Son of Man would suffer and be killed and raised (Mark 8:32). If Jesus had then told Peter, "Go, tell everyone I am the Christ," Peter would have surely preached the wrong Christ. He'd preach Christ without the cross and that is a dangerous message. It also tends to be a nationalistic, prideful, and self-serving message. It's a message Jesus would rather you keep to yourself.

Perhaps Jesus did not want to contribute to false expectations spreading. The mystery of His identity is better revealed through the self-giving love of the cross than miracles and exorcisms. Through the cross the meaning of His exorcisms, miracles, and divine identity come into sharp focus. Without the message of the cross, the disciples would go public with the wrong message about the wrong Messiah. Jesus is not the expected Christ; He is the cruciform Christ.

If you preach Jesus without a cross on your shoulders, you are preaching the wrong Jesus. If you peddle Jesus for extra money or social advancement, you have missed the Messiah. If you proclaim Jesus to further your own reputation or prestige or wealth or political ideology, He would rather you just keep silent. Even if you believe, be sure and tell no one.

Reflection Questions

1. Why do you think Jesus would have kept His identity secret? Why wouldn't Jesus want people talking about His miracles? Why would Jesus then instruct "Legion" to tell his friends and family what great things God did? Can you come up with any other reasons Jesus would have done this? Is there any reason for us to continue this practice today?
2. Why are there so many misunderstandings of Jesus? Are there modern examples of people claiming Jesus for selfish reasons? Can you think of times people might use the Bible, or Christianity, or God to advance selfish agendas? How does the "Messianic Secret" relate to situations like this?

Endnotes

1. Interestingly, the next time Jesus is in Decapolis, He heals a deaf man and "gave them orders to tell no one" (Mark 7:36). The first miracle can be proclaimed in the Decapolis, but the second miracle must be secret. Mark does not tell us why.

REFLECTION 6

AN IMMEDIATE GOSPEL

An Expeditious Gospel

I'VE ALWAYS BEEN a fast talker. If I were to count all the criticisms and complaints I've had about my preaching over the years (which would be a miserable exercise) there is no doubt that the first and foremost complaint is that I talk too fast. It's hard to keep up. I suppose I should work on this. I know I should. Every public speaking class ever taught has emphasized the value of slowing down, pacing your words, speaking clearly and articulately. I know it's important. However, I also know that one of the most common compliments I get about my preaching is that I'm excited about what I'm saying. I'm always afraid if I conscientiously slow down too much it will dull the natural excitement that comes across when I talk about Scripture.

This little problem is why I love preaching the Gospel of Mark. If you're not going fast, you're doing it wrong. It should be fast paced because Mark is fast paced. If ever I feel bad about talking too fast, I comfort myself with the first chapter of Mark. He's going a thousand miles a minute. Mark is excited to tell his story. There is no time to waste. He has a cosmos transforming message, a gospel about a kingdom for a world in desperate need, and it must be proclaimed as quickly as possible, so you better buckle up for the ride.

Immediately

One unique feature of Mark's writing is his continuous repetition of the word "immediately." He uses εὐθὺς ("immediately") eleven times in the first chapter alone and forty-two times throughout his Gospel. Things don't just happen, they happen immediately! At Jesus's baptism, He comes up out of the water *immediately* (Mark 1:10) before *immediately* being cast into the wilderness (Mark 1:12). Jesus *immediately* called His disciples and they *immediately* followed (Mark 1:18, 20). Then Jesus *immediately* went into the synagogue (Mark 1:21) and *immediately* a man with an unclean spirit appeared (Mark 1:23). Then Jesus *immediately* left the synagogue (Mark 1:29). Mark wants you to know that when Jesus hits the scene, things change immediately.

The word εὐθὺς ("immediately") is translated "straightway" in the King James Version. The shortest distance between any two points is a straight line. To do something immediately is to do it straightway, as fast as possible. This is interesting because Mark begins his gospel with a quotation of several Old Testament passages (Mark 1:2–3) which conclude by saying, "Prepare the way of the Lord, make His paths *straight*" (Mark 1:3; Isa 40:3). Guess what word is translated as "straight" in these introductory verses? It's our keyword εὐθὺς, "immediately."

John the Baptist was to prepare the way of the Lord and make His paths "straight" or "immediate." Based on how immediately Jesus does everything in Mark, I say "Well done, John." Isaiah 40:3 is the launching point for the ministry of Jesus and this theme of immediacy that follows. Any time Jesus does something "immediately" it's a subtle reminder that the Lord has come, and His paths are straight.

Mark's repetition of this word creates a sense of urgency throughout the ministry of Jesus. Notice the first words from Jesus's lips in Mark: "The time is fulfilled, and the kingdom of God is at hand; repent and believe in the gospel" (Mark 1:15). Jesus's first words are about how quickly the kingdom is coming. Jesus expects big things to happen soon. The world is changing and you cannot wait. This puts the readers on the edge of their seats as each story immediately leads to the next and the kingdom promptly bursts onto the scene.

This tone of speed and rapidity is furthered by Mark's use of the "historical present" tense. This is clearer while reading in Greek than English, but it makes Mark move even faster. The "historical present tense" is when Mark "begins a narrative in the past tense ('The Pharisees came up to Jesus ...') and then continues it in the present tense ('and they say to him ...'). Mark does this 151 times, enough to drive a grammar teacher mad. Still, as many scholars note, the effect of writing this way is to 'make the past come alive.'"[1] It may not be great grammar, but it intensifies the story. It grabs the past and speeds it right up to the present. All these stylistic features make Mark a compelling, non-stop, fast-paced, action-packed adventure.

Short, Sweet, and Few

Mark not only moves from story to story "immediately," but he doesn't include many of the stories found in the other gospels. Mark offers no narrative of Jesus's birth, no genealogy, no Sermon on the Mount (Matt 5–7) or Sermon on the Plain (Luke 6:20–49), and early copies of Mark do not include any resurrection appearances. Nearly every story in Mark is also in

Matthew and Luke; while Matthew and Luke each contain many stories that are not in Mark. Based on Greek word count, Luke has 19,376 words, Matthew has 18,293, while Mark only has 11,025.[2] Mark only tells what is essential to his story; he has no intention of being long winded.

Here is pretty much everything in Mark that you won't find in the other Gospels: There are two unique sayings of Jesus in Mark: the parable of the seed growing at night (Mark 4:26–29) and a brief description of salt (Mark 9:49, 50b). Those combine for about 5 ½ verses. There are two unique healing accounts: healing a deaf man (Mark 7:31–37) and healing the blind man in stages (Mark 8:22–26). And there is that odd story of a man following Jesus after His arrest who ends up fleeing naked (Mark 14:51–52). That's about it. These few sentences are the only material in Mark that is not also in either Matthew and/or Luke.[3]

When Mark tells the same stories as Matthew and Luke, he often does so with fewer words and details. Consider the temptations of Jesus in the wilderness. Matthew and Luke tell us about his fasting, his conversations with Satan, and three temptations in three different settings. Mark briefly says, "He was in the wilderness forty days being tempted by Satan; and He was with the wild beasts, and the angels were ministering to Him" (Mark 1:13). Mark boils the entire temptation narrative down to one sentence.

This less detailed, quick style of storytelling keeps the reader's attention, but it also creates more questions and fewer answers. In many ways Mark is the most ambiguous of the synoptic gospels. What I mean is Mark does not spend much time clarifying, explaining, or smoothing out difficulties for his reader. Mark expects a lot of his readers. To fully appreciate Mark, the reader must digest a lot of information quickly, before slowing down to spend a lifetime meditating on it.

Ambiguity and Meditation

There are many questions left unanswered in Mark. Matthew and Luke are longer, for one reason, because they try to answer those questions. Here are a few examples (we'll note more as we go through the text):

Mark 1:4 says that John was "preaching a baptism of repentance for the forgiveness of sins." Then Jesus shows up and "was baptized by John in the Jordan" (Mark 1:9). The account is quick, details are limited, and it leaves some big questions in the reader's mind: "Why did John baptize Jesus? Was not Jesus sinless? Did Jesus need to repent and be forgiven?" Mark doesn't answer these questions. There is no conversation between Jesus and John about baptism in Mark. Matthew, however, clarifies the issue by recording a conversation between John and Jesus:

> John tried to prevent Him, saying, "I have need to be baptized by You, and do You come to me?" But Jesus answering said to him, "Permit it at this time; for in this way it is fitting for us to fulfill all righteousness." Then he permitted Him (Matt 3:14–15).

That conversation clarifies some details absent in Mark. Jesus wasn't baptized to be forgiven, but to fulfill righteousness.

Mark 8:15 records Jesus on a boat saying to His disciples, "Watch out! Beware of the leaven of the Pharisees and the leaven of Herod." The disciples fail to understand Him and begin arguing about who forgot the bread. So, what did Jesus mean? Matthew and Luke both take a crack at explaining it. Matthew suggests, "He did not say to beware of the leaven of bread, but of the teaching of the Pharisees and Sadducees" (Matt 16:12). Matthew interprets Jesus's warning to be about "teaching." Similarly, Luke records, "Beware of the leaven of the Pharisees, which is hypocrisy" (Luke 12:1). Luke and Matthew give more information about the meaning of the "leaven" of the Pharisees and Herodians (Sadducees?).[4]

Mark 13:14 makes a veiled reference to the "abomination of desolation standing where it should not be ..." Rather than explaining to us what this means, Mark adds a brief note to the reader, "let the reader understand" (Mark 13:14). This wink to the reader is a cryptic way of teaching an important lesson from the book of Daniel, but he doesn't actually teach us what the abomination of desolation is! Or what it means, "where it should not be." What is it and where shouldn't it be? Matthew does not leave his readers guessing. He records, "the abomination of desolation, which was spoken through Daniel the prophet, standing in the holy place (let the reader understand) ..." (Matt 24:15). Notice, Matthew clarifies that this is a reference to Daniel, and "where it should not be" is "the holy place." Interestingly, Matthew also retains Mark's parenthetical note ("let the reader understand"). Luke is the clearest: "But when you see Jerusalem surrounded by armies, then recognize that her desolation is near" (Luke 21:20). There is no doubt what Matthew and Luke are talking about, but Mark leaves you wondering.

Mark doesn't answer as many questions about Jesus's life as Matthew and Luke. In fact, he creates quite a few. He is more ambiguous, sometimes asks questions without answering them (Mark 2:7; 4:41), and does not always give his readers clarification. Does this mean Mark is a worse writer than Matthew or Luke? Certainly not. In fact, for me, it's quite the opposite. Ambiguity can pull you deeper into the mystery of the story.

I love reading Mark because he forces us to stop and think. He forces us to meditate on the stories and contemplate their possible meaning(s). Mark is full of discussion topics. This makes Mark great to read as a group and wonderful for conversation. A gathered body of believers can read, meditate, discuss, and grow from the text. The author moves at breakneck speed, but to understand him, the reader must slow down. We must pause for reflection. As you read Mark, buckle up for a blazing fast trip, but then slow down for a life-long journey.

Reflection Questions

1. Why would Mark tell his story with such speed and rapidity? What are the benefits of going fast? How might this style of writing help to further Mark's point about the kingdom? Do you think this makes Mark more enjoyable to read?

2. What are the benefits of leaving questions unanswered and making stories ambiguous? What are the pros and cons of this writing style? How would you answer the questions in Mark 2:7, 4:41, and 6:2? Why is it helpful to have four gospels that each take different approaches to telling the story of Jesus? Does this help you in your meditation and reflection upon the life of Jesus?

Endnotes

1. Mark Allan Powell, *Introducing the New Testament: A Historical, Literary, and Theological Survey* (Grand Rapids: Baker Academic, 2009), 131.

2. These figures were taken from D.A. Carson and Douglas J. Moo, *An Introduction to the New Testament* (Grand Rapids: Zondervan, 2005), 96.

3. This list does not include all minor details unique to Mark. For example, all three Gospels tell of Satan tempting Jesus in the wilderness, but Mark is the only Gospel to mention

"wild beasts." Minor unique variations in storytelling are not included, only completely unique stories and sayings. This list of material can be found in Powell, *Introducing the New Testament*, 131.

4. Powell, *Introducing the New Testament*, 133.

REFLECTION 7
MARK'S SANDWICHES: PART 1

Intercalation

INTERCALATION IS a fancy word for when an author begins a story, interrupts his own story with a seemingly unrelated second story, then finishes the first story. The author is "wrapping one story around another to make what some pundits call a 'literary sandwich.'"[1] The final product ends up looking something like this:

- Story 1a (beginning)
- **Story 2** (seemingly unrelated story)
- Story 1b (conclusion)

Once the reader has finished the sandwich, he can then look back in more detail at all he just consumed. What the reader ends up realizing is that those two stories weren't as unrelated as it first appeared. They can be compared and contrasted and by reading them together they shine new light on one another. This is a way of adding depth to each account and giving the reader more for reflection and meditation. Or, in keeping with the "sandwich" language, the reader has more to chew on. In the next two reflections, we will focus on six of these intercalations/sandwiches.[2] We'll see how weaving these stories together produces unexpected contrasts and correlations. We'll study how to consume the sandwiches.

Example #1: A House Divided (Mark 3:20–21 [3:22–30] 3:31–35)

If you read through these verses, you'll notice that they portray numerous responses to Jesus's ministry. At the beginning and end, the "bread" of the sandwich, Jesus's "own people/family" (NASB/NIV; Mark 3:20-21) and "His mother and brothers" (Mark 3:31), are mentioned. Mark lets us know that their visit is not a pleasant one. They are coming to "take custody of Him" because "they were saying, 'He has lost His senses'" (Mark 3:21).

The word translated "take custody" is a word for when someone is arrested (see Mark 6:17 and 14:1). It is difficult to be completely certain who is saying Jesus is "losing His senses" in 3:21. It is possible that His family is coming to take Him because they (His family) think He has lost His mind or it may be that the family wants to take Him because they (the scribes mentioned in the next verse) are saying Jesus has lost His mind, and His family is worried. Either way, Jesus's ministry is creating quite a stir and reflecting poorly (socially) on Him and His family. Ben Witherington III, remarking on this passage, writes,

> Seen from the perspective of honor-and-shame conventions, it is possible to understand the action of the family as an attempt to protect their own family honor ... They did not want him to disgrace the family.[3]

When your son is publicly accused by the authorities of demon possession (3:22), it can be quite concerning.

When the family arrives at the house (3:31), Jesus does not go out to them, choosing to stay with His disciples instead (Mark 3:31–35). Jesus believes He is already gathered with His true family; His true brothers and sisters and mothers are those who do the will of God 3:34–35. If you read Mark 3:20–21 then immediately jump to Mark 3:31–35, skipping everything in between, it would seem like a coherent account of some of the hardships Jesus's ministry created in His family life.

Right in the middle of this story about Jesus's family, however, is an interaction He has with the scribes about demons. This account is the "meat" of the sandwich in between the two slices of bread. The scribes insist that "He is possessed by Beelzebul" and "He casts out the demons by the ruler of the demons" (Mark 3:22). Jesus responds to the scribes in parables (Mark 3:23) and defends Himself admirably with a series of arguments.

Stuck right in the middle of His response is one of Jesus's most popular sayings: "If a house is divided against itself, that house will not be able to stand" (Mark 3:25). Think for a moment about how this statement connects the two stories in this sandwich. We'll look further at this connection as we make our way through Mark's Gospel, but for now, notice that these stories have an important link right in the middle.

Example #2: Parables and the Kingdom (Mark 4:1–9 [4:10–12] 4:13–20)

Another example of this "sandwich" structure is found in Jesus's parables. Jesus is on a boat, speaking to crowds. Jesus begins His parables (the first slice of bread) with an account of what seed does on four different types of soil: road, rocky, thorny, and good soil (Mark 4:3–8). At the end of the sandwich (the second piece of bread), He explains each part of the parable and interprets it for His disciples. He says each of these soils represent how people respond to the "word" (Mark 4:14). People will either never accept it (road), reject it quickly (rocky), accept it fruitlessly (thorny), or absorb it and bear fruit (good soil). There is even diversity within the "good soil" as some will bear more fruit than others (Mark 4:20). This parable is a challenge to the crowd (and reader) to consider how we respond to the words of Jesus, the seed He is sowing.

The entire parable concerns how people respond to the word that is sown. Sandwiched in the middle of this parable and its interpretation is a private conversation between Jesus and His disciples about the purpose of the parables. Jesus speaks in parables because of how people respond to them (Mark 4:10–12). To some the parables will remain an unresolved mystery. They will see but not perceive; they will hear but not understand (Mark 4:12). The seed will be sown, and the word will be taught, but they will reject the parables. They will not produce fruit.

The specific parable of the sower and the overall purpose of the parables are linked in contemplating how people respond to Jesus's teaching. Their application is well summarized by the phrase "he who has ears to hear, let him hear." As different soils respond to seed in different ways, so those who hear Jesus's parables will respond to them differently. The disciples are chosen to be on the "good soil" and produce fruit, and the parables are a way of sifting through and sorting out which kinds of soil the crowds will represent.

Example # 3: Twelve Years a Daughter (Mark 5:21–24 [5:25–34] 5:35–43)

In the third example Jesus disembarks from a boat and is met by a synagogue official named Jairus. Jairus's twelve year old daughter is at the point of death and he needs a miracle. He comes to Jesus to beg for one. Jesus begins passing through a large crowd to find the girl. This is the beginning of the sandwich, the first slice of bread. On His way, the girl dies and the family begins to mourn and lament. The sandwich ends with Jesus raising the young girl from the dead. The meat in the middle is found while Jesus is passing through the crowd. A woman who has suffered from a flow of blood for twelve years is in need of a miracle. She comes to the right place. She reaches out and touches Jesus's garment as He passes. She is healed immediately.

In this case the sandwich is easy to see and the connections between these two stories are numerous. In both instances Jesus miraculously heals someone. In both instances it is a female. In both instances they are nameless and known only as "daughter" (Mark 5:23, 34). In both stories someone falls down before Jesus (Mark 5:22, 33). Both stories mention "fear" and "faith" (Mark 5:33–34, 36). Both miracles happened "immediately" (Mark 5: 29, 42). The most obvious connection is that the woman had a flow of blood for "twelve years" and the girl Jesus raised "was twelve years old" (Mark 5:25, 42). How often do we know the ages of the characters Jesus meets? It's extremely rare. The point of that detail is to weave these two stories together and make a connection.

These two women both had major physical problems, and they both shared the same solution. The woman with the flow of blood was saved only by Jesus and because of her faith. The girl who had died was also saved only by Jesus. I guess we don't know much about her faith; after all, she was dead. Her father, though, was told "only believe" (Mark 5:36). Jairus's act of faith brought healing and salvation to his household. His faith turned death into life. These stories weave together into a powerful narrative of faith, healing, and life that comes from Jesus.

Reflection Questions

1. Why would Mark tell stories in this format? What are the benefits of this literary device? How does this promote further study and reflection? In what ways can reading two stories together provide more depth to each one?

2. Why would Jesus's ministry have been difficult for His family? Why would Jesus teach in parables that many would not understand? In what ways is the twelve year old girl similar to the woman with the flow of blood?

Endnotes

1.Powell, *Introducing the New Testament*, 131.

2. We're focusing on these six, however, others are also proposed throughout Mark, especially grouped together in the Passion narrative of chapters 14 and 15 (Mark 14:17–31, 53–72; 15:40–16:8, etc.). For an excellent study on these issues, see James R. Edwards, "Markan Sandwiches: the significance of interpolation in Markan narratives" in *Novum Testamentum* XXXI, 3 (1989), 193–216.

3. Ben Witherington III, *What Have They Done with Jesus? Beyond Strange Theories and Bad History—Why We Can Trust the Bible* (San Francisco: HarperSanFrancisco, 2006), 119.

REFLECTION 8

MARK'S SANDWICHES: PART 2

Example # 4: Discipleship and Martyrdom (Mark 6:7–13 [6:14–29] 6:30–32):

IN THIS FOURTH EXAMPLE, Jesus sends out "the twelve" by pairs and gives them authority to engage in His ministry. They receive authority over unclean spirits and are to take nothing for the journey except a staff and traveling clothes: no money, no storage, no food, no extra change of clothes. They are to rely solely on the generosity of those responsive to the message and to "shake the dust off the soles of your feet" in the towns that do not receive them.

The disciples then began preaching repentance, casting out unclean spirits, anointing, and healing many (Mark 6:13). That's the first slice of bread in this Markan Sandwich. The second slice is at the end when they return (Mark 6:30–32). They gather with Jesus and report about their experiences. Jesus encouraged them to take some time in seclusion for rest (Mark 6:32). That is the bread of the sandwich. Where is the meat?

In the middle of Jesus sending them out and receiving them back is a different story. It is the story of the martyrdom of John the Baptist. As the disciples go out and preach and heal in the name of Jesus, word begins to spread and rumors emerge. Herod hears a rumor, and believes it, that John the Baptist has risen from the dead. This is terrifying news to Herod because he's the one who killed John the Baptist (Mark 6:16). This is when Mark tells the story of how Herod killed John, the meat of the sandwich.

For historical backdrop: Herod took his brother Philip's wife, Herodias, to be his own and married her (Mark 6:18). John the Baptist saw this as an unlawful union and spoke out against it. This made John some powerful political enemies. Herodias wanted John executed but Herod was unwilling to carry out that wish. He seemed to respect John and enjoyed his preaching (Mark 6:20). A day came, however, when Herod was so enamored by the dancing of Herodias's daughter that he promised to grant her whatever she asked. Herodias told her daughter to ask for John the Baptist's head. Herod regretfully obliged, murdered John, and the decision seems to have tormented him from that point onward.

Now, why would Mark squish the account of John's martyrdom right in the middle of Jesus sending out his disciples? Perhaps the reason is found in the concept of making enemies, persecution, and martyrdom. John's preaching cost him his life. Jesus is very clear that for His disciples to truly follow Him, they must carry a cross (Mark 8:34). Discipleship comes at a cost. James Edwards remarks on this sandwich, "discipleship may lead to martyrdom. The disciple of Jesus must first reckon with the fate of John. Thus, John's martyrdom not only prefigured Jesus's death, but it also prefigures the death of anyone who would follow after him!" The disciples are beginning to follow in John the Baptist's footsteps. They are beginning to follow in the footsteps of Jesus.

Example # 5: The Season for Figs (Mark 11:11–14 [11:15–18] 11:19–21)

In this sandwich, Jesus has finally arrived in Jerusalem. His crucifixion is imminent. The first thing He does upon entering Jerusalem is have a look at the temple (Mark 11:11). He "cases the joint" because He's preparing for something monumental the next day. Then He turns and goes back to Bethany (Mark 11:11). The sandwich begins the next morning when Jesus is walking back to the temple with His disciples. He becomes hungry and finds a nice, leafy fig tree, but upon closer inspection, "He found nothing but leaves, for it was not the season for figs" (Mark 11:13). Jesus then curses the fig tree so that it never produces figs again, "and His disciples were listening" (Mark 11:14). This is the first slice of bread.

A little later comes the second slice of bread at the end of the sandwich (Mark 11:19–21). Jesus and His disciples are again walking by this same fig tree which was "withered from the roots up" (Mark 11:20), and Peter comments on it. What an odd story. Why would Jesus use His divine powers to curse a fig tree? Is this (as some have claimed) just a whiny, petulant response to not getting His way? The tree didn't do anything wrong; it wasn't even in season. Would not a better miracle have been to make the out of season fig tree produce figs? This scene only makes sense when read as a sandwich.

Right in the middle of this fig tree cursing is an account of Jesus back at the temple. This is the meat of the sandwich. He begins "to drive out those who were buying and selling in the temple, and overturned the tables of the money changers and the seats of those who were selling doves; and He would not permit anyone to carry merchandise through the temple" (Mark 11:15–16). We will further discuss the significance of this in a later reflection, but for now, notice how this relates to the fig tree.

The fig tree was leafy and looked productive, but upon closer inspection it was producing no fruit. It was out of season and as a result, it was cursed and would never produce fruit again. Similarly, the temple looked like an active place of worship. There was a lot of hustle and bustle and buying and selling, but then Jesus stopped the temple proceedings. Everything halted because of Jesus. I think the point is that the temple was out of season, and while it looked productive, it wasn't accomplishing what God intended. Rather than being "a house of prayer for all the nations" it had become "a robber's den" (Mark 11:17). The temple had leaves, but it produced no fruit.

Creating this disturbance at the temple, which ceased all the purchasing of animals, was a planned, intentional prophetic demonstration of what the temple had become and a picture of what the future of the temple would look like. Jesus will soon go on to discuss the destruction of the temple. He didn't childishly lose His temper and start throwing tables in a tantrum as He didn't curse the fig tree because He didn't get His way. These were prophetic signs, demonstrations of reality as God sees it, and pictures of what the future holds. The temple, like the fig tree, is out of season and not fulfilling its God-given task. This is a symbolic depiction of the destruction of the temple; the temple is the withered fig tree.

Example #6: Betrayal and Anointing (Mark 14:1–2 [14:3–9] 14:10–11)

Finally, our last example is found in Mark 14 as the Passion Narrative is beginning to unfold. Our passage begins, as Passover draws near, with the chief priests and scribes conspiring to secretly kill Jesus (Mark 14:1). They must do it in secret otherwise the crowds would become scandalized and begin rioting (Mark 14:2). This is the first slice of bread. If you skip down to verse 10, for the second slice, we find that Judas is the key to the secret arrest of Jesus. Judas knows where Jesus stays and he agrees to betray Jesus for money. He begins seeking "an opportune time" (Mark 14:11). If you read Mark 14:1–2 and immediately skip to verses 10–11, it seems like one coherent paragraph.

The meat of this sandwich is verses 3–9 where Jesus is anointed by an unnamed woman. This woman gives her absolute best and most precious gift to honor Jesus. She brings Him "an alabaster vial of very costly perfume of pure nard; and she broke the vial and poured it over His head" (Mark 14:3). This is an extraordinarily expensive gift worth over three hundred denarii (estimated to be a whole year's income). She gave up wealth for Jesus, to honor Him with the best she had.

In this sandwich the stories are best read in contrast to one another. Judas, named prominently as "one of the twelve" (Mark 14:10) betrays Jesus for money. This woman, whose name isn't even mentioned, gives up a tremendous amount of money just to honor Jesus. Compare the priorities, discipleship, greed, selflessness, and devotion of these two people. Judas is forever remembered as the betrayer, while Jesus says of this woman, "wherever the gospel is preached in the whole world, what this woman has done will also be spoken of in memory of her" (Mark 14:9). Judas chooses money over Jesus; she chooses Jesus over money.

Jesus forces us to make decisions and choose sides. Judas sided with the chief priests and scribes to secretly betray the Lord under cover of night. This wonderful woman chose to anoint Jesus with her most precious gift, even in the face of scorn, because He meant so much to her. What does Jesus mean to you? How much is He worth to you? What decisions will you make regarding Jesus?

Reflection Questions

1. In what ways is the mission of the disciples similar to the martyrdom of John the Baptist? Why is it important that John was killed for preaching truth to the powers and authorities of his day? What other examples can you think of where Jesus or His disciples were persecuted for standing up against wicked rulers?

2. In what ways is the fig tree analogous to the temple? Can you think of any modern examples where something might "look the part" spiritually, but in reality is unfruitful? Can we fall into this trap ourselves? How might John 15:5–11 relate to this passage?

Endnotes

1. Edwards, "Markan Sandwiches," 206.

REFLECTION 9
THE LORD IN THE WILDERNESS

Mark 1:1–13

The Wilderness in the Bible

ONE OF THE most familiar biblical settings is "the wilderness." Countless important events, stories, and biblical metaphors take place in the wilderness. The Hebrew word for wilderness, מִדְבָּר (midbar), is found roughly 270 times in the Old Testament. The Greek word for wilderness, ἔρημος (erēmos), is used about 50 times (and almost 340 times in the LXX). The point is, if you read your Bible, you'll spend a lot of time in the wilderness. It will help you to know something about it.

Israel has a profound "wilderness" history. When Hagar flees Abram's household (the first time) she was found by God "by a spring of water in the wilderness" (Gen 16:7). God saw her and cared for her in the wilderness. The second time, when Hagar and her child were banished from the family, God heard weeping "in the wilderness" (Gen 21:14, 17), and again cared for her. Her son, Ishmael, grew up and "lived in the wilderness and became an archer" (Gen 21:20–21). Later in Genesis, when Joseph's brothers plotted against him, they decided to throw him down into a waterless pit "in the wilderness" (Gen 37:22–24).

In these stories, "wilderness" is a dangerous and deserted area where resources are limited and wild animals roam free. The wilderness is where humans did not, and often could not, live. That Ishmael lived in the wilderness tells you something about his tenacity and resourcefulness. God had to intervene to save Hagar from the wilderness, and Joseph only survived because he was sold into slavery.

The wilderness takes on monumental significance in the Exodus narrative. Leaving Egyptian bondage, the children of Israel enter the wilderness and wander for 40 fateful years. So difficult is their wilderness experience that they long for the life they had back in Egypt where they were beaten, enslaved, and their children were massacred. They prefer slavery and death to the wilderness. The wilderness so distorted their memories and perceptions that they cried out, "in the land of Egypt ... we sat by the meat pots and ate bread to the full ... you have brought us out into this wilderness to kill this whole assembly with hunger" (Exod 16:3).

Without the Lord's provision, they could not have survived the wilderness. He gave them mysterious bread from heaven and quail (Exod 16:1–21), and water from a rock (Exod 17:1–7; Num 20:8–12). If survival depends upon bread from the sky and water from a rock, it probably means your resources are scarce. The book of Numbers details many of their hardships suffered in the wilderness. Surviving the wilderness depends entirely upon God's grace (Deut 8:15–17).

Blessing and Curse in the Wilderness

The wilderness is not one specific geographic location. It is any uninhabitable, inhospitable territory where humans can't survive. Other beings could survive and even thrive in the wilderness. In some Jewish thought the wilderness was a dwelling place for demons and frightening spiritual beings. It is also often pictured as the home of wild beasts and untamed animals. Among those wild animals listed in the wilderness are jackals, lions, serpents, ostriches, mountain goats, and wild donkeys.

Through unbearable pain, Job laments, "I have become a brother to jackals and a companion of ostriches" (Job 30:29). That seems like an odd complaint until you realize those are wilderness animals and the wilderness is the scary, desolate, chaotic, uninhabitable land overrun with wild animals and evil spirits. That's what Job's world has become; his life is the wilderness.

An important development of this wilderness theme is that God has plans for healing it. Ezekiel 34:25 promises a day when God will set a good and fair shepherd over His people, and He will "make a covenant of peace with them and eliminate harmful beasts from the land so that they may live securely in the wilderness and sleep in the woods." God promises to remove those wild beasts from the wilderness (which, like Daniel 7, Ezekiel uses to represent world empires) and make all creation, even the wilderness, a place to live in safety and peace.

The wilderness lacked sources of water, sufficient rainfall, and proper vegetation. God has plans to change that. Isaiah 35 promises, "The wilderness and the desert will be glad, and the Arabah will rejoice and blossom; like the crocus it will blossom profusely and rejoice with rejoicing and shout of joy" (Isa 35:1–2). The wilderness will be blessed with trees like Lebanon and will see the glory of the Lord. When this happens, the blind will see, the lame will leap, the deaf will hear, the mute will shout for joy, "for waters will break forth in the wilderness" (Isa 35:5–7).

Then, Isaiah continues, there will be a highway in the

wilderness, "a roadway, and it will be called the Highway of Holiness ... No lion will be there, nor will any vicious beast go up on it" (Isa 35:8–9). Wisdom says one should avoid traveling through the wilderness because of the great danger associated with it, but in the day of God's promise, there will be a highway in the wilderness and the wild beasts will no longer be a threat.

This wilderness theme recurs throughout Isaiah (especially chapters 40–55):

"Clear the way for the Lord in the wilderness; make smooth in the desert a highway for our God" (Isa 40:3).

> I will make the wilderness a pool of water and the dry land fountains of water. I will put the cedar in the wilderness, the acacia and the myrtle and the olive tree; I will place the juniper in the desert (Isa 41:18–20).

> I will even make a roadway in the wilderness, rivers in the desert. The beast of the field will glorify Me, the jackals and the ostriches, because I have given waters in the wilderness and rivers in the desert, to give drink to My chosen people (Isa 43:19–21).

> Indeed, the Lord will comfort Zion; He will comfort all her waste places. And her wilderness He will make like Eden, and her desert like the garden of the Lord; Joy and gladness will be found in her, thanksgiving and the sound of a melody (Isa 51:3).

These quotations, especially Isaiah 51:3, provide an important image of new creation. The pre-Eden world of Genesis 2:5, with no rainfall or vegetation, could be thought of as a wilderness. In Genesis 1, God brings order and life to the dark chaotic sea (Gen 1:2) and in Genesis 2 God brings a garden and life to the barren wilderness. In Genesis 2, God turns the wilderness into a beautiful, life-giving garden, and promises to do the same throughout Isaiah.

The wilderness is the anti-Eden. When God blesses His people, the wilderness becomes like a new Eden (Isa 51:3). Conversely, in Genesis 3:17–19 the fruitful ground is cursed to be like the wilderness. Adam is banished from the garden, back to the wilderness where the land is inhospitable and harsh and thorns and thistles grow. Joel depicts God's judgment in this same way: "the land is like the garden of Eden before them but a desolate wilderness behind them, and nothing at all escapes" (Joel 2:3). In blessing, God turns the wilderness into Eden and in curse, God turns Eden into the wilderness.

According to Isaiah, a day of blessing is coming when the wilderness will be turned back to Eden, the dry land will flow with water, trees will fill its landscape, and even the animals will rejoice and praise God. Unlike the tragic Exodus story where the children of Israel wandered aimlessly and died in the wilderness, or the Eden story when Adam and Eve were banished from the presence of God to the wilderness, the prophets hope for a new and better Exodus and a day of New Creation (Isa 65:17; 66:22), where the wilderness will become life-giving, peaceful, and secure, with water, vegetation, and a highway for the Lord.

The Wilderness in Mark

The Gospel of Mark begins in the wilderness. In fact, Mark introduces John the Baptist with the aforementioned quotation from Isaiah 40:3: "The voice of one calling in the wilderness, make ready the way of the Lord" (Mark 1:3). That means the Isaiah wilderness theme should be firmly planted in your mind as you begin Mark. You must not miss this scene. The Lord will visit the wilderness and there will be blessing and new life; even the wild animals will no longer be a threat.

Mark combines Isaiah's quote with other Old Testament citations: "Behold, I send My messenger [ἄγγελόν, angel] ahead of you, who will prepare Your way" (Mark 1:2). Mark borrows this language from Exodus 23:20, "Behold, I am going to send an angel [ἄγγελόν] before you," and also Malachi 3:1, "Behold, I am going to send My messenger, and he will clear the way before Me." In Greek, Mark resembles the LXX of Exodus 23:20 more closely than Malachi 3:1. The context of Exodus 23:20 is that the Lord's messenger/angel will protect Israel from their enemies, leading them through the wilderness and into the Promised Land.

By combining wilderness images from Exodus and Isaiah, Mark prepares the reader for something remarkable to happen in the wilderness. A new Exodus is about to take place. A highway is being prepared for the Lord's return. Before the Lord comes, a messenger will prepare the way. In Mark's narrative, John the Baptist fulfills the role of the messenger (literally "angel"), and Jesus fulfills the role of the Lord. Throughout Mark's Gospel Jesus will fulfill the role of the coming of the Lord, acting with the Lord's divine authority, and doing what only the Lord can do.

Before Jesus arrives, embodying the return of the Lord, God's messenger, John, goes ahead to the wilderness to prepare His highway: "John the Baptist appeared in the wilderness preaching a baptism of repentance for the forgiveness of sins" (Mark 1:4). It is in no way insignificant that John offers forgiveness in the wilderness. John does not preach that one must go to the temple to receive forgiveness (like perhaps his priestly father would have, Luke 1:5ff), but to go out to the wilderness. That's the last place you'd expect to find the blessings of God. In the introduction to Mark, the wilderness is becoming a place of forgiveness and divine presence.

John is introduced dressed as a true wilderness man. His clothes resemble Elijah, that troubler of Israel (compare Mark

1:6 and 2 Kigs 1:8) who himself spent time in the wilderness (1 Kigs 19:4ff). This description hints that John is the fulfillment of Malachi 4:5–6 (see Mark 9:11–13).

Among those coming out to John to be baptized was Jesus. "Immediately" following His baptism, the Holy Spirit "casts Him out into the wilderness" (Mark 1:12–13). Jesus experiences all the hardships that the wilderness has to offer. The 40 days and trials in the wilderness should remind you of Israel's 40 years of trials in the wilderness. Unlike Israel, however, who rebelled against God in the wilderness, Jesus overcomes the wilderness. He overcomes temptation, the powers of darkness, and Satan himself. Jesus emerges from the wilderness trials victoriously.

Mark gives significantly less detail about this wilderness experience than Matthew and Luke. Mark does not mention any specific temptations or conversations with Satan, or even that Jesus was fasting. Mark does mention something unique, however. Mark is the only Gospel to mention the "wild animals" with Jesus in the wilderness. Taken together with the quotation of Isaiah's wilderness theme, which Mark already quoted, it seems Mark is envisioning Isaiah's vivid depiction of peace with the animals in the wilderness.

Peace with animals is imagined all the way through Isaiah, both in the return from Babylon and in the future glorious age (Isa 11:6–10; 65:25). Like Adam in the garden of Eden, Jesus can live in peace with even the dangerous wilderness animals. He can make even the wilderness look like Eden again. He can overcome the tempter (unlike Adam and Eve) and bring blessing to the most unexpected places.

Launching the gospel of Jesus in this wilderness setting symbolizes a fresh start for God's people, a true victory over the wilderness, a new Exodus, and perhaps a new Eden. A time of blessing and forgiveness and a better future is on the horizon. The Lord is found in the wilderness.

Reflection Questions

1. How is God's creation central to the ministry of Jesus? How does the wilderness relate to God's creation? Why is it important that Jesus overcomes the hostilities of the wilderness? How is the curse in Genesis 3:17–19 related to the wilderness?
2. How do the wilderness scenes in Mark relate to the Exodus story? Why is it important that Jesus defeated temptation in the wilderness before beginning His ministry? What is the significance of the wild beasts? What times and seasons in your own life are like the wilderness?

REFLECTION 10
BAPTISM AND CRUCIFIXION

Mark 1:9–11

Baptism and Crucifixion

ALL FOUR GOSPELS record Jesus's baptism. There are interesting similarities and differences in each account. A unique feature in Mark is that the baptism is at the very beginning of the Gospel. Matthew and Luke begin their Gospels with virgin birth narratives that prepare the reader to identify Jesus as the "Son of God" (Luke 1:35) and "God with Us" (Matt 1:23). John begins with the pre-existent "Word" who became flesh (John 1:1, 14). Mark, however, begins with a voice from heaven calling Jesus His beloved Son (Mark 1:1, 11).

Remembering that the term "Son of God" has royal and kingly implications (Ps 2:6–7; 2 Sam 7:14; 1 Chr 28:6; John 1:49), Mark begins his Gospel with inauguration day. This is the day that God proclaims Jesus to be His "Beloved Son" and anoints Him as King.

David was anointed king years before he finally took the throne (1 Sam 16:1–13; 2 Sam 2:7; 5:4). Similarly, Jesus is anointed with the Holy Spirit and proclaimed to be the Son of God at

His baptism, but only later does He receive His crown and royal robes (Mark 15:17–18). It is on the cross that the plaque is placed above His head: "The King of the Jews" (Mark 15:26). The Gospel of Mark takes us from inauguration (baptism) to coronation (cross), and ultimately exaltation (resurrection).

Jesus's baptism and crucifixion (Mark 1:9–11 and Mark 15:37–39) bookend, or sandwich, His entire ministry. They also share the same imagery, vocabulary, and theology. During His baptism, the heavens are "*torn*" (σχίζω) open, the Spirit (πνεῦμα) descends upon (εἰς) Him, and a voice (φωνή) from the heavens says, "You are My beloved Son (υἱός), in You I am well-pleased" (Mark 1:9–11). This short section introduces you to the divine Sonship and launches the ministry of Jesus.

While on the cross Jesus "*uttered a great voice*" (φωνὴ) and "*breathed His last*" (ἐξέπνευσεν). The veil of the temple was "*torn*" (σχίζω) from top to bottom and the centurion at the cross said, "Truly this man was the Son (υἱός) of God" (Mark 15:37–39). These two paragraphs share much in common and echo each other in their use of the words: voice, torn, Spirit/breath, and Son.

The word "torn" is especially pertinent in the baptismal account because the common word for the heavens opening in a prophetic vision is *anoigo* (ἀνοίγω see Matt 3:16). Mark, however, uses the more violent word for "rip" or "tear" (*skizo*). He only uses this word two times in this entire Gospel: once at Jesus's baptism (Mark 1:10) and again at His crucifixion (Mark 15:38). In Jewish thought the veil in the temple was representative of the heavens, both of which contained the presence of God on the other side (Heb 9:1–10; Josephus, *Antiquities* 3.6.4), and both of which are torn open during the baptism and crucifixion of Jesus.

These paragraphs also share a form of the word "Spirit/breath." In Jesus's baptism the Spirit (noun, *pneuma*) is going into (εἰς) Him but in the crucifixion, He breathed (verb, *epneusen*) out (ἐξ). *Pneuma* in at baptism and *pneuma* out at crucifixion.

Furthermore, baptism is when the voice from heaven calls Jesus God's Son and the crucifixion is the first time a human character calls Jesus God's Son. The proclamation of Sonship is rare in Mark's Gospel and intentionally introduces and concludes Jesus's ministry from baptism to cross. Jesus is God's Son from God's voice in the heavens all the way to man's voice at the foot of the cross.

The baptism and death of Jesus is intricately linked to His divine Sonship. By linking the crucifixion to Jesus's baptism, Jesus's death looms over the entire gospel and is the clearest image of what it means that Jesus is God's Son.

Baptism and Psalm 2

There are several important Old Testament allusions in Mark's brief depiction of Jesus's baptism. We already said that this baptism is presented as inauguration day and connected with Psalm 2. Psalm 2 is regularly cited throughout the New Testament in connection with Jesus (Mark 1:11; Matt 3:17; Luke 3:22; Acts 4:24–26; 13:33; Heb 1:5; 5:5).

Psalm 2 begins with the nations raging and plotting against God and His chosen king (Ps 2:1–2). This king is referred to as God's "Anointed" (מָשִׁיחַ - *Messiah*; Χριστός - *Christ*). When God hears the puny tremors of rebellion, He scoffs at human pride and frailty. In rage He terrifies them, saying, "I have installed My King upon Zion, My holy mountain" (Ps 2:6). God has installed, or inaugurated, His chosen and anointed king and no one can overthrow him.

The king tells us exactly what God decreed: "He said to Me, 'You are My Son, Today I have begotten You'" (Ps 2:7). What day is "Today"? It's the day He was begotten and became God's son. The day that God "installed" His king (Ps 2:6–7). It is inauguration day. The Psalm ends with a warning to all nations and kingdoms of this world to show discernment, take warning, and come before God and His Anointed with reverence and worship.

When the Lord decrees, "You are My Son" to His Anointed (Christ/Messiah) King, on inauguration day, the connection of Mark 1:11 is impossible to miss. In Greek the phrases are almost verbatim the exact same. The LXX of Psalm 2:7 says, "υἱός μου εἶ σύ" (*My Son you are*) and the Greek text in Mark 1:11, says, "σὺ εἶ ὁ υἱός μου" (*You are My Son*). Except for word order and an additional definite, it is the exact same sentence. Mark's version adds the description *"the beloved"* (ὁ ἀγαπητός) right after that phrase, so that it would literally read, "You are My Son, the beloved."

Mark 1 and Isaiah

Another passage we might also consider is Isaiah 42:1 which describes God's servant who will bring justice to the nations. This servant is a major figure in Isaiah 40–55 (Isa 41:8–9; 42:1, 18–19; 43:10; 44:1–2, 21, 26; 45:4; 48:20; 49:3–7; 50:10; 52:13–53:12) and we commonly call Him the "Suffering Servant." Sometimes this servant is presented as Israel (Isa 41:8; 44:1–2, 21; 45:4; 48:20; 49:3); sometimes he is someone who acts on behalf of Israel (Isa 49:5–7). Ultimately, this servant "will justify many, As He will bear their iniquities" (Isa 53:11). This servant does no violence, and no deceit is found in His mouth (Isa 53:9). This servant "poured out Himself to death, And was numbered with the transgressors; Yet He Himself bore the sin of many, And interceded for their transgressors" (Isa 53:12).

In the same way that "son of God" in the Old Testament refers both to Israel (Exod 4:22–23) and a person (the king), so the Suffering Servant both refers to Israel and some unidentified person. His identity has long been debated.

Now, why discuss this servant of Isaiah? Because Jesus is not only introduced at His baptism as the Son of God, but also as the servant. Isaiah 42:1 says, "Behold, My Servant, whom I uphold; My chosen one in whom My soul delights. I have put My Spirit upon Him; He will bring forth justice to the nations." The imagery and language of this passage appear in Mark 1:11. Isaiah describes a servant who receives God's Spirit and is the one "in whom My soul delights." Mark describes a chosen king who receives God's Spirit and is the one in whom "I am well pleased."

Since Mark opens with a quotation from Isaiah 40 (Mark 1:3), perhaps we should read Mark (especially the introduction in Mark 1:1–15) with Isaiah in mind. If we do, we'll see connections between Jesus and the Suffering Servant, and deeper significance to the wilderness setting. We'll understand more clearly the Gospel that Jesus preached (Mark 1:14–15; Isa 52:7) and the theme of Jesus bringing the "return of the Lord to Zion" (Isaiah 52:8). We may also note Isaiah 64:1 which pictures God "tearing the heavens" and "coming down" to be with His people, is the same imagery as the heavens being torn open and the Spirit coming down as a dove in Jesus's baptism.

To summarize, Jesus's baptism is a powerful moment where He is anointed as God's Spirit-filled chosen king. This moment looks backwards to Psalms and Isaiah and looks forward to the cross. From this point onward, we should see Jesus as God's Son, His Servant, and the chosen king destined for shame and glory.

Reflection Questions

1. Why is it significant that Mark bookends the ministry of Jesus with declarations that He is the Son of God at His baptism and crucifixion? In what

ways do you see baptism and the cross related? How might Romans 6:3–8 tie the cross and baptism together?

2. How is Jesus understood as God's Son through His death? How is Jesus like the Suffering Servant of Isaiah 40–55? How might we demonstrate obedience, faithfulness, and love through suffering?

REFLECTION 11
THE COMING KINGDOM

Mark 1:14–45

The Euangelion of God

AFTER HIS BAPTISM, the Spirit "cast Him out" (ἐκβάλλει) into the wilderness to face His first major test as the anointed King. As God's Son and Servant (both terms in the Old Testament can refer to Israel) Jesus must overcome Israel's past failures and be victorious where Israel was defeated. He must fulfill Israel's calling in Himself. He overcomes the wilderness faithfully in 40 days (unlike Israel who failed for 40 years), prevails over Satan's temptations, and is unharmed by the wild beasts. Like Israel, ministering angels support Him through the harsh wilderness test (Mark 1:13; Exod 14:19; 23:20–25).

After emerging victorious from the wilderness, it's time to enter the promised land and promote the new and coming kingdom. His proclamation is set "after John had been taken into custody" (Mark 1:14). We are not given any further details about John's arrest until Mark 6:14–29. John, who was introduced as the faithful forerunner to the Lord (Mark 1:2–3), a humble preacher (Mark 1:7), the 2nd coming of Elijah (Mark

69

9:13), and a topic of contention later in the ministry of Jesus (Mark 11:27–33), is persecuted and imprisoned by the rulers of the kingdoms of men. He is later executed by the beasts (Dan 7) because of His righteousness and their sinful, lustful, violent, rebellious pride. That Jesus enters Galilee "preaching the gospel of God" is temporally linked to the arrest of John the Baptist might be a subtle image of the contrasts between the kingdom of God and the kingdoms of this world. It may also be a warning that God's kingdom does not come without conflict and suffering.

Mark 1:14–15 contains language that would be familiar to anyone acquainted with the Roman Empire. Each of the words has an important political meaning. This section of Mark is contrasting the politics of Jesus with the politics of the empire.

The word "preaching" (κηρύσσων) suggests an official, royal proclamation that would be made on behalf of a king. A "preacher" (κῆρυξ -kerux) was a herald of the king who proclaimed official messages with the authority of the king. By the way, preachers, make sure you represent King Jesus with honor, fastidiousness, and clarity when you speak on His behalf.

The "gospel" (εὐαγγέλιον) was announced by kings when they finally came to the throne, conquered their enemies, and brought peace and salvation to the land. This word and examples of its usage are given in the first reflection.

The word "kingdom" (βασιλεία) obviously is the same word used to describe kingdoms of the earth. This word is used of the Roman Empire.

The imperatives "repent" (μετανοεῖτε) and "believe in the gospel" (πιστεύετε ἐν τῷ εὐαγγελίῳ) would also be used by political authorities. They are not merely religious or Christian words, especially not at the time Jesus is using them. It would be anachronistic to read these as "Christian" words. This message would be heard as something like, "change your loyalties and give your alliance to a new reign." For example, if a New Englander was loyal to the British crown, after the American Revolution, he would be expected to repent (change loyalties) and believe (give allegiance)[1] to the good news (independence and freedom).

Jesus is calling upon His listeners to prepare for a new kingdom bursting onto the scene, they need to change their whole way of thinking and switch allegiances. There is a new King and a new way of doing kingdom. Unlike the "gospel" of Caesar Augustus, Jesus proclaims the "gospel of God" which He immediately connects to "the kingdom of God." The Gospel of God is that His kingdom is at hand, so amend your ways of thinking and give your loyalty and allegiance to this gospel.

Isaiah 52:7–8 and the Gospel

The language Jesus uses again reaches back to the book of Isaiah. The gospel in Isaiah 52:7 was the proclamation that "Your God reigns" (Isa 52:7) and on the horizon the watchmen could see, "the return of the Lord to Zion" (Isa 52:8). God's return echoes back to the beginning of Mark, where the voice in the wilderness must "prepare the way of the Lord, make His paths straight" (Mark 1:3; Isa 40:3). The gospel of God is the Lord's return through the wilderness to Zion as king. In Mark, watch and see if anyone begins in the wilderness, travels to Jerusalem, and takes His place as king (He may receive His crown in surprising fashion).

In Isaiah 52, God had plans to comfort His people, redeem Jerusalem, and show the power of His salvation to all the nations (Isa 52:9–10). Israel is told to "Depart, depart, go out from there" (Isa 52:11). The context of Isaiah 52 is leaving Babylonian captivity; Israel is to "shake yourself from the dust and arise; be seated, O Jerusalem; loose the bonds from your neck, O captive daughter of Zion" (Isa 52:2).

The wonderful gospel message of Isaiah is that Babylonian captivity is over! It's like a second Exodus is taking place, this time they are leaving Babylon instead of Egypt. When they left Egypt, they did so in haste, unable to even let the Passover bread rise. When they leave Babylon, however, "you shall not go out in haste, and you shall not go in flight, for the Lord will go before you, and the God of Israel will be your rear guard" (Isa 52:12). God will protect Israel from the front and behind, leading them safely home.

Jesus's first words in Mark announce a new kingdom, the end of an old regime, the promise of a better day and the abolition of oppression and misery. Egypt, Babylon, and Rome will no longer be your king because something new is taking over the world. And unlike Egypt, Babylon, and Rome, this kingdom does not come through violence and economic oppression. It will not come with harsh injustice or force and will not "lord it over" and "exercise authority over them" (Mark 10:42). This kingdom comes in a new way. How will it come? That's what the rest of the Gospel of Mark is about.

When Jesus said the "time is fulfilled" and this "kingdom of God is at hand" He sure wasn't kidding. It's happening "immediately." That statement begins a series of events that demonstrate the power of the coming kingdom. The rest of Mark 1 is a whirlwind of the ministry of Jesus and no opposition can stand before Him. Crowds gather from all over as He teaches, heals, and casts out demons with unparalleled sovereignty.

Glimpsing the Kingdom

Jesus's first actions begin the formation of a new Israel (Mark 1:16–20). He will call twelve men (the first four are introduced here) who will symbolically represent the new twelve tribes of Israel. Our next reflection will be dedicated to understanding a little more about these twelve.

Then Mark 1:21–22 demonstrates the powerful and authoritative teachings of the kingdom. Jesus is an electric teacher and the amazed crowds flock to Him. In the synagogue man arrives with an unclean spirit arrives (Mark 1:23–26) who recognizes Jesus as "the Holy One of God!" (Mark 1:24). Jesus rebukes the spirit and casts him out with an authority never before seen. The authority of His teaching (Mark 1:22) was confirmed by His authority over the spiritual forces of darkness (Mark 1:27). All who see Him are amazed (Mark 1:22, 27) and "Immediately the news about Him spread everywhere into all the surrounding district of Galilee" (Mark 1:28).

Jesus immediately goes from the synagogue to Andrew and Simon's house. Simon's mother-in-law is sick with a fever and Jesus "raised her up, taking her by the hand" (Mark 1:31; compare Mark 5:41–42). News was spreading and by the time evening came, people were flocking to the house, bringing the sick and demon possessed. The whole city was there. Jesus was working and healing and casting out demons with authority over physical illness and spiritual beings.

All this teaching, healing, casting out of demons, and gathering large crowds has just been one Sabbath day in Jesus's ministry (Mark 1:21–34). The kingdom is erupting before their eyes. When God reigns, sickness is healed, and Satan loses his grip on the world.

Mark 1:35 begins early the next morning, "while it was still dark," and Jesus arose to go pray by Himself. Simon and others woke up and when they found Jesus, they said, "Everyone is looking for you" (Mark 1:37). The beginning of Jesus's ministry is a nonstop adventure without a moment to rest. Jesus can't even find uninterrupted private prayer time.

Jesus takes His disciples to nearby towns to preach and repeat the same actions (Mark 1:38–39). Notably, Jesus says, "This is why I came" (Mark 1:38). Jesus is said to "preach" (κηρύσσω) three times in Mark 1 (Mark 1:14, 38, 39). John the

Baptist preaches (κηρύσσω) in Mark 1:4, 7. And a cleansed leper "preaches" (κηρύσσω) in Mark 1:45. Jesus is "preaching" the gospel of the coming kingdom of God and needs to do that in all the towns of Galilee.

Jesus was "moved with compassion" (Mark 1:41) when he saw the man with leprosy. There is a peculiar textual variant here. Some early manuscripts say that Jesus felt "anger" instead of "compassion" when he healed the man. It's easy to see why Jesus would feel compassion for the leper, but harder to figure out why He might be angry.[2] If anger is the correct reading, Jesus may have been angry about the harm and pain caused by the leprosy, or that this man had been socially ostracized.

To heal him, Jesus touches a man (Mark 1:41) who most people avoided, and "immediately" the leprosy leaves. Jesus warns him to be silent and not tell anyone about this healing. We discussed the secretive nature of Jesus's ministry already and it will pop up all over the text of Mark (it's already appeared in Mark 1:25, 34, 43). Jesus tells this leper to go show himself to the priest and to follow the customs of Moses for cleansing. Instead, this man preaches (κηρύσσω) freely everything that Jesus did. And the crowds grow even more.

Based on this first chapter, you'd think the kingdom of God would come quickly, powerfully, and without opposition. There was virtually no conflict, everyone was amazed, the authority of the King was evident, and the masses were flowing to Him. Jesus can't even enter a town, so He stays in the unpopulated areas, and everyone goes out to find Him (Mark 1:45). This is an amazing introduction to the kingdom. Surely, things will stay this positive forever, right?

Reflection Questions

    1. How is the ministry of Jesus political? How is it

different from the politics of His (and our) day? Why is it important that our words like "repent," "belief/faith," "King," "kingdom," "gospel," "church," "preach," "Lord," "Son of God," were all used to describe aspects of politics in the Roman Empire? If we thought of the kingdom of God as our political affiliation and the teachings of Jesus as our political platform, how would that change your politics?

2. How is the kingdom of God seen in the first chapter of Mark? How is the kingdom of God seen through teaching? Casting out demons? Healing?

Endnotes

1. For a helpful book demonstrating the idea of "faith" as "allegiance" read: Matthew W. Bates, *Salvation by Allegiance Alone: Rethinking Faith, Works, and the Gospel of Jesus the King* (Grand Rapids: Baker Academic, 2017).

2. As a general rule, textual scholars prefer more difficult readings, because they are less likely to be a scribal innovation. It seems counter intuitive, but think about it, why would a scribe purposefully make something less clear? The tendency among scribes is to make the text clearer and easier to understand. So usually, the more difficult reading is the original one.

REFLECTION 12
CALLING OF THE TWELVE

Mark 1:16–20; 2:13–17; 3:13–19

Calling the Twelve

FOUNDATIONAL to this coming kingdom is that Jesus garner a following of devotees (Mark 1:16–20). Jesus calls two brothers, Simon and Andrew, and two other brothers, James and John. These two sets of brothers were fishermen. Reading Mark alongside John would give the impression that this was not technically Simon and Andrew's first time to meet Jesus (that meeting is in John 1:35–42), but Mark mentions no previous relationship.

Mark portrays a coming kingdom and four men who "immediately" leave everything behind, their fishing equipment, their boat, and even their own father, to follow Jesus. They heard the announcement and immediately followed. That is what it means to "repent" and "believe." They changed what they were doing (fishing) and they began to follow (allegiance/belief).

This is the first of three scenes where Jesus calls and adds followers (Mark 1:16–20; 2:14; 3:13–19). In the first instance, Jesus calls these four fishermen. They are uneducated men, probably struggling to make ends meet. The second call is to Levi, a wealthy tax collector with a large house and many wealthy friends (Mark 2:13–17). Levi and his friends were hated by many, including the religious leaders of the day. The third and final call is when Jesus appointed twelve men, out of a larger group, so "that they would be with Him and that He could send them out to preach, and to have authority to cast out demons" (Mark 3:13–15).

Who Were These Men?

Mark 3:13–19 mentions names, and nicknames, for all twelve, but whenever we compare these lists to the other Gospels, it gets confusing. They do not always line up easily.

- Simon—Best known as Peter. He heads every list of the disciples we have. John 1:42 also calls Him Cephas. This is the name Paul generally uses for him (1 Cor 1:12; 3:22; 9:5; 15:5; Gal 1:19; 2:9, 11, 14) but Paul does use the name Peter in Galatians 2:7, 8. Peter is the Greek word which means "rock" and Cephas is the Greek transliteration of an Aramaic word meaning "rock." Peter (or Cephas) is a nickname given to Simon (sometimes spelled Simeon) by Jesus.
- James and John—These brothers were fishermen, called by Jesus, and given the nickname "Sons of Thunder." John is traditionally thought to be the "Beloved Disciple" of the Gospel of John. The name James, in Greek, is Ἰάκωβος (Iakōbos) and he is probably named after the patriarch Jacob. This

James is not the brother of Jesus or author of the book of James. This James was martyred by King Herod in Acts 12:1–2.

- Andrew—This is Peter's brother. He has a Greek, rather than Jewish, name that means something like "manly." Jesus spends time at his and Peter's house in Mark 1:29 with James and John. His largest role is in the Gospel of John where he is instrumental in bringing Peter to meet Jesus (John 1:40–42) and he appears a few other times (John 6:8; 12:22). In Mark, he joins Peter, James, and John to ask Jesus privately about the destruction of Jerusalem (Mark 13:3–4).

- Philip—Philip is mentioned in all four Gospels but is featured most prominently in John (John 1:43–48; 6:5–7; 12:21–22; 14:8–9). He is from the same city, Bethsaida, as Andrew and Peter (John 1:44) and he brings Nathanael to Jesus (John 1:44–45). Like many of the apostles, references to him fade away after the first chapter of Acts. Later Gnostic Christianity connected several writings to Philip, like the *Gospel of Philip*, the *Acts of Philip*, and *The Letter of Peter to Philip*.

- Bartholomew—He is mentioned in Matthew, Mark, Luke, and Acts but he is absent in John. John, however, speaks of a "Nathanael" (John 1:44-51; 21:2) who is absent in the synoptics. Nathanael (in John) and Bartholomew (in the Synoptics) are connected to Philip when mentioned, which has led some to believe that they are the same person, meaning, Nathanael is another name for Bartholomew.

- Matthew—When read alongside the other Gospels, one learns that Matthew is probably the tax collector also called Levi (Matt 9:9; 10:3). This would give him the honor of having the least popular profession among the twelve, but probably the most money.

- Thomas—The name "Thomas" is a Semitic word meaning "twin" and is probably a nickname. Another nickname he has is Didymus (John 11:16; 20:24; 21:2), which is a Greek word also meaning "twin." Apparently this guy has a mystery twin. We do not know Thomas' first name. Gnostic Christianity had some fun with this fact and supposed his first name was actually Judas (*Gospel of Thomas*) and that he was the identical twin brother of Jesus (*Acts of Thomas*).

- James—This is a second James (Ἰάκωβος), known as the "son of Alphaeus," which distinguishes him from the first James, the Son of Thunder. This Alphaeus seems to be a different person than Levi's father who is also called Alphaeus (Mark 2:14). Some believe this is the one called "James the Less" in Mark 15:40. "The Less" probably means "the younger" in distinction from the other James who is older. Some suppose that it could be a reference to height instead of age, which, if true, is a little funny.

- Thaddaeus—This one is tricky. Thaddaeus is mentioned in Mark 3:18 and Matthew 10:3 but is not mentioned in Luke/Acts or John. Instead, they mention another Judas (John 14:22) who is a relative of someone named James (possibly James the Less? Son of Alphaeus? Or an unknown James? - Luke 6:16; Acts 1:13). Thaddaeus probably, like so many of the apostles, is known by a second name, Judas. But to call him Judas would create confusion with the more infamous Judas, so Matthew and Mark call him Thaddaeus. Luke calls him Ἰούδαν Ἰακώβου "Judas of James" (possibly "son" or "brother" of James. "Son" seems the most likely implication, but then we're left to guess who this James could be), and John calls him Judas "not Iscariot."

- Simon—We also have another Simon, but this one is not called "rock," rather he's called "the Zealot." This is not the normal word for zealot/zealous (ζηλωτής) used in New Testament passages like Luke 6:15; Acts 1:13; Acts 22:3; Galatians 1:14. This word is Καναναῖον and is only used here and in Matthew 10:3. It's the word for Canaanite. It also means zealot which seems to be how Luke interprets it (Luke 6:15). Josephus describes "zealots" as a fourth sect of Judaism (Pharisees, Sadducees, Essenes, and Zealots). Zealots were violent revolutionaries who wanted to overthrow the Roman Empire and free Israel from Roman oppression. Their origins can be traced back to Judas of Galilee who led a revolt against Rome (mentioned in Acts 5:37) during the childhood of Jesus. While he was killed, some followers remained (but were scattered) and it's possible Simon was one of them. However, some scholars argue that the "zealots" didn't become a recognizable and distinct political group until closer to AD 70.

- Judas—Known as "Iscariot," which may be a Greek rendering of the Hebrew phrase "man from Kerioth" (איש־קריות). His father is called "Simon Iscariot" in John 6:71. Judas is always mentioned at the end of these lists, as he is the one who betrayed Jesus. This blunt detail reveals the direction this story will turn in the ensuing chapters. Mark wants us to immediately read Judas' name with suspicion and keep his sinful end in mind from the beginning.

Working through all those names and nicknames and descriptions is never an easy task and they don't always line up perfectly in each of the four Gospels. What is clear is that Jesus chooses twelve disciples to send out as apostles. Some manuscripts of Mark 3:14 say, "whom also he named Apostles." This phrase is included in the ESV and NIV, but absent in the NASB and KJV. Most Bibles will include a footnote about the phrase, whether they include it in the text or not. Other than possibly this verse, the only time Mark calls the twelve "apostles" is in Mark 6:30. Mark usually calls them "the twelve" or "disciples."

Diversity and Discipleship

In Mark 1:16–20 Jesus calls the first four of these apostles. They are brothers, from the same region, with the same profession. You may expect Jesus to be putting together a somewhat homogenous group. By the end, you can see that this is an incredibly diverse group of men. That may be the point.

The fact that Mark calls them "the twelve" so regularly suggests something significant about that number (Mark 3:14, 16; 4:10; 6:7; 9:35; 10:32; 11:11; 14:10; 17, 20, 43). The number "twelve" also pops up in other contexts throughout Mark (Mark 5:25, 42; 6:43; 8:19).

It seems that by calling twelve men, Jesus is intentionally mirroring of the twelve tribes of Israel. He even goes on a mountain, like Moses, to call the new Israel (Mark 3:13), but unlike those twelve tribes of old, these twelve are not all brothers. They represent different families, education levels, professions, politics, and socioeconomic backgrounds. You have Jewish fishermen, tax-collectors, and zealots here. This may be the only group in world history where men of these three professions/worldviews willingly spent time together, shared meals, and taught the same message.

Jesus's kingdom will be like a new, revived Israel, but it will extend beyond family and genealogy. It will expand Israel to be as diverse as the world. In Mark 3, Jesus calls the twelve and sets them apart as apostles and it is no coincidence that Mark 3 ends by redefining family to include all who do the will of God, regardless of genealogy and nationality (Mark 3:35). In Jesus's kingdom, family is about a common commitment to God, rather than blood, social similarities, or shared political affiliations. Jesus shows through these men the radical unity that can be achieved with and through diversity.

He centers this unity around a common mission: to preach and demonstrate the kingdom of God. To the fishermen, he promises to make them "fishers of men" (Mark 1:17). They have been fishing their entire lives, but now they will begin fishing for what truly matters.

These would not be most people's first choice. They are not the most important, educated, polished, popular, and respected, but the power of the kingdom rests not in human talent and ability, but in God's reign. We cannot create God's kingdom on our own, God can, even with this ragtag crew of disciples.

Reflection Questions

1. Why do you think the disciples were so diverse? How important is diversity within a church? In what ways were the disciples diverse and in what ways is your church family diverse? What can you do to facilitate a church environment where diverse groups of people feel welcomed?

2. If diversity matters, why would Jesus have chosen

twelve Jewish men to be His disciples? Could there be any important Old Testament backdrop to this number of men? In what ways is Jesus like Israel? In what ways is Jesus refining Israel and in what ways is He formulating a new Israel?

REFLECTION 13
ACCUSED OF BLASPHEMY

Mark 2:1–12

Conflict Stories

CONTROVERSY ALWAYS FOLLOWS the kingdom of God. In Mark 1, Jesus preached, gathered a large following, healed many, and cast out demons. He exercised power over this world and the spiritual forces of darkness. Nothing in the heavens or on earth can stop Him now! Well, let's just wait and see how the story goes.

Every step forward for the kingdom is met with struggle and conflict. These conflicts escalate throughout Mark, culminating in the cross, where the conflict rages to its most intense and vile height. The kingdom is forged through suffering, and it all begins right here.

Mark 2 initiates the conflicts that will follow. Mark 2:1–3:6 contains a series of five conflict stories, each in response to a kingdom moment. These stories escalate to the point that, "The Pharisees went out and immediately began conspiring with the Herodians against Him, as to how they might destroy Him" (Mark 3:6).

During these stories Jesus is accused of blasphemy, fellowship with scoundrels, failure to produce spiritually mature followers, having followers who break the Sabbath, and breaking the Sabbath Himself. Each conflict centers around an important question that arises because of Jesus:

1. "Why does this man speak that way? He is blaspheming; who can forgive sins but God alone?" (Mark 2:7).
2. "Why is He eating and drinking with tax collectors and sinners?" (Mark 2:16).
3. "Why do John's disciples and the disciples of the Pharisees fast, but Your disciples do not fast?" (Mark 2:18).
4. "Look, why are they doing what is not lawful on the Sabbath?" (Mark 2:24).
5. "Is it lawful to do good or to do harm on the Sabbath, to save a life or to kill?" (Mark 3:4).

The fifth and final question is distinct from the previous four, because Jesus asks this one. The other questions are asked (either verbally or mentally) by the accusing scribes and Pharisees, but the final question is an offered by Jesus. Tensions rise with each conflict. The next few reflections will focus on these conflict stories and what they tell us about Jesus and His kingdom.

Getting through the Crowds

Mark 2:1 reports that Jesus He went back home after His travels. This is probably Jesus's own home in Capernaum. The crowds have been following and growing, and now that Jesus is home, they all show up to see Him. Earlier "the whole city had gathered at the door" (Mark 1:33), but now "there was no longer any room, not even near the door" (Mark 2:2). The kingdom is impacting the city. Jesus uses this opportunity to speak "the word" to them (Mark 2:2; see Mark 4:14).

While the teachings of Jesus are certainly wonderful, most people come to Him for the healings. This occasion is no different. Four men come to His house, carrying a paralyzed man. We know little about these four, but it's noteworthy that they care deeply for their paralyzed friend and trust in Jesus's power to heal.

A problem arises because of the growing crowd. The growing numbers have been mentioned several times already in Mark 1, but this is the first use of the word ὄχλος, "crowd." This is a keyword in Mark's Gospel and becomes part of many stories (Mark 2:4, 13; 3:9, 20, 32; 4:1, 36, 5:21, 24, 27, 30, 31; 6:34, 45; 7:14, 17, 33; 8:1, 2, 6, 34; 9:14, 15, 17, 25; 10:1, 46; 11:18, 32; 12:12, 37; 14:43; 15:8, 11, 15). From beginning to end, the crowds play a role in almost every story of Jesus.

These four men cannot carry their friend to the door because of the crowd, so they take matters into their own hands. Like the raucous crowds of shoppers on Black Friday, these crowds at Jesus's house will not move out of the way for a paralyzed man to be carried through. The four men climb to the top of the house, remove the covering, and begin to dig a hole large enough to fit their friend through Jesus's roof.

Roofs in the ancient city of Capernaum were quite different from roofs on our modern houses. They were held up mostly by logs and sticks which supported enough tightly compacted and hardened earth to keep rain and moisture out. These four had to remove the fixtures and "dig" through His roof to get their friend inside. This is not a nice thing to do to somebody's house, but they were desperate. Hopefully, they would have been willing to fix the roof before they left, but still, they broke social protocol to get their friend to Jesus. I don't know that I would respond as well as Jesus. He doesn't even care about the hole in His roof; He cares about their faith.

Forgiveness of Sins and Blasphemy

"Son, your sins are forgiven" (Mark 2:5). That remarkable declaration is the first thing said when they come in through His roof. Some listening may have thought Jesus meant, "even though you destroyed my roof, I forgive you." Others heard something much deeper than that. They heard some human claim to forgive sins. Forgiving sins is God's job. The scribes are well aware of passages like Isaiah 43:5: "I, even I, am the one who wipes out your transgressions for My own sake, And I will not remember your sins" and Exodus 34:7 where the Lord "forgives iniquity, transgression, and sin."

Perhaps Jesus was only declaring something God had done and not claiming to do it Himself? For example, if I see someone receive baptism and I tell them, "Congratulations, your sins are forgiven," I did not claim to be the one who forgave them, I only said what God did. If Jesus were doing this, it wouldn't be blasphemous, but it would still be problematic.

It would be a problem because this person didn't go to the temple or offer sacrifice. While there is precedent for it in the Old Testament (1 Sam 12:13), forgiveness apart from the temple would be a challenge to temple authority. Similarly in Mark 1, John the Baptist was preaching a new way of forgiveness, apart from the temple and sacrificial system (Mark 1:4). Jesus is suggesting forgiveness comes by their faith. Would that not be presumptuous to offer a new method of forgiveness unstipulated by God?

The scribes take this statement by Jesus to be more than presumption. They take it to be blasphemous. They think Jesus is claiming to forgive sins as God. It turns out they are right. That is exactly what Jesus did. The scribes think to themselves ("reasoning in their hearts") that Jesus is blaspheming. Jesus can only claim to forgive sins if Jesus is also claiming to be God, because only God can forgive sins (Mark 2:7).

Jesus was immediately aware of their thoughts. Imagine that. The man who forgives sins also knows the thoughts of the heart of man. It sounds a little bit like the Lord is returning to His people and forgiveness and healings are spreading (Mark 1:3). Jesus responds to their question by asking, "Why are you reasoning about these things in your hearts? Which is easier, to say to the paralytic, 'Your sins are forgiven'; or to say, 'Get up, and pick up your pallet and walk?'"

How would you answer that question? What would you think is easier to say? It's impossible for me to do both. I suppose I think it's easier to say, 'Your sins are forgiven.' Guilt and forgiveness are invisible. The only way we know our sins are forgiven is by trusting God. If I tell someone that they are forgiven, I may be right or wrong. You'd have to ask God. If I tell a paralyzed person to get up and walk, it becomes obvious to everyone that I'm a huckster and a charlatan, selling what I cannot provide.

So, how can Jesus demonstrate that His words have authority? Since forgiveness is invisible, how can He prove the forgiveness is real? How will anyone know? He proves it by healing the man, saying, "'So that you may know that the Son of Man has authority on earth to forgive sins' — He said to the paralytic, 'I say to you, get up, pick up your pallet and go home'" (Mark 2:10–11).

Immediately, the paralyzed man does this exactly. He stands (for the first time in who knows how long) and picks up his own pallet (instead of being carried, he can now carry things), and he walks home through the crowds (so that everyone can see what Jesus has done). When this happens, the crowds begin to glorify God, shouting, "We have never seen anything like this!"

(Mark 2:12). By the way, this sounds a lot like the beautiful wilderness picture of Isaiah 35:5–7.

Reflection Questions

1. Why is it important that Jesus heals both physically and spiritually? How can helping someone physically give you more credibility as a spiritual help? What connection is there before "your sins are forgiven" and "take up your bed and walk" in the kingdom of God?

2. What does this text reveal about the identity of Jesus? How is the Son of Man able to forgive sins? How would you answer the scribes' question, "Who can forgive sins but God alone? (Mark 2:7)? How does this passage relate to Mark 1:3 (Isa 40:3)?

REFLECTION 14
JESUS'S EVIL COMPANY

Mark 2:13–22

The Innocence of Jesus

IF you really want to find fault with me, you'll probably succeed. My failures as a Christian, minister, husband, father, and human can be detected if you search hard enough. That's one reason I hope I never find myself with the enemies Jesus had. Mark 2:1–3:6 illustrates the constant scrutiny Jesus was under. His enemies fixated on His every action, interpreting them in the least charitable light possible, and still they were unable to develop any credible accusations. There was just no legitimate dirt to find on Jesus.

In the first conflict story, Jesus was considered a blasphemer because He forgave sins. While blasphemy is certainly a serious charge, He didn't do anything immoral. In fact, He forgave and healed somebody. If you look at my life and forgiveness and healing are the worst things you can find, I must be doing well. Jesus's unparalleled goodness quickly leaps off the page in the second chapter of Mark.

The next three conflicts aren't even about Jesus's actions per se, but about those with whom He associates. They find nothing bad about Jesus, so they accuse Him of spending time with bad people. He has meals with sinners (Mark 2:16), His disciples don't fast (Mark 2:18), and His disciples picked and ate some heads of grain on the Sabbath (Mark 2:24). These accusations are about His disciples and His company, rather than Him. In each instance, Jesus defends His company and still comes out spotless.

The fifth and final conflict in this series, in Mark 3:1-6, is another example of Jesus healing someone. In that scene Jesus healed someone on the Sabbath Day. That was His big crime. The innocence of Jesus is remarkable to watch throughout the story of His life. No matter how hard the search, they find no sins to pin on Jesus.

Bad Company

When you drive on a major highway in Texas, you'll probably have to pay a tax (generally you'll get a bill in the mail which you better pay quickly before they slap fees on top of the toll). Jesus traveled a lot, often with crowds, all throughout Roman occupied Galilee (Mark 2:13). When you do that, the odds are pretty good you'll be stopped at some checkpoint and forced to pay a tax. Jews couldn't even walk around their own land without Rome taking their money. They hated being bothered and burdened by paying these taxes and they especially hated the people who collected them. Multiply that hatred exponentially when that tax collector is a fellow Jew.

Jews were not supposed to take your money and give it to the Romans; that was the ultimate act of disloyalty. Tax collectors were hated because they supported Rome with their brother's money and would often get rich in the process. Sometimes they even cheated their fellow Israelites just to pocket a little extra (Luke 19:8). Imagine selling out your own country, supporting your national enemy, and cheating your neighbor to get rich. That's a tax collector.

Jesus sees this tax collector named Levi sitting at his booth and Jesus, rather than being disgruntled and cursing at him, calls to him, "Follow me." That's jaw dropping. This is the same call He made to the fishermen in Mark 1:17. Levi had no idea when he got ready for work that day that His life would never be the same again.

After calling Levi, Jesus goes to his house for a meal. This is apparently a grand house. It holds Jesus, His disciples, and "many tax collectors and sinners." The shindig was so large that it caught the eye of the "scribes of the Pharisees" who would never dine with a group like that. They interrogate Jesus's disciples, asking, "Why is He eating and drinking with tax collectors and sinners?" (Mark 3:16).

Jesus's Answer

While the disciples were asked the question, Jesus is who answers it. His answer is simple, succinct, and powerful: "It is not those who are healthy who need a physician, but those who are sick; I did not come to call the righteous, but sinners" (Mark 2:17).

Jesus has a clear purpose and mission in mind. He also has a specific audience; He calls sinners rather than the righteous. Hearing the call of Jesus necessitates the humility to recognize our sinful state. In the beatitudes, Jesus says, "blessed are they who hunger and thirst after righteousness" (Matt 5:6). I only hunger and thirst when I am hungry and thirsty. If I am full, I don't hunger and thirst. If I think I am full of righteousness, I won't hunger for it. If I think I am healthy, I won't seek a doctor. It's only when we recognize our sinful condition that we'll find Jesus.

This is a powerful reminder and a difficult challenge to the church. Churches are tempted to look for that happy, well-dressed, spiritual, preferably wealthy, young family that will strengthen the youth program, give you some extra Bible teachers, maybe a song leader or two, help with the budget, and can be great friends with the other young families. We see them enter and everyone crawls over themselves to meet them, welcome them gladly, and make them feel right at home. By the way, that's entirely appropriate. It's not a problem at all. We should do that.

But what we shouldn't do, is prioritize them over the sinner who stumbles into a church building with nowhere else to go. What about that man who walks in and looks like he's never stepped inside a church building before? He looks like he's struggled to keep a job, has lived a rough life, has no family, and probably won't be teaching Bible classes in the foreseeable future. Maybe he's struggled with addiction. Maybe he's struggled to find a shower. Maybe he will take constant effort and vigilance. What if always needs rides to church and help with food? What if he's always behind on his bills, and he adds nothing to the church budget, youth program, or worship and education ministries?

Isn't it a little easier to let someone like that slip away? Maybe we don't call them as much. Maybe we even feel a little bit of unspoken relief that we can relax and get comfortable again. Unlike the Pharisees who would turn their back on that sinner, Jesus specifically reaches out to him. Unlike that poor sinner, however, in this passage Jesus spends time with wealthy sinners. Tax collectors are oppressors, rather than the oppressed.

We ordinarily think of Jesus reaching out to the poor miserable wretch (which happens often), but in this scene Jesus is in the nice house with the wealthy people who cheated their way to the top. Jesus could easily be accused of playing favorites and trying to make friends with money, even if they are sinners.

Jesus tarnishes His own reputation to eat and drink with them. He is a physician. He doesn't pick and choose which sickness He will heal. Jesus intends to heal and transform the oppressed and the oppressor, the wealthy and the poor, the top and the bottom, tax collectors and prostitutes. Jesus does the exhausting, painful work of ministry.

Sometimes we must get our hands dirty even if our reputations are tarnished. Sometimes we must reach out to those in genuine need, leaving the comfort of the church building to enter the homes of sinners. Sometimes we need to find the sick, rather than waiting on them to find us. Sometimes we need to prioritize those lacking righteousness over those who are filled. As followers of Jesus, we must take our work as physicians seriously. As followers of Jesus, we must learn to love and serve without prejudice, favoritism, or partiality.

Reflection Questions

1. Why would Jesus spend time with tax collectors and sinners? Do you think Jesus had fun at these gatherings? Why would Jesus let His good name get dragged through the mud to spend time with outsiders?

2. Are you more likely to be judged because of your company or to judge someone because of their company? How often do you reach out across moral, political, and religious aisles to eat and drink with people? What does it mean, "I came not to call the righteous, but sinners"? In what ways is Jesus like a physician? In what ways are you sick?

REFLECTION 15
FASTING AND RIGHTEOUSNESS

Mark 2:18–22

His Disciples Don't Fast

THE THIRD CONFLICT is about fasting, or more accurately, the lack of fasting. Jesus's disciples are not fasting like some think they should. Who are these disciples? We've seen Him call Simon, Andrew, James, and John (Mark 1:16–20) and Levi (Mark 2:14), but many others are following Him (Mark 2:15) and the crowds keep growing.

The disciples of John and the Pharisees were in the strict habit of fasting. Luke 18:12 describes a Pharisee who fasted twice weekly. John the Baptist lived an ascetic life and apparently passed that along to his disciples, whereas Jesus did not. John the Baptist abstained from wine and food (Matt 11:18), although he'd still enjoy a fine meal of locust and honey (Mark 1:6), while Jesus ate and drank and was called a drunk and a glutton (Matt 11:19). Everyone could see they lived different lifestyles. John's disciples and the Pharisees practiced a strict lifestyle of rigorous fasting; Jesus's disciples did not.

Jesus took fasting seriously and saw the value in it

(according to Matthew and Luke). Although, interestingly, Mark never mentions Jesus fasting. Even in the wilderness for those 40 days, Mark says nothing about fasting (Mark 1:13). The Pharisees wonder, if Jesus is a spiritual leader, why doesn't He act like it? Why are His disciples less righteous than the Pharisees? Shouldn't Jesus be producing spiritually mature followers? They don't even fast. So, they ask, "Why do John's disciples and the disciples of the Pharisees fast, but your disciples do not fast?" (Mark 2:18).

Jesus's Response

Jesus responds to this with a brief little story (Mark 2:19-20). The basic point is this: the wedding is not the time to fast. While the bridegroom is with you, it's time to prepare and it's time to celebrate. It would be foolish to plan your spiritual fast for the day of the big wedding you planned. If you're the best man or maid of honor at a friend's wedding, choose a different day to fast. Jesus says the day for fasting will come later: "But the days will come when the bridegroom is taken away from them, and then they will fast in that day" (Mark 2:20).

Jesus does not deny the value of fasting; He says there is a time and a place for it. While He is ushering in the kingdom of God on earth, it's not the time. Jesus will not be around forever and when He is "taken away" (an early allusion to His destiny), the time will arrive for fasting. As Christian readers, the implication seems to be that right now is our time for fasting. If you never practice fasting perhaps you need to awaken to what time it is.

Jesus's point is made clear in two illustrations. First, judging Jesus based on preexisting molds of what you think He should be is like sewing a new patch on an old piece of clothing. You'll accidentally destroy both the new and the old. New pants often shrink when washed for the first time. If they have already shrunk, and you patch a hole in them with new, unshrunk cloth, when they are washed, the new cloth will shrink, but the old pants will not, so the patch will rip at the seams causing an even bigger hole.

Secondly, wineskins expand as the wine ferments. If the wineskins, which have already expanded, are filled with new wine, they'll expand beyond their limit. They'll burst and spill the wine and ruin the wineskin. Make sure you put the new wine in new wineskins.

Something New is Here

Observing this section, it makes me wonder if there is an intentional chiastic structure to these five conflict stories. A chiasm is a literary device using a specific pattern of repetitions in the way a story is told. Usually, the beginning and the end of a story mirror each other in some way. Then the second part of the story will mirror the second to last part of the story. And they build towards the middle. For example, in these five conflict stories, the first and last story contain a miracle of healing. The second and fourth conflicts are about eating (eating with sinners and eating grain on the Sabbath). The middle story is about fasting and the arrival of something new. There are different patterns of chiasms that can be found, but for this section of Mark it will look like this:

A. Jesus heals a paralyzed man.
B. Jesus eats with sinners.
C. The disciples don't fast because something new is here.
B. The disciples eat on Sabbath.
A. Jesus heals a man with a withered hand.

If this style is intentional, the chiasm is designed to bring your attention uniquely to this middle story, where we find the main principle. This may serve as the primary interpretive principle for all five conflicts. The point is that Jesus is doing something new, rather than something old. You cannot fit Jesus or His ministry or His kingdom into any pre-existing paradigms. Forget what you thought you knew about forgiveness, fellowship, acts of piety like fasting, and Sabbath Day (the last two conflicts), Jesus is the new paradigm. Jesus provides a new lens through which to see the world and answer all these questions.

This central conflict is key to understanding the other conflicts. It is key to understanding the problem Jesus faces throughout the entire Gospel of Mark. His opponents are trying to box Him in and judge Him based on preconceived notions of what they were expecting. Their old expectations of the Messiah and the kingdom of God are blinding them to the new, amazing, world transforming events happening in front of them.

Some have open eyes and see the new taking place. They follow Jesus and say things like: "What is this? A new teaching with authority!" (Mark 1:27) or "We have never seen anything like this!" (Mark 2:12). That's right, you have never seen anything like this. This is a new teaching. This is a new authority. The world is changing and it's time to get out of the way, stop trying to control it, and hop on board ready to see and follow wherever it goes.

Reflection Questions

1. Do you ever fast? Does your church ever fast? Does Jesus expect us to fast? What are some potential benefits of fasting? How can fasting help you

remember the poor and be more generous? How can
fasting make you more thankful?

2. In what ways are the teachings of Jesus new? In what
   ways are the teachings of Jesus ancient? How does
   the "new piece and cloth" and the "new wine"
   symbolically represent the ministry of Jesus? How
   can we make sure we are ready to receive it as "new
   wineskins"?

REFLECTION 16

BREAKING SABBATH AND EATING GRAIN

Mark 2:23–28

The Importance of Sabbath

THE FINAL TWO conflicts concern Sabbath regulations. Sabbath was a big deal. In the Bible, the sanctity of Sabbath originates long before Judaism, all the way back at creation: "Then God blessed the seventh day and sanctified it, because in it He rested from all His work which God had created and made" (Gen 2:3). Before Abraham was called, Israel became a nation, or the 10 commandments were given, the Sabbath was set apart by God and made special and significant. In fact, rather than humanity being the climax of the creation week, all things build to Sabbath.

Part of the purpose of the Sabbath day was to imitate God. God rested on the seventh day, and He instructed His people to as well. Why? There are numerous benefits to Sabbath that God wanted to share with His people. For one, it is a reminder that life is not all about work and toil. As Americans we can benefit from this lesson. We take so much pride in our work ethic. There's a running competition about who works the most and is the most exhausted. When one person describes how hard he's been working, another jumps in to show how his life is even harder. We certainly don't want people thinking we're lazy, so we work and toil and labor and our spouses and children and peace are all neglected. God warns us against falling into that trap. There is more to life than work.

Sabbath is also a reminder that there is more to life than money. If you worked on that 7th day, you could provide even more money for your household, build bigger barns, and get a little more security for the future. But it would never be enough. You'd still work for more, crave more, and strive for more. God wants us to be content and trust in Him, so He mandates from the beginning, to set aside time for not making money. Set aside time to remember and reflect on the good things God has provided and then enjoy them. Experience contented peace and rest with God.

Perhaps most important, however, is that Sabbath is the great equalizer. Sabbath keeps justice in the land. No matter how wealthy or important you are, or how poor or wretched, Sabbath is for you. In the bitter misery of Egyptian slavery, the Israelites were denied Sabbath. God wants Israel to remember that misery and never deny Sabbath to anyone else again. Every human deserves rest.

In Deuteronomy's retelling of the 10 commandments, Moses details the reasoning for Sabbath:

> the seventh day is a sabbath of the LORD your God; in it you shall not do any work, you or your son or your daughter or your male servant or your female servant or your ox or your donkey or any of your cattle or the sojourner who stays with you, *so that your male servant and your female servant may rest as well as you.* You shall remember that *you were a slave* in the land of Egypt, and the LORD your God brought you out of there by a mighty hand and by an outstretched arm; *therefore*

the LORD your God commanded you to observe the sabbath day
(Deut 5:14–16).

Sabbath was a gift for Israel, their servants, their sojourners, and even their animals.

At times, the joy and peace of Sabbath became a burden. People tend to prefer money to rest. Some couldn't wait for Sabbath to end and work and wealth to begin again: "Hear this, you who trample the needy, to do away with the humble of the land, saying, 'When will the new moon be over, So that we may sell grain, And the sabbath, that we may open the wheat market ...'" (Amos 8:4–5). Greed caused them to hate Sabbath. Sabbath matters because everyone matters. Sabbath matters because justice matters. God was determined to make Israel a Sabbath people, a people of justice, equality, fairness, peace, and rest. Sabbath was a call for Israel to imitate and enjoy God.

Sabbath Traditions

The Pharisees were serious about Sabbath. They knew how important Sabbath was to God and how important it was for Israel. They were scrupulous and meticulous to make sure Sabbath was not violated in any possible way. As life in Israel continued after Moses, it's easy to imagine how many disputes arose concerning Sabbath: "What exactly counts as 'rest' and 'work'? If I bring a book to my neighbor on Sabbath, does that count as work? What if he lives uphill and I break a sweat on the way? Does any physical exertion count as work? Am I really resting if I visit my neighbor?"

Answers to these, and millions of other questions, were intentionally and particularly parsed out over the years. Sabbath developed countless traditions associated with it. This was probably done with good and honest intentions, but the intention of Sabbath was sometimes left behind.

In the Old Testament you can find some specific Sabbath violations:

1. Cooking (Exod 16:23)
2. Plowing and harvesting (Exod 34:21)
3. Gathering wood and kindling fire (Num 15:32; Exod 35:3)
4. Carrying loads into/out of Jerusalem for selling in the marketplace (Jer 17:19ff; Neh 13:15ff).

Notice that helping someone in need, feeding the hungry, or healing isn't listed above. Sabbath was certainly never intended to keep you from loving your neighbor.

Breaking Sabbath?

The next conflict in Mark happens on Sabbath Day while Jesus and His disciples walked through a grain field. One of the laws in Torah, for the benefit the poor and hungry, was to leave the borders of your property unharvested, so that the needy could come by and eat from your field (Lev 19:9–10; 23:22).

You were supposed to share your harvest. As the hungry disciples walked through a field, they picked a few heads of grain and ate. This is what Deuteronomy 23:24–25 is specifically allowing. You can eat grapes from your neighbor's vineyard and handpick grain from your neighbor's field (just don't bring tools or fill up buckets to take home). This is a perfectly legitimate action six days of the week. What about the seventh?

The Pharisees don't think so. They say to Jesus, "Look, why are they doing what is not lawful on the Sabbath?" (Mark 2:24). Could this technically be considered harvesting? I suppose so if you want to be stingy, which apparently these Pharisees do. They are just looking to pick a fight with Jesus. They are trying to find fault in any way possible. So, they find fault with, not

Jesus, but His disciples hand picking some grain on the Sabbath.

Jesus gives three quick responses to their accusation. The first comes from I Samuel 21:1–6 when David and his men were hungry and needed food. They meet up with a priest named Ahimelech ("in the time of Abiathar" in Mark) but he has no bread for them. He only has the consecrated bread for the priests from the table of presence. It is clearly unlawful for David or his men to eat this bread (Lev 24:5–9), but they were desperate, hungry, and ate it anyway. David, God's anointed, and his men were in need (Mark 2:25), so they ignored a technicality in the Law of Moses.

David was probably given a special privilege because he was David. He was hungry and the priest had bread. That bread is technically only for the priests, but certainly the purpose of that law is not to deny food to the hungry. A situation arose where feeding the hungry and caring for the Lord's anointed was more important than following protocol. So technically, yes, they did something unlawful, but the intention of the law was not broken and a greater law, "love your neighbor as yourself" was followed. Even though David acted unlawfully, the Pharisees still revere him and consider him a great king and man of God. Jesus, the Anointed Messiah, and His disciples are given no such grace.

The second response comes by pointing out the intention of the Sabbath: "The Sabbath was made for man, and not man for the Sabbath" (Mark 2:27). Remember, the Sabbath was intended to be a blessing, not a burden. It was a reminder of rest, freedom from slavery, justice, and equality for everyone. It was given to bless Israel, their servants, their animals, and their land. It was a time of peace and joyful fellowship with God the Redeemer. It was a reminder that life is not about work, money, or fancy cars, but peace with God.

Sabbath was certainly not designed to turn people against

each other, critiquing, criticizing, and condemning others over minor (questionable) transgressions. There is nothing in the texts about Sabbath that would indicate some hungry men couldn't pick a head of grain as they walked through a field. Should they have grabbed tools and spent the day harvesting and storing up grain for the future? Obviously, no. But they didn't do that. They simply grabbed some food. Sabbath was made to bless you, not keep you hungry and weighed down with unreasonable burdens. It was made for you; you were not made for it.

Finally, Jesus's third response is that "the Son of Man is Lord even of the Sabbath" (Mark 2:28). This passage, like Mark 2:10, ascribes to the Son of Man authority that only belongs to God. What mere man could be Lord of Sabbath? The Son of Man, from Daniel 7, not only receives a kingdom and shares the throne room with God, but according to Mark 2, He can forgive sins and is Lord of the Sabbath. The promise of God returning to His people is happening in Jesus Christ (Mark 1:3; Isa 40:3; 52:8). When we go back and read about Sabbath, even back in Genesis 2:3, perhaps we ought to begin seeing the Son of Man in those passages. He is the ruler and master of the Sabbath Day. Instead of criticizing Him for not following Sabbath our way, perhaps we should learn from Him and start following Sabbath His way.

Reflection Questions

1. What are some ways we might miss the intention and purpose of God's teaching? How was Sabbath being misunderstood? How might we turn God's blessings into burdens? What can we do to make sure this does not happen?
2. Do you practice any form of Sabbath in your own

life? Is it still important to take time to stop working and take time for rest? Do we make sure others can experience rest also? How often do you spend quality time with family and loved ones? Does Jesus call us to abandon Sabbath or enter into Sabbath?

REFLECTION 17
TO KILL OR SAVE?

Mark 3:1–6

When Jesus Gets Angry

THIS SCENE IS AGAIN SET on the Sabbath Day. Everything about Sabbath noted in the previous reflection still applies. Jesus enters a synagogue and sees a man with a withered hand. Others are watching also. They are watching Jesus, not to see Him perform some miraculous act of mercy or kindness, not to worship Him or learn from Him, but to accuse Him. Jesus is fully aware of their hearts, and He decides to challenge them.

He calls the man up in front of everyone and starts asking some questions. The scribes and Pharisees have asked their questions (Mark 2:7, 16, 18, 24), now it's Jesus's turn: "Is it lawful to do good or to do harm on the Sabbath, to save a life or to kill?" (Mark 3:4).

The answer to this question is simple. Every person there should be able to answer it. "Well, Jesus, obviously, it's lawful to do good and to save life, not to do harm and kill." Boom. That's the answer. That's all they had to say. Easy question with a simple answer. They don't say it. They cannot answer. They are experts on the Law and care deeply about Sabbath, but they kept silent, and Jesus gets angry (Mark 3:5).

Why couldn't they answer that question? Their problems with Jesus have escalated to the point that they cannot think properly about Scripture. Sabbath has become a weapon against Jesus. Remember, Sabbath was never intended to keep you from helping someone. Sabbath was not to be used as a trap. Sabbath was never about ignoring a man with a withered hand, but the Pharisees cannot see that now. Hatred has a way of blinding us and hardening our hearts.

The word translated "anger" (ὀργῆς) in Mark 3:5 is rarely used about Jesus. It's not used when He flips the tables in the temple, or when Peter denies Him, or when He's mocked, beaten, and crucified. Jesus doesn't get angry when He is being mistreated, but when spiritual leaders don't care about their people, when they neglect and ignore a man in need, or use him as a prop in some sick vendetta, Jesus gets angry. When men are so hard-hearted that they'd rather see their Sabbath tradition upheld, than a person in need be healed, Jesus gets angry. When adherence to custom is placed above love for one another, Jesus gets angry.

Then Jesus lashes out in His anger. Most of the time when someone lashes out in anger, people get cursed or punched or something bad, hurtful, or violent happens. When Jesus lashes out in anger, somebody gets healed. This passage shows how deeply Jesus cares about those in need. It shows that Jesus gets angry at injustice and hard hearts.

Save a Life or Kill?

Remarkably, this passage also shows us that to Jesus, ignoring and walking past a man in need is the same as "harming" or "killing." Think about it, Jesus asks, "Is it lawful on the Sabbath to do good or to do harm, to save life or to kill?" (Mark 3:4).

Who said anything about harming or killing anyone? The Pharisees don't want Jesus to harm or kill the man with a withered hand, they want Jesus to ignore him. At least for a day. Just wait 24 hours and heal him tomorrow.

Jesus doesn't see that as an option. For Jesus, to ignore those you could help, is to harm them. When we care more about our extra food, second cloak, and bigger barns than feeding the hungry, clothing the naked, and helping the poor, we contribute to their pain and suffering. We are not bystanders but perpetrators. Jesus will not ignore this man. He will not neglect, harm, or kill. He will save.

One time I heard someone make a fascinating connection between this passage and an account in 1 Maccabees 2:29–48. In 1 Maccabees 2, Israel, while being attacked on the Sabbath Day, refused to fight. They choose to die rather than violate Sabbath. This is honorable and noble, but also unsustainable. Opposing armies could always just wait until Sabbath to attack and there would be nothing you could do. The Jews recognize that if they all died and lost the war, they couldn't keep Sabbath anyway. They had to fight on Sabbath to protect Sabbath!

They decided that, to protect the people and honor the name of God, they must fight on the Sabbath. When Jesus asks if it is lawful to save life or to kill on Sabbath, I wonder if anyone thought about this Sabbath exception. This is an instance where Israel decided it was lawful to kill on Sabbath. If the need is big enough, they can wage war, fight, and kill on the Sabbath.

When is the need big enough to save on the Sabbath? This is the question they cannot answer. They do not think the man with the withered hand is important enough to be healed on Sabbath. They'd rather follow their customs no matter who suffers from them.

Why Heal on the Sabbath?

The fact that Jesus so often heals on the Sabbath, rather than waiting until the next day, suggests two important truths. The first is that Jesus cares. He really cares and doesn't want to see anyone suffer one more day than necessary. The second is that Jesus uses tension to create teaching opportunities and to test hearts. If Jesus heals somebody, but it's on the Sabbath, now you have a choice to make. Will you marvel at the gracious act of miraculous deliverance? Or condemn Him for breaking the Sabbath? When Jesus casts out demons, will you marvel at His authority over the forces of darkness, or say "He casts out demons by the ruler of the demons"? Healing on Sabbath, speaking in parables, casting out demons are all ways that Jesus tests the hearts of those around Him. He sees who is sincere, who has ears to hear, and who is blind.

Jesus tests to see who really cares about people, the kingdom of God, and authority from on high. He also sees who really cares about Sabbath. Jesus did not come to destroy or abolish Sabbath. Jesus isn't making Sabbath less important, but more important. As followers of Jesus, we live every day like Sabbath, like Jubilee. We celebrate peace with God, we demand justice for all, we rejoice in our freedom from slavery, we help the poor and needy, and we remember that money is not what life is all about. We live daily the message of Sabbath because when we follow Jesus, we are following the "Lord of Sabbath." He's not Lord of Sabbath because Sabbath is unimportant, but because Sabbath is intensely important, and the glories of Sabbath are taking over God's world.

The man Jesus healed will always remember that Sabbath day. Maybe every Sabbath day thereafter will be a reminder of God's healing and grace to him through Jesus. God's love was seen, Jesus's authority was experienced, a man was delivered from suffering, and maybe that's what Sabbath is all about.

Reflection Questions

1. What makes Jesus angry? How did Jesus respond to anger? What makes you angry? How do you respond to anger? When are some appropriate times for anger? Is this possible to harmonize with Matthew 5:21–22?
2. How might we also interpret God's word for our convenience? In what ways do we make exceptions to "kill on the Sabbath" but not to "heal on the Sabbath"? How important is helping people? Are there any commands we should put above helping, loving, and service others?

REFLECTION 18

THE KINGDOM GROWS AS A HOUSE DIVIDES

Mark 3:13–35

Jesus's Family

WE REFERRED to this passage earlier when we were discussing the "Markan Sandwich" literary device. If you read Mark 3:20–21 and then skip down to finish verses 31-35, you'll get a brief coherent story concerning Jesus and His family. While Jesus is home (Mark 3:20) the crowd gathers again. The crowd is present at the beginning (Mark 3:20) and end (Mark 3:32) of this sandwich. Also present are Jesus's "own people" (Mark 3:21) or "his family" (ESV, NRSV, and NIV) who, at the end of the sandwich, are called "His mother and His brothers" (Mark 3:31).

They think Jesus has "lost His senses" (Mark 3:21) and they come to "take custody" of Him. The word translated "to take custody" or "to seize" is κρατῆσαι. It is used in Mark 6:17 to describe John the Baptist's arrest and in Mark 12:12; 14:1, 44, 46, 49 of the arrest of Jesus. It's also used for that naked guy in Mark 14:51. Jesus's family wants to "arrest" Him, to grab Him and stop His ministry because He has lost His mind.

Jesus's family is presented rather negatively in this passage. They are contrasted with those who do the will of God (Mark 3:31–35). His family is struggling with His ministry. I suppose that makes sense. The religious leaders of the day are saying Jesus is influenced by evil spiritual beings. The most trusted spiritual authorities in all the land think He is in cahoots with the ruler of the demons (Mark 3:22). Their words have influence.

Plus, Jesus has not been acting like a typical firstborn son. He has not taken a wife and He's neglecting the family business. He left His family home, spends His time with 12 strange men, and is constantly causing friction with the leaders of Israel. Rumor has it, He carouses with drunks and sinners, breaks Sabbath repeatedly, and may even have committed blasphemy (Mark 2).

Trying to place myself in the shoes of His family, I understand their struggle. His brothers clearly don't believe in Him (John 7:5). It would be upsetting to see your brother take off on some itinerant mission and leave the family behind, especially when everything He does shines a negative light on your household and destroys your reputation.

Even Mary is struggling with Jesus. Joseph is not mentioned anywhere and many suspect he died earlier in Jesus's life. Mary was probably a relatively young widow, maybe in her mid-40s. She has at least five sons and two daughters (Mark 6:3) with the firstborn being about 30. Jesus, the oldest son, would be expected to work and support his mother and family. Instead, He embarks on a life of poverty and conflict. That must be hard and confusing. Surely, she remembers His miraculous birth and the vision from the angel 30 years earlier (Luke 1:26–38; but not mentioned in Mark). She's seen Him perform miracles (John 2:1–10). She must remember and trust and have faith, but even the most faithful can be tested, and doubt, and struggle.

You could definitely imagine Mary thinking: "Why did He have to leave now? Why is He so controversial? Why do they say He is in league with demons? Why are they saying such horrible things about Him? Why are there so many horrifying rumors? Do people really want to kill Him? He's my Son; I just want to make sure He's okay. I want to make sure He's not in over His head or mixed up in anything dangerous. Let's just get Him back home."

Maybe Mary only wants to take Him away from the crowds and the controversy and the craziness. Maybe she wants to learn more about what He was doing from His own lips. This is her Son; her special, miraculous, firstborn Son. She's probably worried sick about Him and wants to help Him through whatever is going on in His life. In Mark 3 we may have a concerned, loving, mother wanting to save her Son.

Jesus and the Demons

After Jesus's family is introduced, we run into another conflict story (just add it to the list that started back in Mark 2). Jesus has cast out many demons by this point and it must be explained somehow. Certain scribes come from Jerusalem (Mark 3:22), perhaps sent by the Sanhedrin, to investigate the radical Rabbi in Galilee.

There is a certain logic to their accusation if you grant their primary premise. The primary premise is that Jesus is a sinner. He breaks Sabbath, spends His time with drunks, and blasphemes! He is obviously not on the side of the Pharisees, Torah, Moses, or God. He is dangerous and leads people astray, but He also keeps casting out demons. He also heals. How can He do it?

If Jesus is a sinner, His power certainly isn't from God. God wouldn't bless a sinner with these miracles. So, the power must come from some other source. What source, other than God, has power over nature, demons, and spiritual forces of darkness? The ruler of the spiritual forces of darkness! This is the only other answer I can think of. This is the only answer that cures their cognitive dissonance. Since Satan is in charge of the demons, he can send them wherever He wants. Jesus surely got His powers from Satan!

The name "Beelzebul" (Mark 3:22) likely derives from a pagan Canaanite god, Ba'al, who later came to be associated with the ruler of demons and Satan himself. The pagan gods surrounding Israel and their idols were usually considered to represent real demons and evil spiritual beings (Deut 32:17; 1 Cor 10:20–21). In the mind of many Israelites, these gods were not "non-existent" but were demons who sometimes really did exercise power (like those Egyptian sorcerers in Exodus). Jesus must be worshipping those gods/demons and getting his power from them. This is how He can sin, break Sabbath, and blaspheme, but still do miracles and have authority over demons.

There are some huge problems with this theory. For starters, the first premise is wrong. Jesus is not a sinner and has not blasphemed or broken Sabbath (in any way that violates the original intention of Sabbath). And secondly, the idea that He gets His powers from Satan ignores that He has been working against Satan. He has not been sending demons into people but casting them out. Jesus is cleaning the world of demonic wickedness and clearing the path for the kingdom of God. Jesus is not fighting for Satan, but directly and obviously against Him.

Therefore, Jesus argues,

> How can Satan cast out Satan? If a kingdom is divided against itself, that kingdom cannot stand. And if a house is divided against itself, that house will not be able to stand. And if

Satan has risen up against himself and is divided, he cannot stand, but is coming to an end. But no one can enter a strong man's house and plunder his goods, unless he first binds the strong man. Then indeed he may plunder his house (Mark 3:23–37).

When Jesus casts out demons, it is not evidence that He is working with Satan, but that He is Satan's even stronger adversary. Satan is the "strong man" with many possessions (people with unclean spirits), but Jesus is stronger. He bound Satan and is plundering him. Jesus is overpowering and demolishing the work of Satan and putting an end to the devil himself. Jesus's words give us reason to celebrate that God is taking over this world and Satan is finding less room to work. Just when Satan takes ownership of somebody, he is bound, and his possession is set free.

Jesus's True Family

As this passage concludes, Jesus's mother and brothers arrive outside the house and call for Him. He doesn't go. He stays with His followers and teaches them about family. Jesus redefines family to be those who obey God, rather than those who share blood (Mark 3:35).

Later in Mark, Jesus will say,

There is no one who has left house or brothers or sisters or mother or father or children or lands, for my sake and for the gospel, who will not receive a hundredfold now in this time, houses and brothers and sisters and mothers and children and lands, with persecutions, and in the age to come eternal life. But many who are first will be last, and the last first (Mark 10:29–31).

There may be times that living for the kingdom disturbs and disrupts your family life, but Jesus offers a truer and larger family among the people of God.

This whole "sandwich" deals with loyalty and division within kingdoms and families. Division destroys kingdoms and houses. This is true in both kingdoms of the earth and the kingdom of God; this is true in our flesh and blood families and the family of God. When Jesus redefines family and kingdom to be God's reign and those who live within His reign ("do His will"), it changes the way we read His words: "If a kingdom is divided against itself, that kingdom cannot stand. And if a house is divided against itself, that house will not be able to stand" (Mark 3:24–25). Just as Satan cannot be divided against Satan, so the family of God cannot be divided against itself.

This passage (Mark 3:21–35), when taken as a sandwich, becomes a call to obedience and unity for the family of God. Jesus's earthly family was divided, but His kingdom family is not. The concluding sentence of the story becomes our interpretive key. By redefining His family as "whoever does the will of God" (Mark 3:35), the lens shifts away from Jesus's divided house, away from Satan and the demonic, and away from the scribes' accusations, to the spiritual household of God. Unity is essential for any kingdom and any household, especially God's.

Reflection Questions

1. How important is unity in the family? How important is unity in the kingdom? Has Jesus ever caused strife in your family relationships? Has there ever been strife within your church family? What can you do to work towards unity? How is the church like a family?

2. Why would some discredit the exorcisms of Jesus? Why would the scribes be threatened by the authority of Jesus? Why would Jesus's ministry be so hard on His family? Why would Mary be confused about what Jesus is doing?

REFLECTION 19
UNFORGIVABLE SIN

Hard Hearts

IMAGINE BEING SO blind you attribute Jesus's miracles and exorcisms to Satan. This is the pinnacle of a hard heart. The miracles and exorcisms of Jesus function similarly to His parables. His parables divide honest seekers from those who have ears but don't hear. One story could elicit two starkly different reactions. Similarly, the miracles can either cause you to rejoice and worship or grow angry and bitter. The scribes could not deny the miracles, but they could deny the source and goodness of it.

They thought Jesus was a blasphemer and through their malice and blindness, they became the blasphemers. God is usually willing to forgive blasphemy. If you blaspheme the sons of men, He will forgive, but blasphemy against the Holy Spirit is an eternal sin that is never forgiven (Mark 3:28–30). Wow. That's a really hard statement, and I'm not sure exactly what to do with it. So, let's discuss it.

Jesus begins this statement in verse 28 with the word "Truly" (or "Verily" if you prefer the KJV). This is a Greek word that virtually everybody knows. It's the word Ἀμὴν or, in

English, *Amen*. This word is traditionally used at the end of a sentence or prayer. Jesus is unparalleled in ancient Judaism by using it to introduce, rather than conclude, His words. This reversal of linguistic norms is a strategy to ensure the importance of what follows is not missed. It tells us to listen up because something important is coming. So, whatever we do with this statement, we better not ignore it.

What is an Eternal Sin?

What does Jesus mean? Is there really an eternal sin that God will never forgive? That's hard to fathom. God is repeatedly, shockingly, overwhelmingly forgiving throughout the Bible. Let's look at a few common attempts to make sense of this passage.

i. Hypothetical Sin: Some suppose this may be more of a hypothetical statement, than an actual legal decree. What I mean is, there were certain sins that leaders in Israel deemed "unforgivable." There were certain sins that received swift and decisive punishment (like the death sentence) rather than forgiveness. In Israel, there were capital sins.

In his commentary on Mark, William Lane draws a parallel between the "unforgivable sin" and a passage in the Jewish writings known as Sifre, which says: "The Holy One, blessed be he, pardons everything else, but on profanation of the Name [i.e. blasphemy] he takes vengeance immediately" (Sifre, on Deut 32:38 [end]).[1] This passage describes blaspheming the name of God as met with vengeance rather than pardon.

With this idea in mind, some think Jesus is saying something like, "If you believe that blasphemy against God is an unforgivable sin, then you are the ones guilty of it! If you link the Holy Spirit to Satan, you have committed the ultimate blasphemy, the ultimate 'unforgivable sin.'" If this is the case, Jesus may not be making a decree about literal unforgivable sins, but illustrating the hypocrisy of the Jerusalem scribes: "If you scribes believe in unforgivable sins, then you are the ones guilty of them!"

2. *Specific Sin:* Another interpretation emphasizes the historical situation in which this one specific sin occurred. It may be that the only way to blaspheme the Holy Spirit is with this exact specific sin. Meaning, to commit this sin, Jesus must appear before you and cast out a demon, and you must attribute that exorcism to Satan. That one sin is the eternal sin of blaspheming the Holy Spirit.

3. *Heart Condition:* Another explanation is to emphasize the heart of the scribes. Their hearts were so hard, they became unforgivable. Think about this: if you are so stubborn that you would reject Jesus right in front of you, even after His miracles and exorcisms, then nothing else on earth will ever convince you to repent. Nothing Jesus could say or do would ever bring you to Him; in fact, they would only drive you farther and farther away. You could reject everything and attribute it all to Satan. You could even attribute the resurrection to Satan.

This means you will never seek repentance, so you have sinned irreversibly. An eternal sin is committed when your heart becomes so hard that you will never, ever turn to God in repentance. If someone sincerely wants to repent, they must not have committed the eternal sin, because their heart isn't eternally hard. This means the "eternal sin" is not a specific sin, but a specific heart condition. Those who commit eternal sin will eternally have a hard heart.

Can We Do This Today?

There may be some truth in each of those responses, but the big uncomfortable question many have about this text is whether we can still blaspheme against the Holy Spirit and commit an eternal sin today. If today you said that Jesus had an unclean spirit or that His miracles were the work of Satan, is there no hope for you? Could you say something so rotten about God or the Holy Spirit that you are eternally sealed for damnation even if you sincerely wanted to repent?

When I've been asked that question, my answer is to always trust in the goodness and forgiveness of God and repent if you know you should. That is never the wrong thing to do.

I do not believe there is anyone who desperately longs for forgiveness and repents and proclaims and submits to the Lordship of Jesus, who God will reject because of a foolish statement made earlier in life. I wonder if Paul ever discredited the miracles of Jesus when He was a "blasphemer, persecutor, and insolent opponent" (1 Timothy 1:13)? I bet he did, and I know God forgave him. If you have a sincere heart that truly longs for God, God knows that. To borrow the "hard heart" interpretation, this may be an eternal sin because they made an eternal decision to reject Jesus. To eternally reject Jesus, is an eternal sin. If you want Jesus and approach God for forgiveness, you have not committed an eternal sin. I believe there is always hope with God.

Let me end with this word of caution: be extremely careful what you say and what you close your mind to. I believe there are people so hardened that nothing will ever cause them to turn to God. I've heard of people who wanted witnesses at their deathbed to prove that they died rejecting God to the end. There are people unconvinced by Jesus's miracles and exorcisms, they don't believe Moses and the prophets, and "neither will they be convinced if someone should rise from the dead" (Luke 16:30). They are so hardened that nothing will change them.

We have the potential to delude ourselves, sear our consciences, and foolishly live in our own pride and blind wisdom. We can find ourselves so distant that we never want to come back, so blind that we never truly see again, and so hardened that our hearts will never soften to the will of God. We may reach a point where we never return, not because God won't let us or wouldn't forgive us, but because in our sinful arrogance we constantly grow more resentful and bolder in our rejection of God so that even the Holy Spirit becomes indistinguishable from Satan. Be sure you do not start down that path. It's frightening, dangerous, and damning.

Reflection Questions

1. What is an "eternal sin"? Is there such a thing as a "point of no return"? Does God keep anyone from repenting? Can a person reach a point where nothing will ever cause them to repent? What can you do to make sure you do not go down this dangerous path?
2. What are some of the most surprising and encouraging examples of repentance in the Bible? Are there examples from your own life and experiences of someone repenting that you never thought would? Should the church ever assume someone is incapable of repentance? When will God stop wanting to forgive?

Endnotes

1. William L. Lane, *The Gospel according to Mark: The English Text with Introduction, Exposition, and Notes* (Grand Rapids: Eerdmans, 1974), 97.

REFLECTION 20

"ON THE SOIL"

Mark 4:1–34

"On the Soil"

AS MARK CONTINUES, the crowd reappears and has become "very large" (Mark 4:1). The crowd is so large that Jesus must enter a boat to create a little distance so He can teach them (see Mark 3:9; 4:1). It's important that Jesus is teaching them from a boat while they remain "by the sea on the land" (Mark 4:1). "On the land" is an interesting little description. It seems unnecessary. I mean, where else would they be? I think this phrase may be added for a specific illustrative purpose, which we will now explore.

In Mark 4, Jesus gives three parables about seed and soil. One parable describes a sower who throws seed on four different kinds of soil, each providing a different environment for the seed, with only one, "the good soil," producing fruit. The second parable is about seed sown "on the soil" by a man who then goes to sleep. While he is sleeping, without his knowledge, the seed sprouts and the soil produces a crop. The third parable is about a mustard seed which is thrown "on the soil," and though the seed is tiny, it produces the largest plant in the garden. These three parables are all connected by the "seed" which is thrown "on the soil."

The reason I think Mark intentionally locates Jesus's listeners as "on the land" (ἐπὶ τῆς γῆς) is because that same phrase pops up in each of these parables. The word "soil" and the word "land" are the same Greek word (γῆς). Some English Bibles translate Mark 4:1 with the phrase "along the shore" (NIV), so it's easy to miss, but literally the people are standing "on the soil" while Jesus preaches about seed landing "on the soil."

The phrase ("on the soil" or ἐπὶ τῆς γῆς) appears in Mark 4:1, 8, 20 (Verses 8 and 20 add the adjective "good" to describe the soil), 26, and 31 (twice). It's the key phrase in this chapter; it's no accident that these parables are introduced and spoken to people "on the soil." The audience of Jesus, by standing on the soil, become active participants in His parables. They are the main point in the parables.

If "sowing the seed on the soil" represents bringing the "word" of God to people (Mark 4:14–20; 33–34; see also Mark 2:2; 7:13; 8:38; 13:31), Jesus fulfills the role of the one sowing the seed. He brings the word/seed to those "on the soil" and each parable is about what the soil does with the word. Each listener must ask, "What am I doing with this seed and on what soil am I standing?"

The Purpose of Jesus's Parables

In Mark 4:10–12, Jesus shockingly reverses the well-known purpose of parables. Ordinarily, parables served to clarify and simplify teaching. In Rabbinic literature, parables are commonly used this way. They appear all over the Talmud and Mishnah to aid your understanding of God. For example, read this fascinating conversation in the Talmud between Rabbi

Gamliel and a pagan philosopher about idolatry. The Rabbi uses a series of parables to answer questions and illustrate his point:

> A certain philosopher asked Rabban Gamliel: It is written in your Torah with regard to the prohibition against idol worship: "For the Lord your God is a devouring fire, a jealous God" (Deuteronomy 4:24). For what reason is He jealous and does He exact vengeance from the idol's worshippers, but He is not jealous of the idol itself and does not destroy it?
>
> Rabban Gamliel said to the philosopher: I will relate a parable to you. To what is this matter comparable? It may be compared to a king of flesh and blood who had one son, and that son was raising a dog. And the son gave the dog a name, naming him after his father. When the son would take an oath, he would say: I swear by the life of the dog, my father. When the king heard about this, with whom was the king angry? Is he angry with the son or is he angry with the dog? You must say that he is angry with the son. So too, God is angry with the worshippers who attribute divinity to objects of idol worship and not with the objects of idol worship themselves.
>
> The philosopher said to Rabban Gamliel: Do you call the idol a dog? But the idol truly exists, i.e., has power. Rabban Gamliel said to the philosopher: And what did you see that caused you to believe that the idols have power? The philosopher said to Rabban Gamliel: A fire once broke out in our city, and the entire city was burned down, but that temple of idol worship was not burned down.
>
> Rabban Gamliel said to the philosopher I will relate a parable to you. To what is this matter comparable? It may be compared to a king of flesh and blood whose province sinned against him. When he wages war, does he wage war against the living or does he wage war against the dead? You must say

that he wages war against the living. God punishes the living worshippers and not the idol, which is not alive.

The philosopher said to Rabban Gamliel: You call the idol a dog; you call the idol dead. If it is so, let God remove it from the world. Rabban Gamliel said to the philosopher: Were people worshipping only objects for which the world has no need, He would eliminate it. But they worship the sun and the moon, the stars and the constellations, and the streams and the valleys. Should He destroy His world because of fools? (Avodah Zarah.54b 18–22).

In this example, Gamliel's answers are insightful, helpful, and clear. Jesus does not claim to teach in parables this way. He instead uses parables to cloud perception and dim understanding. All His listeners have ears, not all have "ears to hear" (Mark 4:9). Jesus wants to speak in a way that confuses the hard hearted but draws sincere listeners to Him. He wants to see what kind of soil they are standing on. This takes precision to accomplish.

Seeing and Hearing

The word "hear/listen" is central to understanding Mark 4 (Mark 4:3, 9, 12, 15, 16, 18, 20, 23, 24, 33). It appears repeatedly, even more than the words "soil" and "seed." Jesus begins this set of parables with a 2nd person plural imperative, commanding everyone to "Hear!" (Ἀκούετε). This is common in the Old Testament (see Deut 6:4–6). Then He teaches in parables "as far as they were able to hear it" (Mark 4:33). He challenges His listeners, "He who has ears to hear, let him hear" (Mark 4:9, 23). The four types of soil in Mark 4:14–20 are differentiated by their response to "hearing" the word (Mark 4:15–20). Jesus calls us to be good and productive hearers.

Mark 4:24 contains a fascinating phrase: "Take care what

you listen to" (NASB) or "Pay attention to what you hear" (ESV). The Greek expression is: βλέπετε τί ἀκούετε. The first word is an imperative, meaning, "See!" Literally, it says, "See what you hear." It's often translated as "Take care" or "Pay attention," which is a fine translation, but that disguises the grammatical connection between Mark 4:24 to Mark 4:12: "They may indeed see but not perceive, and may indeed hear but not understand." Jesus speaks in parables to keep people from "seeing" and "hearing" (4:12), but then commands them to "see what you hear" (Mark 4:24). There's a paradox in the parables. Jesus wants us to "see" and "hear" and be good soil, and the parables are a test to see who will and who will not.

This mysterious and hidden teaching style is not supposed to last forever. Jesus tells His disciples:

> A lamp is not brought to be put under a basket, is it, or under a bed? Is it not brought to be put on the lampstand? For nothing is hidden, except to be revealed; nor has anything been secret, but that it would come to light. If anyone has ears to hear, let him hear (Mark 4:21–23).

These parables are not meant to always keep people blind or deaf or unrepentant (Mark 4:11–12). They are a momentary test.

Jesus does not want us being "blind" or "deaf" to His teaching. A major irony in Mark is that His chosen disciples remain blind and deaf to near everything He does. Jesus lets them in on the secrets of the parables, but they still fail to understand them. They see his miracles but do not gain insight (Mark 6:52). They have hardened hearts. Jesus finally asks them: "Do you not yet see or understand? Do you have a hardened heart? Having eyes, do you not see? And having ears, do you not hear? And do you not remember ... Do you not yet understand?"

(Mark 8:17–21). The disciples are not much better than anyone else at comprehending the cryptic Jesus.

Mark records the parables and some of their interpretations for us. He also details all the "secret" things of Jesus. Mark purposefully reveals the secrets and bringing to light what had been hidden. We receive that benefit. Let's make sure we honor it with open eyes, listening ears, and willing hearts. Let's stand on the good soil as we take in the words of Jesus.

Reflection Questions

1. What is the significance of the listeners standing "on the soil"? When you read Mark 4, what kind of soil are you on? What kind of a hearer are you? How does this connect to the unique purpose of the parables in Mark 4:11–12?

2. Why would Jesus keep the meanings of His parables secretive? How can you make sure you have "ears to hear"? Does Jesus want people to misunderstand Him? When does Jesus want the secret and hidden things to be "made manifest" and "come to light" (Mark 4:22)?

Endnotes

1. To find this translation online: https://www.sefaria.org/Avodah_Zarah. 54b.19?lang=bi&with=all&lang2=en.

REFLECTION 21
THREE SEED AND SOIL PARABLES

Mark 4:1–34

Parable of the Soils

JESUS'S first parable describes four environments on which a seed can land. The first is beside a road. Nothing grows there. Before any growth occurs, birds come and steal away the seed. The second is a rocky area where no roots can grow and firmly grip. There may be some quick rapid sprouting, but the lack of root will be the death of the plant. It is quickly scorched by the sun and withers away. The third is a thorny area. The plant can grow here, but the thorns choke it out and make it unproductive. It exists, but it serves no valuable purpose and produces no fruit. Finally, the fourth is "the good soil." Here the seed remains, takes root, and nothing chokes it out. It can grow and flourish and produce. Some produce thirty, sixty, or one hundred-fold.

Thankfully, this is a parable where Jesus explains each part. I wish He did that with more of His teachings, but this interpretation provides clues for how to understand His other parables also. This parable is about hearing and responding to the word of God.

Intentionally sandwiched in between the parable and its explanation, is a purpose statement for all the parables which we discussed some in the previous reflection. This is one of those "Markan Sandwiches" where the middle should be interpreted in light of the beginning and end. The parable of the sower (or the soils) helps us understand the overall purpose of Jesus's teachings/parables. Just as this parable speaks of good and bad soils, so the parables as a whole fall upon good and bad listeners.

Explanation of the Parable

The seed is the "word," and in this context, Jesus is the one sowing it. Later it will be His disciples, and today it should be us. Some of that seed (God's word) will land on the road (hearers), where birds (Satan) will come and snatch it away. This means some people will never respond positively to the word, even for a minute. They have ears, eyes, and hearts owned and protected by the wicked one.

The seed that falls on the rocky soil is loved and accepted. Those who received it begin to grow in it, but something quickly shifts. The persecution and affliction surrounding God's kingdom finds them. Jesus is emphatic that the blessings of the kingdom will come "along with persecutions" (Mark 10:30), that to follow Him means self-denial, carrying a cross, and death (Mark 8:34–38). Jesus, as the forerunner of the kingdom, suffers persecution, carries a cross, and dies miserably. Some will follow Him, but those on the rocky soil will smile politely, slowly back away, shaking their heads and saying, "No thanks. That's not for me."

The seed that falls in the thorny area is heard and accepted and endures. These grow and they develop roots, but those thorns in their lives constantly compete with the kingdom. Those thorns are the worries of the world, deceitfulness of riches, desires for other things (Mark 4:19). These thorns choke out the word and it never produces anything. You may see these people at church on Sunday morning. They've been baptized and regularly eat the Lord's Supper and read their Bibles, but the kingdom rarely influences their decisions. They don't sacrifice for the kingdom. They are more concerned with IRAs and 401ks, jobs, status, property, vacations, and wealth. They may hang around the kingdom their entire life, but matters of this world (politics, occupation, security, retirement) consume and worry them. They believe the lie that wealth will bring them satisfaction and peace. This is one of the major concerns about living in the "Bible Belt" or in a "Christian Culture" where Christianity fits snugly into the background of your life.

Finally, we get to that good, productive, fruitful soil. This seed takes root, endures, grows strong, and produces fruit. Not all soil produces the same amount of fruit. Some good soil produces thirty, some sixty, and some one hundred, but it's not a competition and comparison is not the point. It is one thing to accept the word of God, but it is another to obey, repent, and produce.

Jesus is not specific about what this fruit is. Even His explanation of the parable leaves the meaning of the fruit vague. So perhaps we can see diversity here. This fruit may include evangelism, service to others, and integrity in your own life and family. We know fruit is healthy and life-giving, and that is what the word can produce in us.

Parables of Mysterious and Impressive Growth

Mark 4:26–29 and Mark 4:30–32 contain two more, much shorter, parables about the kingdom. They both focus on kingdom growth but in different ways. The first story compares the kingdom of God to a man who sows seed "upon the soil" and then goes to bed. He awakes and sleeps and lives his life day after day while the seed is hard at work. It sprouts and grows and eventually produces. This man doesn't know how the seed sprouts and he certainly cannot make it sprout: "The soil produces crops by itself" (Mark 4:28). Growth is beyond his control, yet he reaps the benefits: "when the crop permits, he immediately puts in the sickle, because the harvest has come" (Mark 4:29).

The final parable begins in verse 30 where the kingdom is compared to a mustard seed. The mustard seed is "smaller than all the seeds that are upon the soil" but it "becomes larger than all the garden plants and forms large branches" (Mark 4:31–32). The growth of a mustard seed is unprecedented and remarkable. The kingdom of God, which at this point looks entirely unimpressive, especially when compared to the might and grandeur of the Roman Empire, will eventually become the largest plant in the garden.

A relatively small group of Jews following an unknown Rabbi who is easily arrested and shamefully crucified isn't the type of problem that Rome loses much sleep over. To Rome, Jesus was a small problem, and His crucifixion was a small event, but that small mustard seed grew and eventually transformed the entire world. Both in the personal life of a follower of Jesus and in the kingdom of God on a global scale, God provides growth that is both mysterious and impressive.

The branches are so large, the parable continues, that birds make homes in its shade (Mark 4:32). The language used in this description is borrowed explicitly from a promise made by God in Ezekiel 17:23. In Ezekiel's image, however, this tree is a mighty cedar planted on a mountain top. Mark borrows Ezekiel's language and in a surprise twist, substitutes a lowly mustard seed in a garden. Remarking on this twist, Richard Hays comments,

To be sure, the manner in which the fulfillment occurs is surprising, as suggested by the transformative metaphorical substitution of an inauspicious mustard seed for Ezekiel's noble cedar. That is why Jesus's hearers continue to be baffled and the message of the kingdom remains mysterious.[1]

In other words, comparing God's kingdom to a cedar makes far more sense to Jesus's hearers, especially those who catch the reference to Ezekiel 17, than comparison to a mustard seed. The cedar tree is what you expect; the mustard seed is what you get. Similarly, the kingdom being inaugurated through some powerful conquest would make far more sense than inauguration on the cross. This may be why so many became deaf and blind to His parables and the kingdom. You expect the kingdom of God is like a mighty army, or a massive cedar, or a tidal wave, but Jesus likens it to a tiny mustard seed tossed on the soil.

Taken together, these three parables offer a word of encouragement for those seeking the kingdom but not finding it. Don't look for the cedar, look for the mustard seed. It may be small and seem insignificant, but the growth will blow your mind. It's growth is not dependent upon your cleverness, rhetoric, or abilities, but on God. In fact, it may grow while you are in bed asleep. You can sleep, wake up, go outside, and be amazed at what God has done. While this happens, do not be shocked when others walk away from it; not everyone with ears has ears to hear the message of the kingdom. Satan, persecution, and the concerns of this world are all out to silence the message, but that doesn't mean the kingdom is not all around us.

We cannot make the kingdom grow. We cannot control how large it grows. We cannot predict what the kingdom will do or look like, we cannot force people to be good hearers or to produce one hundred-fold, but we can obey, follow, commit, watch, and rejoice as God remakes the world. We can work and be part of God's plans. We can enjoy the harvest when that day comes.

Reflection Questions

1. How do you know if you are on good soil? Are you a Christian? Are you bearing fruit for the kingdom? Specifically, what does that fruit look like? How often do you worry about the temporal things of this world? How much time do you spend serving/working for money? Do you agonize over politics, wealth, or status? How can these things "cares of the world" render you unfruitful in the kingdom?
2. In what ways has the kingdom unexpectedly grown more than you anticipated? Are you ever surprised at what God accomplishes? How is the parable of mysterious growth applicable to the church and ministry? What do you think the future of God's kingdom will look like?

Endnotes

1. Hays, *Echoes*, 31.

REFLECTION 22
CALMING STORMS

Mark 4:35–41

A Few Helpful Psalms

I WANT to begin this study of Mark 4:35–41 by reading a few selections from the Psalms which serve as a helpful backdrop to this story.

> Psalm 65:5–7: By awesome deeds You answer us in righteousness, O God of our salvation, You who are the trust of all the ends of the earth and of the farthest sea; Who establishes the mountains by His strength, being girded with might; *Who stills the roaring of the seas*, The roaring of the waves, And the tumult of the peoples.

> Psalm 89:8–9: O LORD God of hosts, who is like You, O mighty LORD? Your faithfulness also surrounds You. You rule the swelling of the sea; *When its waves rise, you still them.*

> Psalm 107:23–30: Those who go down to the sea in ships, Who do business on great waters; They have seen the works of the

LORD, And His wonders in the deep. For He spoke and raised up a stormy wind, Which lifted up the waves of the sea. They rose up to the heavens, they went down to the depths; Their soul melted away in their misery. They reeled and staggered like a drunken man, And were at their wits' end. Then they cried to the LORD in their trouble, And He brought them out of their distress. *He caused the storm to be still, So that the waves of the sea were hushed.*

During Creation: Psalm 104:5: He established the earth upon its foundations, So that it will not totter forever and ever. You covered it with the deep as with a garment; The waters were standing above the mountains. *At Your rebuke they fled*, at the sound of Your thunder they hurried away (See also Job 26:10–12).

During Exodus: Psalm 106:8–10: Nevertheless He saved them for the sake of His name, That He might make His power known. Thus *He rebuked the Red Sea and it dried up*, And He led them through the deeps, as through the wilderness.

In these verses, notice that God "rebuked" the water during the creation week so that the waters fled and hurried away (Day 3), and God rebuked the waters during the Exodus, so they dried up and the Israelites crossed on dry ground. The waters respond to the rebuke of God. Notice also that it is God who can "still" and "hush" storms (Ps 89:9; 107:30). It is God who rules the seas and the wind and waves obey Him.

The Sea in the Bible

In Mark 4:35–41, Jesus finished teaching His parables and evening has come. He entered a boat to travel from Galilee to the region beyond the sea. They are leaving Israelite territory.

As they sail across the sea of Galilee a terrifying storm arises on the waters and Jesus falls asleep. The waves are crashing over the sides of the boat which is being tossed around helplessly upon the violent sea.

The sea, in the Bible, is not a friendly area. The Israelites are not a water-loving people. The sea is like the liquid wilderness. Read everything the Bible says about the sea and the deep waters and you will find mostly chaos, fear, and shipwrecks. The sea is full of creatures, like Leviathan, terrible and fierce, fire-breathing, multi-headed enemies, both untamable and unimaginably dreadful. God is the only warrior mighty enough to conquer these monsters (Ps 74:12–14; Job 41:1–34; Isa 27:1).

Before Day 1 there was nothing but darkness and sea (Gen 1:2). God took control of the darkness by saying, "Let there be light." He "rebuked" the sea, saying, "Let the waters below the skies be gathered into one place, and let the dry land appear" (Gen 1:9; Ps 104:5). Old Testament scholar John Walton reminds us that in the ancient Near East, "*chaos* is the opposite of *cosmos*" and that the "primordial sea" is "the principal element of the precreation condition."[1] In other words, in Genesis 1, when God rounded up the waters so that dry land appeared, God created cosmos out of chaos.

The waters were then used to judge the world during the great flood. In the flood, the world was destroyed by water and brought back to the pre-creation state of Genesis 1:2 (see 2 Pet 3:5–7). Almost every boat story in the Bible is about storms and fear and shipwreck and death (Remember Noah, Jonah, Jesus, Paul, etc.).

It's no wonder that in the New Creation, with the new heavens and the new earth, one description is that "there is no longer any sea" (Rev 21:1). In the Bible the "sea" is like the wilderness. In Genesis 1–2, God turns the wilderness into a garden and the sea into fruitful land. The sea represents chaos, fear, monsters, and death. These themes merge together in

Mark 4 when the disciples' worst fear is realized. Fishermen would know this fear well. They are convinced that finally the sea will conquer them.

"Hush, Be Still"

While the storm rages, the sea consumes, and the disciples fear for their lives, the Lord calmly sleeps. He is at peace. Remember, it was evening and He had been walking and teaching all day; Jesus is tired. That the Lord got tired and fell asleep is a touching reminder of His humanity. Yet, while He sleeps, His people are in dire need and great distress. They woke Him and cried out: "Teacher, do You not care that we are perishing?" (Mark 5:38).

For the disciples, it seems that chaos, danger, and fear are taking over their world, death is hurtling towards them, and the Lord is unconcerned. He sleeps rather than saves. There are numerous calls in the Bible for God to "Wake up!" and save His people (Psalm 7:6; 35:22–23; 44:23–26). This is one of them ... kind of. They don't technically ask Jesus to save them. At this point they might not know that's an option. They at least want His help though. They want Him to be concerned. They are in no way prepared for what happens next.

Jesus arises and, like the Psalms say, He "rebukes" the wind and speaks to the waters, "Hush, be still." The wind and water promptly and reverently obey. The unruly sea, in an instant, becomes perfectly calm. A storm vanishes. Chaos is overcome, and cosmos is restored.

For the disciples, the fear remained even though the storm ceased (Mark 4:40–41). Fear will define the disciples (and others) throughout most of the ministry of Jesus (Mark 4:40–41; 5:15, 33, 36; 6:50-52; 9:32; 10:32; 11:18, 32; 12:12, and 16:8). "Fear" is one of the most common responses to Jesus and is a major theme in Mark's Gospel. In fact, it's what the Gospel of Mark ends with in many of the earliest copies of it (Mark 16:8). The hope is that this fear will lead you to come trembling before Jesus, to seek Him, grow closer, and turn that fear into faith. Often, however, fear leads to flight and fear leads to silence.

In fear, the disciples begin to wonder who it really is in this boat with them? They ask each other, no doubt in hushed tones, "Who then is this, that even the wind and the sea obey Him?" (Mark 4:41). Jesus does not answer. Mark does not answer. The story ends with this ambiguous question. That is why we started this study off by reading through those important passages in the Psalms. They help provide the answer. Who rebukes the wind and waves? Who hushes and stills the seas? The mysterious identity of Jesus is understood in answering those questions.

Richard Hays eloquently sums up the ramifications of the miracle thusly:

> What is unmistakably clear, however, is that Jesus's mastery over the wind and waves demonstrates that he is the possessor of a power that the Old Testament consistently assigns to the LORD God alone. It is God who rebuked the waters and formed the dry land, God who parted the sea for Israel, God who made the storm to be still.[2]

Mark began His gospel with a prophecy admonishing, "make ready the way of the Lord" (Mark 1:3). I think at this point it's safe to assume He has arrived.

Reflection Questions

1. How is Jesus calming the sea similar to Him overcoming the wilderness? How is this story another example of the Lord returning to His

people? What does this passage tell us about the
authority and power of Jesus?

2. Do you ever feel that God sleeps during the storms
   of your life? What storms has Jesus helped you
   through? In what ways can Jesus bring peace and
   calm to this world? What is the relationship
   between faith and fear?

Endnotes

1. John H. Walton, *Ancient Near Eastern Thought and the Old Testament: Introducing the Conceptual World of the Hebrew Bible* (Grand Rapids: Baker Academic, 2006), 184–185.

   2. Hays, *Echoes*, 69.

REFLECTION 23

GOODBYE LEGION

Mark 5:1–20

Jesus over Legion

UP to this point in Mark's Gospel, Jesus has taught with divine authority, healed many, and calmed storms. He also cast out demons and exercised authority over unclean spirits (Mark 1:24–27; 34; 3:11). Jesus is demonstrating the coming kingdom of God (Mark 1:14–15). So far, this has all been accomplished in Galilee. We're about to leave Israel and enter the land of the Gerasenes.

On the way to this new territory, Jesus "rebuked" the sea. Let's talk about the word "rebuke" for a minute. Earlier in Mark, Jesus "rebuked" (ἐπιτιμάω) unclean spirits (Mark 1:25 and 3:12). This same word is used when Jesus rebukes the stormy sea (Mark 4:39). This subtly connects the casting out of demons to the calming of the storm. That connection becomes sharper when you realize the verb translated "Be still" in Mark 4:39 is the same word translated as "Be silent" in Mark 1:25 (φιμόω). In both instances, Jesus uses it as an imperative.

Mark 1:25 and 4:39 are grammatically and thematically

parallel. Calming the storm was supposed to remind us of Jesus casting out demons. Jesus can rebuke and calm spiritual chaos (demons) and natural chaos (storms). Jesus has authority over the storms of life caused by demonic forces of evil in the same way that He has authority over the storms on the sea. All the world's chaos turns to peace in Jesus. You'll need to know that as we begin this next story.

Chaos Among the Gerasenes

Now that Jesus leaves the boat (on calm waters), entering a new geographical territory, He meets chaos again. Jesus has shown His power and authority over demons throughout Galilee and now it's time to show it extends even beyond the sea. Jesus is entering unclean Gentile lands. It's time to show His dominion has no borders: the wilderness, Galilee, the sea, the country of the Gerasenes, the human and demonic realms are all under His authority. As they dock in the country of the Gerasenes, Jesus is immediately challenged in new and extraordinary ways in foreign and unknown places.

This new region has tombs, swine, and a man more powerful than any we have seen so far. He comes charging up to Jesus from the tombs. This man's supernatural strength allowed him to tear apart chains and shackles. Nothing can bind him. He spent his life screaming among the dead and gashing himself with stones. He was powerful, terrifying, and completely out of his mind. He's entirely unpredictable and dangerous. Like the raging storm in the middle of the sea, this man is out of control and untamable. Who can calm, quiet, and give peace to this maniac overflowing with darkness and demons? Who can rebuke the spirits, exercise authority, and give some relief? Who can calm this storm?

This demoniac runs up to Jesus and falls down before Him. Like the other demons we've met so far, he knows exactly who

Jesus is. The disciples just witnessed the unquestionable divine power of Jesus on the sea and, in fear, asked the question, "Who then is this, that even the wind and the sea obey Him?" (Mark 4:41). This Gerasene demoniac knows the answer. He knows exactly who Jesus is, and He knows exactly what Jesus can do. He answers, saying, "Jesus, Son of the Most High God" (Mark 5:7). The disciples are slow to understand, but this raving lunatic, across the sea (in Gentile territory) recognizes Jesus instantly. He begs Jesus, by God Himself, not to torment him.

His name is Legion, and within him are many demons. Legion is an important name because it doubles as a military term in the Roman army. At the time of these events, a Roman century would have been about 100 men. A cohort would have been five centuries. And a legion would have been 10 cohorts. This would make a Roman legion about 5,000 men. This man is possessed (and oppressed) by a legion of unclean spirits. A demonic army has taken residence within him.

With unparalleled power, Jesus casts these spirits into a massive herd of swine on a nearby mountain who run down the mountain into the sea and drown. There were about 2,000 of them. Isn't it interesting how Jesus saved his disciples from drowning on the way here, but Legion meets his fate by drowning. Jesus produces peace out of chaos in both stories. Jesus demonstrates power and authority in both passages. If you ignore that chapter break, the stories of calming the sea and casting out Legion flow beautifully into one another.

For a helpful Bible study tip, in Mark, play close attention to what Jesus does while traveling. On His way to cast out Legion, He calms the storm. On His way to raise Jairus' twelve-year-old daughter, He heals a woman with a twelve year flow of blood. On His way to the temple, He curses the fig tree. On His way to Jerusalem, He predicts and describes His crucifixion and resurrection. The travel stories are often the key to interpreting what Jesus does on arrival.

What Does this Mean?

An important theme is emerging in this passage that will be developed further in later texts of Mark's Gospel. Jesus just entered Gentile territory. The term "Legion" describes a massive Gentile army. 2,000 swine, unclean animals, who often represent unclean Gentiles, were filled with a legion of unclean spirits in this unclean land. Basically, there is a lot of unclean stuff happening right here.

One of the key takeaways from this passage is that the authority of Jesus is not limited to Galilee and is not just for Israel. Gentiles will have their place in the kingdom of God. Geography and nationality cannot contain God. Like the parable of the mustard seed (the last thing Jesus taught before crossing the sea—Mark 4:30–32), the growth of the kingdom is beyond imagination. Jesus is Lord of all people, no matter what side of the sea they live.

The kingdom of God will cross the sea, overcome the spiritual forces of darkness, exercise power over Legions, and even Gentiles will hear the great works of Jesus. As those stormy waters became calm and clear, after meeting Jesus, this crazed man was "sitting down, clothed and in his right mind" (Mark 5:15). If Jesus can give peace to the storms on the sea and to this lunatic who was completely overcome by the powers of evil, Jesus can bring peace to you.

The power of Jesus once again caused fear and everyone "became frightened" (5:15; see 4:41). They are so frightened that they try to kick Jesus out of this area (Mark 5:17). They were "imploring" (παρακαλέω) Him to leave the region (Mark 5:17). The kingdom of God is always met with resistance and the peace of Jesus is often rejected. Many people would rather dwell in chaos than welcome Jesus. Many would rather live among the tombs, screaming into the night, and gashing themselves with stones, than to fall before Jesus with humility and worship. Many would rather nail Jesus to a cross than follow Him and count the cost.

But there are some, like this previously demon possessed man, who runs to Jesus "imploring (παρακαλέω) Him that he might accompany Him" (Mark 5:18). The Greek word for "implore, beg, urge, beseech" is used in verses 17 and 18 (it's also used by Legion in Mark 5:10, 12), to describe two opposing responses to Jesus. The masses begged Jesus to leave, and one man begged to follow.

Jesus didn't let him follow. Instead, Jesus sent him on a mission. Mark 5:19 is the first time in Mark that Jesus sends someone to go speak about Him. Jesus responds, "Go home to your people and report to them what great things the Lord has done for you, and how He had mercy on you." Normally, Jesus tells people to remain silent. In fact, He does it later in this same chapter (Mark 5:43). In this foreign land, however, Jesus commands for the news to spread. Perhaps Jesus is preparing the soil in this region as a future mission field. Perhaps He is demonstrating that even Gentiles can come to faith.

To conclude, it's important to see what happens in Mark 5:19–20. Jesus sends this man home to report "what great things the Lord has done" (Mark 5:19). When the man does this, he proclaims "what great things Jesus had done" (Mark 5:20). Jesus is the Lord who has done great things. Again, Mark begins with a call to "prepare the way of the Lord" (Mark 1:3) and repeatedly demonstrates that through Jesus, the Lord has arrived.

And the Lord comes with an important message: there is no man, storm, army, legion, geography, unclean spirit, or force of evil in this world Jesus cannot overcome. Jesus can bring peace to chaos, order to disarray, a right mind to the maniac, and calm to the raging waters. This was demonstrated 2,000 years ago, and it is just as true today. The kingdom of God continues to reach new areas, overcome obstacles, conquer forces of darkness, save people's lives, and set the world right. The kingdom still brings peace through the unstoppable mission of Jesus.

Reflection Questions

1. How does geography impact the interpretation of this story? How does the casting out of Legion relate to the calming of the storm? How does the word Legion relate to the Roman Empire and military? Why are "pigs" a good resting place for Legion? How is the authority of Jesus demonstrated in this passage?
2. What is the significance of the contrast between Jesus saving His disciples on the sea and the pigs drowning in the sea? What is significant about the demon-possessed man's strength? What is significant about the fact that he lived among the tombs? Why did this man "fall down before" Jesus?

REFLECTION 24
TWO DAUGHTERS

Mark 5:21–43

Daughters in Need

JESUS DOESN'T STAY in Gentile territory long (but He'll be back in Mark 7). He soon returns to Galilee and is met by another crowd (Mark 5:21). A man from the crowd named Jairus, a synagogue official, runs up to Jesus and falls at His feet (compare Mark 5:6 and Mark 5:22), and "implores" (παρακαλέω - see Mark 5:17–18) Jesus to come heal his daughter who is on the verge of death. Jesus sees him, hears him, and follows him. The crowd also follows. It's so congested that everyone is shoulder to shoulder, touching and pressing up against Jesus from every direction.

This story is arranged in Mark's popular "sandwich" style. As Jesus works His way through this crowd, a second story begins, and another life is changed by Jesus. Press the pause button on Jairus and his daughter for a moment as a new character is introduced.

Being Unclean

A woman has suffered with a flow of blood for twelve years. She has done everything in her power to stop this. She agonized at the hands of doctors and physicians and spent her every penny on medical treatment. Nothing has helped. Instead, it's gotten worse.

Imagine this woman's life right now. She has a serious medical ailment filling her world with misery and despair. She's in constant discomfort. She's now in poverty. She wasted all her money on treatments that did not work. She sinks into hopelessness. Having spent her money, the basic necessities of life are a struggle for her. Marriage and childrearing are no longer an option in her life. Any kind of meaningful relationship is impossible for her because this flow of blood renders her in a perpetual state of uncleanness. The book of Leviticus addresses what to do in her situation and the ramifications for her life are abysmal:

> When a woman has a discharge, and the discharge in her body is blood, she shall be in her menstrual impurity for seven days, and whoever touches her shall be unclean until the evening. And everything on which she lies during her menstrual impurity shall be unclean. Everything also on which she sits shall be unclean. And whoever touches her bed shall wash his clothes and bathe himself in water and be unclean until the evening. And whoever touches anything on which she sits shall wash his clothes and bathe himself in water and be unclean until the evening. Whether it is the bed or anything on which she sits, when he touches it he shall be unclean until the evening. And if any man lies with her and her menstrual impurity comes upon him, he shall be unclean seven days, and every bed on which he lies shall be unclean.
>
> If a woman has a discharge of blood for many days, not at

the time of her menstrual impurity, or if she has a discharge beyond the time of her impurity, all the days of the discharge she shall continue in uncleanness. As in the days of her impurity, she shall be unclean. Every bed on which she lies, all the days of her discharge, shall be to her as the bed of her impurity. And everything on which she sits shall be unclean, as in the uncleanness of her menstrual impurity. And whoever touches these things shall be unclean, and shall wash his clothes and bathe himself in water and be unclean until the evening (Lev 15:19–27).

This woman has done nothing wrong. It's not a sin to have a flow of blood or to be unclean. Uncleanness happens to both men and women for very natural, morally neutral, events in life. The remedy for uncleanness sometimes involves washings, sacrifices, and waiting for a few days. When that uncleanness never departs and lasts year after year, when there is nothing you can do to be cleansed, it becomes an unbearable, hopeless, miserable existence.

This woman is in poor health, discomfort, and poverty, and because of her uncleanness, she is an outcast, lonely, and contagious. She is barred from the congregation and the synagogue and temple (she's the exact opposite of Jairus in every way). Others must keep their distance from her. Not only can she make you unclean, but anything she touches also can make you unclean.

The Faith to Touch Jesus

Then she touches Jesus. She does not speak to Him. She does not ask His permission. She does not touch His skin. She knows the whole crowd is pressing in all around Him and she also knows she isn't supposed to get in crowds. She's supposed to stay away and should never start touching people, but this is her chance. Maybe she can sneak up behind Him and "just touch His garments" (Mark 5:28) and no one will ever know. Granted, Leviticus 15 says that would make the clothing and whoever wears them unclean, but this is her only chance. Maybe this will be the event that heals her and changes her whole world.

She gave in and touched Him and "Immediately the flow of her blood was dried up; and she felt in her body that she was healed of her affliction" (Mark 5:29). She gambled on Jesus (which is always a smart bet), and she was healed immediately. Then something else also "immediately" happened: Jesus felt some of His power transfer into her. He turned and faced the crowd, asking, "Who touched My garments?" (Mark 5:30). She secretly touched Him and was healed, but she didn't get away with it.

The disciples think Jesus is asking an absurd question. They wonder, "Who touched you? The whole crowd touched you. Everyone is touching you. You're pressing your way through a huge group of people." Jesus ignores them and focuses His attention on the woman who would much rather be left unseen. She broke all the social customs and legal expectations, selfishly touching a man in her uncleanness. This woman put "touching Jesus" above doing what was "right." Jesus focuses on this woman and turns the entire crowd's attention to her.

Does Jesus need to go change clothes and bathe and wait until the evening to be clean again? That's what Leviticus 15:27 says He must do. Does He rebuke her? Does He embarrass her? She just put her own needs above Leviticus. That's a bold move. How will Jesus respond?

She responds with fear and trembling (like 4:41 and 5:15). She knows she did something wrong; she tried to be inconspicuous but couldn't fool Jesus. She tried to sneak up behind Him and only touch His clothes (Mark 5:27). She was in such a hard spot. She didn't want to be a problem or a burden or disobedient, but she needed to be healed. She was miserable, and Jesus was a better hope than Leviticus. She fell before Him (like Mark 5:6, 22, 33) and told Him the whole truth. She confessed her transgression.

Jesus responded with love, as a father looks at his daughter (as Jairus looks at his daughter). Would a loving father be mad at his daughter, or would He rejoice that she was finally made well again? Like the Pharisees, Jesus could have rebuked her for a minor infraction, but He doesn't. Those Leviticus 15 instructions are not meant to keep a woman in need from being healed. Jesus is proud of her faith and delighted that she was made well. He looks at her and calls her, "Daughter," saying, "your faith has made you well; go in peace and be healed of your affliction" (Mark 5:34). He gives her love, wellness, peace, and healing.

Notice that it wasn't Jesus' garment that made her well. Soon others will also want to touch the fringe of His cloak for healing (Mark 6:56), but there is nothing special about His clothing. There were countless people touching Jesus in that crowd that day and nothing special happened for them. It wasn't His clothes that did the healing, it was her faith that made her well.

Talitha Kum

The story then shifts back to the other daughter. The twelve-year-old daughter of Jairus. While Jesus stopped to speak to the woman in the crowd, Jairus' daughter died. Her body failed her before He ever arrived. To many, this is the end of hope: "Why trouble the teacher anymore?" (Mark 5:35). Overhearing them, Jesus tells Jairus, "Do not be afraid, only believe" (Mark 5:36).

Jairus, the popular, important, synagogue official, here in his darkest moments, can learn a valuable lesson about faith from that poor, neglected, abandoned, unclean woman in the crowd. He can learn from her faith. Jesus wants him to have her faith.

Jesus brings Peter, James, and John into the house. He tells the mourners that they have no need to mourn. Why mourn for the sleeping? (Mark 5:37–39). After they laugh at His ignorance, Jesus sends them all outside. Entering the lifeless young girl's room with her parents and His disciples, He prepares to change their lives forever.

This father and mother are heart broken. Their whole world came crashing down with the death of their daughter. Like the storm on Galilee, the man possessed with Legion, and even that woman with the flow of blood, they have no control over their lives. There is nothing they can do to solve this problem. Chaos has taken over and, as the climax of these four consecutive stories, death has sunk its teeth into their family. Jesus overcame the powers of darkness in the first three stories: He overcame storms, demonic spirits, and sickness. Now, can He overcome the power of death itself?

Jesus takes her by the hand and says "Talitha kum!" This means "Little girl, I say to you, get up!" (Mark 5:41). "Immediately" this twelve-year-old girl wakes up and begins to walk. "Immediately" they are all astounded. Even death has no power over Jesus. Then Jesus strictly orders everyone to give the girl something to eat and to keep quiet. This scene foreshadows the ultimate victory of Jesus and sings forth the wonderful kingdom truth: Death is defeated in Jesus.

Reflection Questions

1. How many ways can you compare and contrast the two females in this story? Do you think the mourners found out the girl was raised back to life?

Or did they believe Jesus was right that she was just sleeping? How would these events have changed the characters from this day forward?

2. When is it most difficult to place your trust in Jesus? How can the woman with the flow of blood be an example for us? Did she do the right thing by touching Jesus in her uncleanness?

REFLECTION 25

TOUCHING THE UNCLEAN

Touching the Unclean

LET'S slow down and take a break from Jesus's nonstop ministry to consider an important theme that has been emerging. Jesus just got off the boat in Galilee after visiting a Gentile city, and the first two things He does are make contact with unclean people. We already addressed that the woman with the flow of blood was unclean, but notice also that Jesus takes the dead child "by the hand" in Mark 5:41. Numbers 19:7 says, "Whoever touches the dead body of any person shall be unclean seven days." Both stories should render Jesus unclean at the end of Mark 5.

One of the most important and controversial aspects of Jesus's ministry is His interaction with the Law of Moses. In Mark, Jesus regularly bumps up against the Law of Moses (or at least popular interpretations of it). He and His disciples are accused of breaking Sabbath on numerous occasions. He will soon declare all foods clean (Mark 7:19) which directly overturns what Moses wrote. He also consistently ignores purity rituals about "clean" and "unclean." Jesus moved with compassion and touched people who are otherwise ignored.

In Mark 5 He touched a dead girl, and His clothes were touched by the woman with the flow of blood, both should render Him unclean. In Mark 1:41 He touched a leper (see Lev 5:3). Remarkably, when Jesus touches the leper, He says, "be clean" (Mark 1:41). That's not the way "clean" and "unclean" are supposed to work. You don't touch a leper and give cleanness, rather you touch a leper and you become unclean.

Contagious Cleanness

Ordinarily, uncleanness spreads and contaminates, but with Jesus, the opposite occurs. Uncleanness did not spread to Him, rather His cleanness spread to others. There is an important oracle in the book of Haggai that discusses how "clean" and "unclean" ordinarily work.

Haggai is a short book containing four oracles (Hag 1:1, 2:1, 10, 20). The third is a question to the priests: "If a man carries holy meat in the fold of his garment, and touches bread with his fold, or cooked food, wine, oil, or any other food, will it become holy?" The priests correctly answer this question in the negative. It will not become clean (Hag 2:12). Then a second question is asked, "If one who is unclean from a corpse touches any of these, will the latter become unclean?" And the priests correctly answer in the affirmative, "It will become unclean." (Hag 2:13).

The point of the oracle is that the children of Israel are living unclean lives but then working on rebuilding the temple. Rebuilding the temple (the clean thing) does not spread to purify their sinful lives (the unclean thing). Rather, their sinful lives (the unclean thing) spreads to contaminate and defile the temple (the clean thing). So, before famine hits, O Israel, consider your ways, repent, and build the temple with clean hands! Haggai's point only works if uncleanness is contagious, but cleanness is not.

Even in our day we easily understand this point. If a sick person and a healthy person take turns breathing on each other's faces (which would be odd and gross), who will affect the other person? Will the healthy person's germs heal the sick person? No, obviously, you cannot heal the sick by breathing on them. Can the sick person's germs spread to the healthy person? Yes, that happens all the time. In the age of COVID we are all well aware that sickness spreads and health does not.

Imagine a cup of nice, pure, clean ice water and imagine next to it is a hunk of raw, gross, slimy, chicken breast. What happens if you put that chicken in the cup of water? Will the water purify the chicken so that it's healthy to eat? Obviously not. It will certainly make the water undrinkable though. Why? Because unclean spreads, clean does not.

Mark points out repeatedly that during the ministry of Jesus, this natural rule is reversed. Jesus takes the uncleanness of the world into Himself and sends it back out in purity. Jesus heals the uncleanness of the world, not by shunning, avoiding, and escaping it, but by pursuing, touching, and cleaning it. Rachel Held Evans writes about these stories, saying,

> the point isn't just that Jesus healed these people; the point is that Jesus touched these people. He embraced them just as he embraced other disparaged members of society, often regarded as 'sinners' by the religious and political elite—prostitutes, tax collectors, Samaritans, Gentiles, the sick, the blind, and the deaf.[1]

Jesus reaches out where others pull back.

The Love of Jesus

Jesus lived out the command to "Love your neighbor as yourself" in every way possible. Even when it meant getting His hands dirty. When it was controversial, Jesus still reached out. Jesus healed on the Sabbath because He loved His neighbor as Himself. He ate and drank with tax collectors and sinners because He loved His neighbor as Himself. He touches the unclean because He loves His neighbor as Himself.

If you were injured, paralyzed, or sick, would you want doctors to ignore you because it was Sabbath? Wouldn't you want to be treated with respect, even invited to a meal, although you were a sinner? If you were "unclean" would you want to be ignored, neglected, and forced to the outskirts of society? The way Jesus would answer these questions is the way He treats people.

We don't have the same "clean" and "unclean" rules in our society that existed in ancient Israel, but we do have rules. There are unwritten codes and feelings of disgust we link with certain behaviors. We still, in our own ways, view people we see as "unclean." There are sins that repulse us more than others and we irrationally fear may spread to us if we touch, hug, share a meal, or love the sinner. There are people we avoid and would rather not touch or shake their hand. Would it bother you, in a safe and controlled environment, to hold the hand of a murderer? To hug someone whose sexual lifestyle is ungodly? To wash the feet of a President you didn't vote for?

It is hard not to connect touch with morality, or views of cleanliness. It seems to come from our guts that some people should be avoided. We may know, intellectually, that their moral flaws/sins/dumb decisions/irritating personalities/unchristian worldviews will not actually spread or contaminate us, but still, touch and physical demonstrations of affection can make us cringe. It's easier to touch a good, clean, person that you know and love, than a person you dislike, disagree with, or who is ungodly and sinful. Jesus touched both.

Jesus touched lepers, bleeding women, and the dead. He washed His disciples' feet, even those who would abandon, deny, and betray Him. Jesus didn't violate Moses by affirming uncleanness, rather, He made all things clean. He made all people clean. Gentiles, Samaritans, the poor, the sick, the sinful, Jesus would reach out to them all. He did what others found disgusting because He had compassion, humility, and He understood what it means to love His neighbor.

In the ultimate act of uncleanness, Jesus showed love at its highest level. He became a curse, nailed to a tree, by violent Gentiles, to taste death for all. He didn't only touch the dead, He died. He did not only touch sinners, but "He who knew no sin, became sin, in order that in Him we might become the righteousness of God" (2 Cor 5:21).

Jesus touched the unclean, that they might become clean. He became sin, that we might become God's righteousness. At the end of the story, tax collectors and sinners find their physician, Gentiles receive healing, lepers, bleeding women, and the dead walk away alive and pure, and Jesus emerges victorious over the powers of death to shine forth His life-giving holiness around the whole world. Uncleanness, sin, and death cannot bind Jesus, who conquers and cleanses the uncleanness of this world.

Reflection Questions

1. What do you think about the purity regulations in the Old Testament? Do they make society better or worse? Why could they be beneficial? What is the difference between sin and impurity? How could the purity regulations remind us of the holiness of God?
2. What is the difference between "breaking" the

purity laws and making unclean things clean? How do Jesus's actions relate to Mark 7:19? Why is this so important for the Gentile mission?

Endnotes

1. Rachel Held Evans, *Inspired: Slaying Giants, Walking on Water, and Loving the Bible Again* (Nashville: Nelson Books, 2018), 184.

REFLECTION 26
KINGDOM HARDSHIPS

Mark 6:1–32

Stress

SEVERAL MONTHS AGO, our family moved from Louisiana to Maryville, Tennessee to work with a new church. We said goodbye to many wonderful friends and mentors. We sold a house full of happy memories, where both of our newborn sons came home from the hospital, and transitioned from a church we will love for the rest of our lives. We had to buy a new house, in a crazy market, in Tennessee and begin building new relationships, in a new ministry environment, during the COVID 19 pandemic, with two small children. I could go into detail about the difficulties selling our Louisiana house and how impossible it seemed it would be to find a house in Maryville, but I won't. Anyone who has moved understands the thousands of planned, and unplanned, difficulties and stressors that arise.

On the one hand, the nice sympathetic person will think about how stressful our last few months have been and they may remember their own stressful moving experiences and empathize with us, and pray for us, and wish us the best. Others, however, might read what we've been through and, understandably, not be so touched.

There are many people, in many parts of the world today, in front of whom I would be ashamed to describe my stress. They have fewer options than I do. They can't even dream of the luxuries that I so often take for granted. Or that I delude myself into thinking are necessities, but they are not necessities. In the grand scheme of things, they ultimately aren't even that important. This is my confession and my repentance. I've spent the last few months focused on the wrong things. I am starting a new ministry with exciting new kingdom opportunities. I'm preaching the Lordship of Jesus and the kingdom of God, yet I've had knots in my stomach about my house and bank account and protecting my excess.

Now, I'm not what most in our culture would consider to be "rich," but that exactly illustrates my point. What else should we call it? I do not have to worry about feeding my kids, being homeless (the church even provided housing while we were looking for a home), or freezing with no clothes or blankets to keep us warm. I had everything I needed during the entire moving process, but I worried about school districts, neighborhoods, proximity to parks, number of bedrooms, bathrooms, and a fireplace. I worried about things that wouldn't have even entered the apostle Paul's mind when considering ministry.

You know what Jesus said when He gave His disciples their first preaching commission?

> He instructed them that they should take nothing for their journey, except a mere staff - no bread, no bag, no money in their belt - but to wear sandals; and He added, "Do not put on two tunics." And He said to them, "Wherever you enter a house, stay there until you leave town. Any place that does

not receive you or listen to you, as you go out from there, shake the dust off the soles of your feet for a testimony against them"(Mark 6:8-11).

Imagine that kind of stress. Jesus does not tell them to make sure they set up IRA's and get a good interest rate on their mortgages and find the best schools near the best parks for their kids to play. He said pack nothing and don't wear two tunics. Leave your income and paychecks behind. Remember, some of these men even had families (Mark 1:29-31). Stay where people welcome you, and when they don't welcome you, shake the dust from your feet and move on.

Kingdom Priorities

There is a lesson in this mission about priorities. God's kingdom matters; our wealth, comfort, and security do not. Jesus wants His disciples to learn this message now. Before His death and resurrection, before they take the gospel throughout the world, they need a lesson in kingdom priorities.

The kingdom can make us uncomfortable. Mark 6 begins with the kingdom troubles Jesus faced in His hometown (Mark 6:1-6). He was not believed, many took offense at Him (Mark 6:3 and 6), and it impacted His ministry: "He could do no miracle there except that He laid His hands on a few sick people and healed them" (Mark 6:5). He's already struggling with His family (Mark 3:21) and now we see the problems in His hometown.

The disciples must share these kingdom hardships when they leave home with no money or food or shelter, having no idea what to eat or where to sleep. All that mattered was going forth in the name of the Lord. They could cast out unclean spirits, anoint sick people with oil, and heal them (Mark 6:7, 13), but they couldn't prepare for their own needs or comforts. This mission necessitates selflessness, service, and sacrifice.

The Disciples Return

The disciples left on their mission in Mark 6:12–13 and returned in Mark 6:30–32. This is another one of those sandwiches. In the middle tells the story of the fate, kingdom hardships, and martyrdom of John the Baptist. Our next reflection will focus on the middle of the sandwich, but for now, let's see what happens when the disciples return.

They are weary and no doubt exhausted after their mission. They report to Jesus all they accomplished and taught (Mark 6:30). Jesus listens to them and then gives them one additional order. He doesn't order them to go out and work harder, serve more, or teach with greater fervor. Instead, He tells them to find a secluded place ("wilderness area") by themselves to rest (Mark 6:31–32). They need time for themselves to rest and eat and recover. Jesus often practiced this same form of self-care (Mark 1:12–13, 35). The disciples get in a boat and cross the sea to enjoy some rest.

As a minister and a Christian, I take great comfort in knowing that even Jesus saw the value and importance of rest. No matter what job you have, you need rest. You need to take a break. Nothing on this earth is more important than the kingdom, but even Jesus and His disciples would stop doing kingdom work and rest. Maybe it would be better to say they did the kingdom work of rest. Rest can be a way of serving the kingdom some major benefits.

First, rest is enjoyable, and God wants us to find enjoyment in life. Remember that Sabbath was a blessing to humanity that emphasized, each week, the necessity of rest. Jesus was not against Sabbath or rest, but against a misuse of Sabbath to control others. Life is not all about work, or money, or productivity, or accomplishment. Enjoy time alone, time with your family, and time recovering.

Second, rest makes your kingdom service more effective and fruitful. You are not all-powerful and with time, everyone runs down and grows weary. Take a break from chopping the trees to sharpen your axe. Take a break from your work, ministry, and service, to strengthen and sharpen yourself. Rest is an essential part of being human. You will need it. Your family needs it.

Rest matters because discipleship is hard, and the mission of Jesus is challenging. It was challenging for the disciples, John the Baptist, and Jesus. The call of Christ compels us to carry a cross with a willingness to suffer, bleed, and give it all. The blood of John the Baptist fills the middle of this sandwich because he is a gripping example of giving the kingdom all you have. The comforts of this life ought never be what drives us or fills our hearts with stress, worry, and anxiety. That space in our hearts is reserved for Jesus.

When I consider the suffering of Jesus, John the Baptist, and the disciples, and I prioritize the kingdom of God where it should be, and I remember my mission and allegiance to Christ is to always transcend the comforts of this world, perhaps I can worry a little less about that perfect little house with the manicured lawn and vibrant garden. Perhaps I can worry a little less about my income, savings account, or retirement. Maybe my comfort and luxury will slip further down my priority list and just maybe I could give myself more fully to the ministry of Christ.

Reflection Questions

1. What would be the hardest part of the disciples' mission? How would Jesus's instructions in Mark

6:10-11 teach the disciples to trust? How would it prepare them for life after the resurrection?

2. What are the benefits of rest? In what ways should a Christian rest from ministry? How is this idea related to Sabbath?

REFLECTION 27
HEROD AND JOHN

Mark 6:14–29

Herod's Fear

THE DISCIPLES' mission created such hubbub that rumors began swirling. Jesus has kept most things secretive and close to the vest, but on this mission, His disciples made quite a public stir. Predictably, false ideas about Jesus started spreading.

Some people were saying that John the Baptist, or Elijah, or some other prophet of old was back and had risen from the dead. When Herod heard these rumors, he was tormented by the idea that John the Baptist, who he had unjustly murdered, might have risen from the dead. Herod kept saying to himself, over and over, in a fevered sweat (one could imagine): "John, whom I beheaded, has risen!" (Mark 6:16).

Herod was tormented because he did not want to kill John. He knew John was "righteous and holy" (Mark 6:20) and "was afraid of John" and "kept him safe" and "was very sorry" about the whole thing (Mark 6:20, 26). Herod sacrificed his principles to sacrifice John. Political pressure, arrogance, and pride motivated him more than justice, righteousness, and integrity, so He begrudgingly executed John. The rumors and memories still haunted him though.

These verses remind me of Edgar Allan Poe's "The Tell-Tale Heart." In the poem, a man (the narrator) murders an elderly gentleman because of his "pale blue eye" which looked like the eye of a vulture. The narrator couldn't stop thinking about it, and he began stalking the old man. One night, he entered the old man's apartment and, after hearing the loud beat of the old man's heart, he murdered him, hacked him into pieces, and buried him beneath the floorboards. When the police arrived to investigate, he stayed calm and cool, confident that he covered his tracks perfectly. Then he began to hear it again, from beneath the floor, the loud beating of the old man's heart. Driven to insanity, sure that the police could also hear the heartbeat, he confessed to the murder.

King Herod committed the gruesome murder of an innocent man. John the Baptist's preaching had become a "pale blue eye." Not necessarily to Herod, although it perplexed him, but to Herodias, Herod's wife. She hated John's preaching and wanted him dead, and Herod eventually gave in to her desires.

Mentally and emotionally, Herod couldn't get over the murder. When he heard of miracles and rumors of resurrection, he heard John's heartbeat underneath the floorboard. He immediately assumed John must, in some way, be back from the dead. "John, whom I beheaded, has risen!" (Mark 6:16).

The Backstory

In verse 17, Mark takes us back in time to what really happened with John. Up to this point, we didn't know John had been killed. We learned of his arrest back in Mark 1:14, but now we get the details about it and how it ended with his unjust execution.

Apparently, John kept preaching against Herod and Herodias' marriage. He saw injustice and immorality and he spoke truth to power. John didn't let the status, power, or wealth of any man dictate his message. He preached without a first amendment right to do so, and he was arrested for it.

The events that unfold are a sordid affair. Herod is introduced as "King Herod," although the term "king" seems to be unofficial. Technically, he was a tetrarch. He is commonly known by the name Herod Antipas. He is the son of Herod the Great, who was king when Jesus was born. Mark tells us that Herod Antipas had a brother (half-brother) named Philip (aka Herod II). This is not Philip the tetrarch of Luke 3:1, who was also a half-brother to them. This Philip was married to a woman named Herodias. So, yeah, studying the Herods gets a little confusing.[1]

It seems Herod Antipas had been married for many years to a woman named Phasaelis, before falling for Herodias, his brother Philip's wife. Herodias also happened to be Herod Anitipas' niece by the way. Her father, Aristobulous IV, was also a son of Herod the Great and brother of Herod Antipas and Philip. Aristobulous was in line to be king before he tried to poison his father and was subsequently executed. Herodias was then married off to Philip.

On a trip to Rome, Herod Antipas fell in love with her and they made an arrangement to leave their spouses and she would go back to live with him. She unlawfully divorced Philip, and married her uncle/brother-in-law, Herod Antipas. You got all that? If that seems twisted to you, you're not alone. John the Baptist thinks so too.

John keeps preaching, "it is not lawful for you to have your brother's wife" (Mark 6:18). John doesn't think getting a divorce (Deut 24:1-5; Matt 19:7) automatically makes a new marriage lawful or honorable. He sees injustice and lawlessness taking place in the Herod household, and he speaks about it. He sees lust, deceit, incest, selfishness, sexual immorality, and abandonment. John sees flagrant disregard for Leviticus 18:16, "You shall not uncover the nakedness of your brother's wife; it is your brother's nakedness" and Leviticus 20:21, "If there is a man who takes his brother's wife, it is abhorrent; he has uncovered his brother's nakedness. They will be childless" (Lev 20:21). Herod, the ruler of the Jews, was certainly negligent about the law of the Jews.

Herod's Party and Promise

Mark 6:21 describes a day when Herod bolsters his own name on his birthday (Mark 6:21) by showing the most important people of Galilee all his glory and grandeur. He even has his own stepdaughter come in and dance for the men. This is reminiscent of King Ahasuerus (Xerxes) showing off all his wealth and power and glory for a 180-day feast to "all his princes and attendants, the army officers of Persia and Media, the nobles and the princes of his provinces" (Esth 1:1–5). This is a strategic way to create allies and friendships, strengthen your administration, garner support for future initiatives, and bask in the ambience of your own self-importance.

Herod, like Ahasuerus, provides some female entertainment from his own family. Ahasuerus commanded his wife, Vashti, to dance and parade herself around for these men. She refused and made her husband look like a fool publicly. The embarrassed king, who claims to rule 127 provinces, cannot even rule his own wife. Herod, on the other hand, had his wife's daughter come in and dance. She did not refuse. She danced and Herod and all the men were pleased. Probably intoxicated, full of pride and pleasure, Herod smarts off in front of all the leading men and, in a demonstration of his generosity, offers to grant her whatever she wishes.

Herodias coaxes her daughter to ask, not for wealth or security or territory or a palace, but for revenge. Herodias's rage was so intense that she denied her daughter a generous gift from the king, just so she could murder a good man who was already locked away in prison. Herod, because he had already made the oath in the presence of the most prominent men of the region, saw no way he could back out and save face. To protect his own reputation and to impress those at his banquet, he sent his minions to remove John's head. The executioner found John in prison, hacked off his head, and brought it back up to the party. It was presented "to the girl; and the girl gave it to her mother" (Mark 6:28).

Kings and Kingdoms

John, who came in the wilderness declaring, "Make ready the way of the Lord" (Mark 1:3) was imprisoned for the kingdom of God, and he died alone. His lifeless, headless body lay slumped in a pool of blood on the floor in a dark, grim, dungeon, while the lavish celebration continued. The king and his royal party continued celebrating with luxury and excess. The severed head of an enemy, now adorning the celebration, vividly symbolizes the kingdoms of this world and how they execute their power.

This story, like so many in the gospels, pits the kingdom of God against the kingdoms of this world. It demonstrates the problem that temporal, human, so-called kings tend to have. They are motivated by power, pride, and lust and quickly solve their problems with violence and death. They are the opposite of what King Jesus is all about.

Herod's position and title add an important nuance to this story. Herod Antipas is known as a "king" over the Jews, but is he truly acting like the king of the Jews? John condemns his marriage, not only because it was unlawful, but because a comparison is taking place. Jesus is the true king of the Jews and Herod is the Roman-appointed imposter, and this sham of a marriage proves it. This is the "Son of Man" vs the "Beasts" of Daniel 7 on full display.

N.T. Wright poignantly remarks,

> I don't think he [John the Baptist] was simply concerned with Antipas' immoral behavior, though that was flagrant enough. I think the point was, more tellingly, that anyone who behaved this way could not possibly, not ever, not in a million years, be regarded as the true 'king of the Jews'; Antipas had just demonstrated his utter unsuitability for the position. John pointed this out. Not surprisingly, then, John ended up in one of Antipas's dungeons.[2]

Viewing Herod alongside Jesus in this passage crystalizes the comparison we've been noting throughout this Gospel. Jesus is the true Lord, the King, and the Son of God. He rules the true kingdom, brings the true gospel, and establishes true peace and justice. Jesus dies in shame and agony on a cross for the salvation of those who oppose Him. Herod, on the other hand, imprisons, persecutes, and executes those who oppose him while throwing great feasts in his own honor.

King Herod is but a small picture of Rome, Persia, Babylon, Assyria, Egypt and all the kingdoms who reign by violence, wealth, and pride. John's body was taken by his disciples and placed reverently in a tomb (Mark 6:29). He is a symbol of the kingdom of God. His life and the sorrow of his death foreshadow what the disciples must prepare for (remember this story is sandwiched in between the disciples' first preaching mission), and what Jesus Himself will endure. The kingdoms of this world think they can do as they please and destroy the kingdom of God with prison, armies, swords, and the cross. What they don't understand is that "The blood of the martyrs is the seed of the church."

Reflection Questions

1. Compare and contrast Herod and Jesus as the "King of the Jews." Why did Herod have John the Baptist killed? How did Herod treat his enemies? How does Jesus treat His enemies?
2. How does John's life and death foreshadow Jesus? How does he foreshadow the disciples? What happens when kingdoms are ruled by selfishness, lust, violence, and fear? How do modern politics thrive on these attributes? How does the kingdom of God compel us to avoid these attributes?

Endnotes

1. For further detail, you can read similar accounts in Matthew 14:1–12, Luke 3:19–20; 9:7–9, and in Josephus, *Antiquities of the Jews*, 18.5.

2. N.T. Wright, *Simply Jesus: A New Vision of Who He Was, What He Did, and Why He Matters* (New York: HarperCollins, 2011), 62.

REFLECTION 28
SHEPHERD, COMMANDER, AND LORD

Mark 6:33–44

Shepherding the Sheep

IN MARK 6:30–32, Jesus tells His disciples to rest after their difficult missionary journey, but rest will need to wait. Their mission work was too successful (Mark 6:14–15). The disciples became rock stars over night: rumors swirled and crowds were gathered. These unknown disciples were now recognizable public figures. As they tried to get some rest across the sea, the people saw them, "recognized them," followed "on foot from all the cities, and got there ahead of them" (Mark 6:33). They are like celebrities being hounded by the paparazzi.

When their boat reaches the shore to their secluded place, a large crowd is already there, waiting. Jesus sees the crowd and feels compassion for them (Mark 6:34). Now, I know me. I like to think compassion would be my first feeling here, but I also know what happens when people interrupt my rest because they want something. "Compassion" isn't the best word to describe how I feel.

Jesus has been serving people nonstop and they still won't

leave Him alone. When He tried to pray in seclusion earlier (Mark 1:35–37) the disciples found Him and said, "everyone is looking for you!" Jesus can't get a minute to rest and recuperate and now His disciples can't either. They just returned from a difficult mission trip, their first one, and they are exhausted. But the work continues.

These selfish crowds won't give Jesus or His disciples any rest. Does Jesus respond with anger? Frustration? Does He pretend to walk by without seeing them? Does He tell them to take care of themselves for a change? No. Compassion. He sees them and He feels compassion.

These crowds are following for a reason. They are in need. Jesus likens them to "sheep without a shepherd" (Mark 6:34). Keep that description in mind as you read what follows. Jesus is about to miraculously feed 5,000. This event is in all four Gospels, but Mark is the only evangelist who introduces this miracle by calling the people "sheep without a shepherd." That detail is essential for understanding what follows.

The Lord Is My Shepherd

Mark includes other interesting details also. These "sheep" are standing right beside the water (Jesus sees them as He comes ashore—Mark 6:34). Then Jesus, the Shepherd, makes these sheep "sit down ... on the green grass" (Mark 6:39). It's not common for the text to describe the color of the grass, so why does Mark do it? Maybe it is to let you know the time of year (spring, probably around Passover). Perhaps, it is to remind you of something else also. Perhaps it is intended to remind you of another shepherding passage.

Can you think of any other Biblical image of a Shepherd, leading His sheep beside water, making them lie down on green grass, and then feeding them? Psalm 23 should now enter your mind: "The LORD is my Shepherd, I shall not want. He makes me lie down in green pastures; He leads me besides quiet waters. He restores my soul ... You prepare a table for me ..." (Psalm 23:1–5). Mark wants us to make the connection that Jesus is the Shepherd, the Lord, who cares for the needs of the sheep. This is another demonstration that the Lord has come back to be with His people (Mark 1:3).

Another passage that should come to our minds is Ezekiel 34, perhaps the most detailed discussion of shepherding in the Bible. The leaders of Israel are condemned as rotten and selfish shepherds (Ezek 34:1–10). Their poor shepherding led to the scattering of the sheep. God looks out and sees His people like sheep without a true shepherd. In response, God declares that He, Himself, will become their Shepherd (Ezek 34:11–22). He also promises to raise up another shepherd over them. This later Shepherd will be a servant He calls, "David" (Ezek 34:23).

Ezekiel was written hundreds of years after David's death, so this must be some new Davidic figure who will arise as a Shepherd. Ezekiel 34, like Daniel 7, calls the kingdoms of this earth "beasts" that kill the sheep. The good Shepherd will protect His sheep and "they will no longer be a prey to the nations, and the beasts of the earth will not devour them" (Ezek 34:28).

In Mark 6, when Jesus feeds the sheep who are lying on the green grass, beside the water, He proves to be their Shepherd. He is the shepherd who protects His sheep from the beasts that devour and He compassionately cares, tends, and provides for them. Jesus is the shepherding Messiah.

Feeding the 5,000

Everyone is starving. The disciples haven't had any time to eat (Mark 6:31), and as the sun goes down, everyone is famished. They say to Jesus, "This place is desolate and it is already quite late; send them away so that they may go into the surrounding countryside and villages and buy themselves something to eat" (Mark 6:35–36).

Now it's time to reveal something I didn't mention earlier. The word translated "secluded" or "desolate" in Mark 6:31, 32, 35, is the same word as "wilderness" earlier in Mark's Gospel. This Greek word (ἔρημος) is used three times to introduce the story of Jesus feeding the 5000, and it's also used throughout chapter 1 to introduce Jesus as the Lord who comes through the wilderness to be with His people (Mark 1:3, 4, 12, 13, 35, 45).

As discussed in Reflection 8, the problem with the wilderness is that there is no food there. So, what do you do? The disciples said to send the people out of the wilderness to the populated areas, villages and towns, so they could get some food. Jesus, instead, tells His disciples, "You give them something to eat" (Mark 6:37).

This is an absurd thought. First, there is no food to give them out in the wilderness. Secondly, even if they left the wilderness, found a town, and tried to buy food, there's no way they had enough money to feed 5,000. That would cost "two hundred denarii" (Mark 6:37). That amount of money would be roughly eight months of labor.

Jesus's challenge to feed the people should be read as a test. Jesus was testing His disciples to see how much they understand about His identity. He is the Lord who comes through the wilderness to reunite with His people (Mark 1:3). So, ask yourself, what does the Lord do when His people are hungry in the wilderness? We have an answer to that question back in Exodus 16.

After God rescued the Israelites from Egyptian slavery, they entered the wilderness where there was no food, and they sobbed, cried, complained, and grumbled (Exodus 16:3–4). They even pretended like things were better back in Egypt (how quickly they forgot about slavery and the murder of their children). What does God do when they murmur and complain? He rains down bread from heaven for them.

When the Gospel of John details the feeding of the 5,000, the Exodus narrative is specifically discussed. Mark does not specifically quote the Old Testament, rather he subtly alludes to it. The reader is expected to catch his allusions and dig deeper into the text. Jesus, the Lord, miraculously feeding His people in the wilderness intentionally parallels God feeding the children of Israel in the wilderness.

The disciples only have five loaves of bread and two fish to feed 5,000 men. By the time Jesus finishes this miracle, everyone has been fed and satisfied and there are "twelve full baskets of the broken pieces, and also of the fish" (Mark 6:43). Remember that number of baskets left over; it will come up again later. It also may be an allusion to the Old Testament.

In Leviticus 24:5–9 there were twelve loaves of bread specified for the "Table of Presence" in the tabernacle. Those twelve loaves are believed to represent the twelve tribes of Israel. Since those twelve loaves were in the tabernacle, in the presence of God, it is called the "Table of Presence." They symbolically keep Israel before the face of God. Since the twelve disciples seem to represent a renewed twelve tribes, perhaps these twelve baskets of bread may also represent something similar. With Jesus, they are in the presence of the Lord.

Who is this Jesus?

Consider what this miracle means if Jesus truly is King. The kingdom of God will be the first kingdom in world history without hunger and starvation. Feeding an entire army is no small chore. Imagine a king who can feed an army of 5,000 with only a few loaves of bread. To make sure the reader doesn't miss this point, there is explicit military language used in this story. Jesus "commands" 5,000 people, the size of a Roman legion, to sit in groups of 100s (centuries) and 50s. This is another example, like Mark 5:9-13 where Jesus's authority is illustrated by borrowing the language of the Roman military, then showing Jesus's superiority.

Jesus can feed an army and feed a kingdom. He can cast out a legion into pigs. He can control weather, heal the sick, and even raise the dead. He is a Leader you should want to follow. Jesus is a more perfect King than any Roman who will ever take the throne.

With this mixture of metaphors, Jesus is presented as a commander feeding His troops, a shepherd nourishing His sheep, and the God who provides bread for His people in the wilderness. Jesus the King is commander, shepherd, and the embodiment of God Himself. That's a King who deserves our allegiance.

Reflection Questions

1. Why is it important that this miracle happens in the wilderness? In what ways is Jesus like Moses? In what ways is He greater than Moses? How does John 10:1-30 relate to this passage?
2. What makes Jesus a great king? What makes Him a great Shepherd? What qualities are most important for shepherds? Do you have these qualities?

REFLECTION 29
THE DISCIPLES' HARD HEARTS

Mark 6:45–52

Walking on the Water

"IMMEDIATELY" after feeding the 5,000, Jesus made His disciples get back into the boat and sail over to Bethsaida. He didn't join them. Instead, He stayed back, saw the crowds safely off, until He was finally alone once again. He went up alone on a mountain in the wilderness to pray (kind of like Moses). While Jesus was constantly surrounded by people, He again prioritizes private prayer time.

When Jesus fed the 5,000 it was "already quite late" (Mark 6:35). "When it was evening"[1] Jesus was praying on the mountain. When He finished, He looked out and saw the disciples "straining at the oars, for the wind was against them," and it was the "fourth watch of the night" (Mark 6:48). Dividing nighttime into four "watches" was a Roman practice and became the norm for Jews also. Thus, the use of Roman language continues. The fourth watch would be between 3 and 6 AM. Not only did Jesus's disciples get no rest after they were sent out, but they also pulled an all-nighter, and morning is coming quickly.

He Intended to Pass By Them

The text says Jesus saw them "straining" or "making headway painfully" and "the wind was against them," so He walked out to them. The implication seemingly being that He would help. However, while He is walking out to them, it also says, "He intended to pass by them" (Mark 6:48). What an odd detail. Why would Jesus look out to His disciples as they struggled on the sea during a storm, walk out to them on the water, and then try to pass by without helping?

Why would He want to pass by them? One possibility is that Jesus wants them to solve this problem themselves. When there was no food for the crowds, Jesus told them, "You feed them" (Mark 6:37), but they did not understand. Before He solved the problem, He first challenged them to create a solution.

Could they have really done it? Could they have fed the crowds like Jesus did? Earlier in Mark 6:7, Jesus gave them authority over the spiritual world to cast out demons. Jesus may want them to test the limits of that authority. In Matthew's version of this story, Peter walks out on the water like Jesus. Can the disciples feed crowds, walk on water, or calm this storm? Could they have faith that moves mountains (Mark 11:23–24)? They might be able to, but they don't.

As they struggle in the sea, Jesus walks out to them on the water. He shows complete control over nature. Seeing Him should remind them of what is possible. Seeing Him should remind them that He also already calmed a storm (Mark 4:39–41). Seeing Him should remind them that He is the Lord who just fed the 5,000. He already demonstrated the unfathomable possibilities. Can the disciples share in the power of Jesus? Can they demonstrate faith instead of fear and doubt?

Apparently not. They see Him, think He is a ghost, and become terrified. They misidentify Jesus (which is a common theme) and fail His test. Again, like the first time Jesus calmed the storm (Mark 4:40–41) they respond with fear and confusion.

Who is this Jesus?

Jesus tells them, "Take courage, I AM, do not be afraid" (Mark 6:50). Some Bibles translate the phrase "I AM" with "it is I." But in Greek, that is the exact phrase that God uses from the burning bush in Exodus 3:14. This is yet another subtle pointer to the divine identity of Jesus. It may also be a clue as to why Jesus wanted to "pass by" which is a verb used regularly to describe the I AM's actions in the book of Exodus. The I AM "passes by" Moses numerous times (Exod 33:17–23 and 34:6). Jesus intended to "pass by" (Mark 6:48) while saying "I AM, do not be afraid" (Mark 6:50). Jesus parallels God from Exodus and that's probably not a coincidence.

One final note about this amazing scene comes by connecting it to Job 9:8–11. Richard Hays points out this connection and once you see it, it's hard to ignore. The Septuagint translation of Job 9:8–11 describes God as the One "who alone stretched out the sky and walks on the sea as on dry ground." This is a unique image in the Bible. If Jesus's actions call any Old Testament passage to mind, it is this one in Job. It's the only time we see someone walking on water, and it's God.

It is noteworthy then, that in the context of Job 9, the text also says, "If he passed over me, I would certainly not see him, and if he went by me, I would not even know" (Job 9:11). Job 9 pictures God walking on the sea and he "passed over" and "went by" without notice. The obvious difference in Mark 6 is that the disciples did see Jesus when He intended to pass by, but they still don't know Him. They think He's a ghost. They see Him but cannot recognize Him. Jesus's identity and presence is just as elusive to the disciples as God's is to Job.

Hays writes,

Thus, in Job 9 the image of God's walking on the sea is linked with a confession of God's mysterious transcendence of human comprehension: God's 'passing by' is a metaphor for our inability to grasp his power. This metaphor accords deeply with Mark's emphasis on the elusiveness of the divine presence in Jesus.

Mark, without direct statements like "Jesus is God," subtly points to this truth on nearly every page of his Gospel. This truth is evident to some, but to others, God passes by them unnoticed.

Hard Hearts

When the disciples respond with fear rather than trust, the narrator tells us, "They were utterly astonished, for they had not gained any insight from the incident of the loaves, but their heart was hardened" (Mark 6:52). We learn in Mark 3:5 that the scribes and Pharisees have hard hearts, but that's not supposed to describe the disciples. Here, and in Mark 8:17–21, we discover the shocking truth that the disciples also have hard hearts. They are reluctant to understand and unwilling to believe because of their hearts. This is something Jesus will work to correct.

They were supposed to be learning. They should have learned a lesson from the loaves that prepared them to respond with faith when Jesus walked on the water. They probably also should have learned something the first time Jesus calmed the storm (Mark 4:35–41). Instead, their hearts were hard and they missed the point.

Maybe they were supposed to learn that, through faith in Jesus, they could feed the masses and calm the storms. Perhaps, from the loaves, they were supposed to learn that Jesus is Israel's Shepherd and the God who feeds His people in the wilderness. Perhaps they should have remembered those famous words from Psalm 23, "even though I walk through the valley of the shadow of death, I fear no evil; for You are with me" (Psalm 23:4). Jesus was with them, but they still feared.

They should have learned to trust their Shepherd rather than fear the shadow of death. Perhaps this is why Jesus says, "take courage; I AM, do not be afraid" (Mark 6:50). They were supposed to learn that Jesus is the I AM who walks on the water and passes by in front of them and they can trust Him even in perilous times. They did not learn those lessons. Even when the Lord is with them, they live in fear with hardened hearts.

Reflection Questions

1. What connections can you make between this story and the book of Exodus? Compare and contrast this story with Matthew 14:22–33. What most amazes you about this miracle? What does this miracle teach us about the identity of Jesus?
2. Why would the disciples have hard hearts? What should they have learned from Jesus feeding the 5,000 in the wilderness? What is the connection between Jesus feeding the 5,000 and walking on the water? Why are the disciples still so afraid?

Endnotes

1. Mark 1:32 uses the word "evening" for "after the sun had set." Sunset would begin the first watch of the night.

2. Richard Hays, *Reading Backwards: Figural Christology and the Fourfold Gospel Witness* (Waco: Baylor University Press, 2014), 25.

REFLECTION 30
MISSING THE POINT

Mark 6:53–7:23

The Heart of Man

IT'S MUCH EASIER to influence people's words and actions than their hearts. My two sons are two and four years old, and I can usually control their actions ... kind of. What I mean is when it's time to leave the park, and they begin to cry and scream because they don't want to leave the park, I can still get them in the car. The four-year-old usually will because I tell him to. The two-year-old can be picked up and carried to the car against his will. Ultimately, they both end up in the car. I can explain why we are leaving and usually even get them to say, "Yes Sir!" (Sometimes the two-year-old says, "Yes Ma'am" but we're working on that). Through their tears and tone, it's obvious that their hearts still long for the slide, the rock wall, the green hills, and the stream. They are in the car, but their hearts are far from it.

Sometimes we can practice our obedience and worship this way as well. As followers of Jesus, we may say many of the right words and do a lot of the "Christiany" things, but it's not always representative of where our hearts are. We may be sitting in the pew on Sunday morning, but our hearts are far from God. We may read our Bibles, say daily prayers, attend all of the church events (even wearing a tie), we may teach others, deny ourselves certain pleasures, and live according to the most strict interpretations of the Bible and church practice, but our hearts can still be far from God. Many of the Pharisees, it turns out, were in that situation.

Pharisees dedicated their lives to religious practices and vigilant adherence to a strict interpretation of the Law and its traditions. They looked like the holiest men in all the land, but looks can be deceiving. What's so shocking is how easily all the rule following can distract from our primary objective as believers. This is not always the case, but if we're not careful, it can happen. Strict adherence to the most conservative interpretations of the Bible can potentially lead us farther from God. That seems so counter-intuitive, but like anything else in this world, even something valuable, like obedience and rules, can become dangerous and harmful if done for the wrong purposes. As Jesus will point out, obedience can easily slip into disobedience if we lose track of Who and why we obey. Obedience can become self-serving. Obedience can become an idol.

Tradition, Elders, and Churches

Notice what the Pharisees are obeying in Mark 7:1–13. The Pharisees condemn the disciples of Jesus (remember Mark 2:18 and 24) because they did not wash their hands before eating a meal. "The Pharisees and all the Jews do not eat unless they carefully wash their hands, observing the traditions of the elders" (Mark 7:3). I want to point out just a few things here before we dig deeper.

First, washing your hands is a good thing. The Pharisees, and all the Jews, were practicing something valuable and hygienic (although their purpose was not primarily hygienic). There is nothing sinful about washing one's hands before a meal, obviously. We encourage people to do the same in our culture. Parents teach it to their children, and we look cross at people who refuse to wash.

It could even be valuable to attach religious significance to it. The priests washed before entering the tabernacle (Exod 30:20) as a reminder that they were about to appear before a clean, pure, and holy God. Before eating food, which is given by God, it may be a good idea to approach Him with clean hands and thankful hearts, offering up prayers of gratitude and preparing our bodies before we enjoy His blessings. In our culture we can eat so quickly and mindlessly. Surely adding time for reverence, reflection, and purity before receiving God's blessing of food can be a good idea.

Secondly, this tradition is said to have come from the elders. It is a good idea to listen to your elders. Israel had elders (Exod 3:16; 18:21–26; 24:1; Num 11:16–25) and this practice continued into Christianity. Paul gives descriptions of the type of men these elders are in 1 Timothy 3:1–7 and Titus 1:5–9 and Peter exhorts them to live out their calling as shepherds in 1 Peter 5:1–4.

Elders are shepherds of the people. They have proven themselves to be good fathers and faithful followers, they have gained wisdom and insight, and they have earned an audience by a lifetime of dedication to God. Whether you are a Christian or a Jew, listening to the wisdom of well-respected older people is a good idea. These Jews have been listening to the wisdom and traditions of their elders by washing their hands before meals. There is nothing wrong with this.

Third, only "some of His disciples" were not doing this (Mark 7:2). I wonder why. If washing is something all the Jews do, why did some of Jesus's Jewish disciples not? It's not that hard to wash your hands and it doesn't hurt anyone. Luke 11:38

mentions once at a Pharisee's house Jesus also didn't wash up; did He tell them not to? Were they simply stubborn and obnoxious?

Why couldn't they just be agreeable and go along with the social customs, listen to their elders, and do something harmless like wash their hands before eating? This is the type of stuff that drives people crazy. It drives church leaders crazy: "Just be easy and do what you're supposed to do like everyone else without causing problems! Just wash your hands!"

In my ministry experience, I've seen these types of issues arise repeatedly. Every church develops traditions in how they function. It's impossible not to develop traditions. Many of those traditions are handed down by godly, wise, faithful people, like elders, and they can be good and valuable. Most church members will follow the traditions and keep the peace and help things run smoothly. But some don't. Some eat their meals with unwashed hands. Some refuse to go to our Bible classes. Some do not dress the way everyone else does. Some people are always challenging or "trying to improve" how the church worships, fellowships, and serves the community. Some want to change, ignore, or reject our traditions and practices.

What do you do with those people? Do we kick them out of the church family? Do we talk bad about them behind their backs? Do we try to force them to adhere to our way of doing things? The Pharisees come at Jesus frustrated that His disciples are not following the elders anymore. Every act of open disobedience encourages others to do the same and the elders are losing authority. They storm up to Jesus and say, "Why do Your disciples not walk according to the tradition of the elders, but eat their bread with impure hands?" (Mark 7:5).

False Prophets and Lawmakers

Jesus gives a most unsatisfactory answer. He doesn't rebuke his disciples or tell them, "Just go with the flow and stop being difficult." Instead, He rebukes the Pharisees for focusing on the wrong things. They care more about protecting "their way of doing things" than God's way of doing things. They care more about their control over people than people. They care more about their traditions than God. This is a hard pill to swallow.

This is a trap churches can easily fall into. It's impossible not to develop traditions and many of them are good, defensible traditions, but no matter how good an idea is, or how wise an elder is, or how long something has been practiced, churches cannot enforce laws that don't come from God. You cannot bind people to do church your way. When you do, you put issues above people and yourself above God. Yet, it's easy to do this and feel justified in it. After all, we know it's a good and helpful tradition, we are doing it out of love for the church, and we should learn from our elders. Plus, it's those people being difficult, not us! The Pharisees could say the exact same thing here.

But again, what does Jesus say? If you begin to care so much about your traditions that they matter more than the people who refuse to follow them, you are distancing yourself from God. Jesus reaches back to Isaiah 29:13 and applies this passage to the Pharisees: "This people honors Me with their lips, but their heart is far from Me, But in vain do they worship Me, teaching as doctrines the precepts of men."

If you go back and read Isaiah 29, you'll see it is a woe against the city of Jerusalem. This comes during a series of "Woe" pronouncements that head several chapters in a row (Isa 28:1; 29:1, 15; 30:1; 31:1; 33:1). Judgment is coming for "the city where David encamped" (Isa 29:1).

Isaiah 29 compares false prophets to drunk, blind, and

sleeping men. These prophets are given a scroll of prophecy, but the literate one cannot open the scroll, so the scroll is handed to a seer who can open it, but he is illiterate. No one can see what God is doing, so they make their own plans from their own wisdom. Isaiah 29:14 says, "the wisdom of their wise men will perish" (see 1 Cor 1:19). Those who trust in their own wisdom have no need for God in their plans (Isa 29:15) and like clay that says to the potter "He did not make me" (Isa 29:16). Jerusalem is listening to their blind prophets, and it will bring them destruction.

As listening to false prophets can draw you farther from God, enslaving others to manmade traditions can have a similar effect. The one who creates new teachings and binds them on others is like the false prophet who speaks a word that does not come from God. The Pharisee who condemns a man for not washing his hands, the church who condemns Christians for not adhering to all the traditional procedures, are not better than the false prophet who invents a new path to God. That path always leads only to himself, and his lips and his heart move in opposite directions.

Reflection Questions

1. What are some traditions practiced in your church or personal life that are not in the Bible? What are some of the benefits of those traditions? How can those traditions become dangerous?
2. In what ways can our lips and our hearts say different things? How do man-made commandments render our worship vain? What is a healthy path forward with church traditions?

REFLECTION 31

TRADITIONS, COMMANDS, AND PRIORITIES

Protecting the Law

JESUS DOES NOT CONDEMN the Pharisees for having traditions or for washing their hands. He does not condemn them for listening to their elders. He condemns them for elevating their traditions over people and God. Churches can have traditions and follow them. Many long-lasting traditions that have stood the test of time are meaningful and beautiful. You do not have to change your traditions to suit the whims of every individual, but you cannot define who is a Christian by those traditions. You cannot enslave people to them and judge or condemn those who do not adhere. Jesus does not say their problem is having tradition but violating the commands of God for the sake of their tradition.

These traditions started with honorable intentions and commendable ideas: the law of God is sacred and must be interpreted and applied accurately. Nobody should disagree with that. As time moves forward from the days of Moses, questions about interpretations and applications arose about all sorts of matters of the law. What technically counts as "work" on the Sabbath? What "indecent thing" is meant in

Deuteronomy 24:1? What are the proper ways to "wash" and "be clean" before God? In the Mishnah, you'll find lengthy discussions about every possible way of interpreting the law you can imagine.

Eventually, rabbinic answers to these types of questions became normative, at least among some sects of Judaism. If one obeyed all the traditions, they'd never even come close to breaking the law. The traditions kept you safe from breaking the law. They also kept the law pure and sacred. Traditions were thought to be like a fence that keep one from breaking the law. Fences can be helpful and safe. We want zoos to have fences to keep us safe from the dangerous animals (and to keep them safe from us). Climbing the fence is foolish.

This is how traditions keep us safe from breaking the law. They create some distance between us and sin. Imagine if Adam and Eve built a strong, impenetrable wall around the tree of the knowledge of good and evil. They would have been safe from violation and the world would be a much different and better place. Similarly, Jewish traditions worked to keep people away from violation of the law. Often our church traditions do the same thing.

How Traditions Can Develop

You may have seen this progression happen in churches before. Sometimes we build fences around laws to keep us from violation. For example, church singing described in the New Testament is done without instrumental music. So (many) churches of Christ continue the practice of singing without instruments. "But" one may ask, "what counts as an instrument?" Now we must begin to dissect that question. Do hums and beats produced by the human lips and vocal cords count? What about a pitch pipe to help the song leader? What about hand clapping? Or finger snapping? Is the hand technically an instrument? Is the hand basically a drum? Can one clap during a song? Can one celebrate spiritual things with hand clapping? Can one clap after a baptism? Can one clap after an announcement of good news? Can one clap during a wedding held in the church building? Can you listen to instrumental music during a wedding at the church building? Or a funeral? Can you listen to songs about God, or praising God, with instruments in your car or at home? What if you are not worshipping? Can you clap, or snap fingers, while teaching a new song to help people learn the beat? I've seen each of these questions discussed and even debated about over the years.

By the way, if you are not in churches of Christ, that entire previous paragraph will seem bizarre to you, but every church of Christ has had to answer to those questions. Most churches answer "yes" to some and "no" to others. Some might think those are ludicrous questions while others consider them with utmost seriousness.

I've seen Christians condemn other believers and entire congregations based on how they answer those questions. However, and this is the main point, hopefully we can all see that in answering them, we left the text of the Bible a long time ago. We are now in the realm of interpreting an interpretation of an interpretation and distancing ourselves further and further from the written words of the Bible. This is what the Pharisees did (not to earn salvation, but to honor God and uphold the law). This is how some strange and silly traditions develop (we have them too). Ultimately, they stem from a desire to obey God, but that desire can lead to some weird places.

For many people, these types of traditions become the equal to the law (or even surpass it). If we're not constantly reminded of the difference between traditions and doctrines of God, they always fuse together. At times people will even sin just to keep their tradition pure. They will gossip, become angry, and even condemn fellow believers if they do not follow proper tradition. People will pridefully split churches over traditions. In doing so, they cast aside the Bible for the sake of tradition. Jesus expounds on this point next, giving an example of when the Pharisees cast aside the law of God for their traditions.

The Example of Corban

The example Jesus gives is dedicating your wealth to God instead of using it to help your aging parents. There is nothing inherently wrong with dedicating your wealth to God, but if you say, "My money is Corban [which means given to God], so I can't help you mom and dad," you have replaced the actual command of God to "honor your father and your mother" (Exod 20:12) for the religious practice of the Corban tradition.

To understand this example, we must know that "honoring" our father and mother is not just about saying "sir" and "ma'am." There are financial obligations associated with this command. 1 Timothy 5:3-4 tells the church to "honor" widows who do not have a family to provide for them. This language means to provide financially for them. Jews, in the time of Jesus, had a legal responsibility to care for their aging parents.

The "Corban tradition" seems to be getting in the way of this command. The Greek word Corban [κορβᾶν] is a loan word from Hebrew [קָרְבָּן] which, in the Old Testament, is usually translated as "offering" (it's used almost 80 times in Leviticus and Numbers and only four times elsewhere). It is an offering or sacrifice given to God. Mark 7:11 transliterates the word from Hebrew into Greek. We also find this word discussed in rabbinic literature and the Mishnah. There are two mentions by Josephus, and archaeologists have discovered an Aramaic inscription on an ossuary near the time of Jesus that says: "Everything that a man will find to his profit in this ossuary (is) an offering [Corban] to God from the one within it."

Considering this information, it appears Corban was originally an offering made at the temple, but over time a (controversial) tradition developed of vowing certain possessions or an amount of wealth to God. It's hard to be certain whether those possessions or that wealth had to immediately be given to the temple, but it appears not always. On the ossuary, a man was buried with his "Corban" offering. The Corban vow was like a ban that obligated you to keep your wealth for God, rather than spending it or giving it to others. Those Corban items would be set aside as belonging to God and were off limits for personal use.

This Corban tradition could potentially be a good thing. It could be a way of remembering the generosity of God and giving back to Him. It is a freewill offering of your own goods to the treasury or to God. But, like any good thing, there is the potential for abuse. For instance, if you dedicate your money to God, then it cannot be given to others. You could use a Corban vow as a ban that restricted generosity. Sometimes vows to God can interfere with our obligations to one another (remember Jephthah in Judges 11:29–40?). Jesus accuses the Pharisees of approving of this type of vow.

This vow could be used (even unintentionally) as a loophole to avoid helping others. All you need to do is dedicate your spare funds to God, then when someone is in need, you don't have the money anymore. In the worst cases, it could be devious and intentional. Think of someone budgeting this way: "I know I should give money to God, but I should also help my aging parents. If I do both, I won't be able to afford everything I want. So, what shall I do? I know! I'll give the money set aside for my parents to God instead. Surely my parents cannot complain about me giving money to God. And surely God will be pleased because I am honoring Him with my wealth. And I won't complain because now I get to keep the rest of my money. Plus, I get to look super pious!" Maybe no one schemed in exactly those terms, but that is the type of problem that is arising.

This is a pious way to neglect your parents and to justify it with Scripture: "Do I keep my Corban vow or do I 'honor my father and mother'?" In making a vow to God, you obligate yourself to carry it out (Deut 23:21-23; Lev 19:12). It would be a sin to break your oath, but if you keep your oath, you violate the command to "honor father and mother." In this way, one is setting up two commands of God against each other and using the Law of Moses to justify neglecting their parents.

Corban is a tradition that, through a sketchy interpretive process, can be supported with Scripture and used to neglect the 5th commandment, but God did not ask you to make this vow. Interestingly, Jesus also says you've set aside Exodus 21:17 (see Lev 20:9) which condemns "cursing" or "speaking evil" of your parents. That sin is a capital crime. Financially neglecting your parents is apparently a way of cursing/speaking evil of them.

God did not command Corban vows and He never wants us to neglect our parents. It's important to remember that God would rather us give money to our parents than to Him. The best way to honor God is not to create some new holy act of service or make a vow He never asked for, but to honor your mom and dad.

This is only one example, but Jesus says, "you do many things such as that" (Mark 7:13). It's easy and extremely dangerous to invent holy and righteous sounding traditions and then elevate them over the actual commands of God. If you put a church tradition over the command to "love your neighbor as yourself" I think Jesus is talking to you. If you pride knowledge over love, interpretive exactitude over unity, and comfort over outreach, He may be talking to you too.

Reflection Questions

1. How do traditions become law over time? What role does the Bible, wisdom, and community play in the development of traditions? How should newcomers be expected to respond to church traditions? Should the church reject all traditions? Is that even possible?

2. What does the "Corban" example teach us about traditions? What principles should guide our traditions? How should the command to "love your neighbor as yourself" influence our practice and teachings?

REFLECTION 32

ALL FOODS (AND PEOPLE) CLEAN

Mark 7:14–23

Food and the Heart

JESUS CALLS the crowds back to expound a little further on some of these controversial matters (Mark 7:14). Again, Jesus addresses the "heart." We recently found out that the disciples have hard hearts (Mark 6:52). We also know that the Pharisees care more about their traditions than God's commandments, which distances their hearts from God (Mark 7:6). Jesus wants everyone to understand that the internal heart is more important than external demonstrations of piety.

This is among Jesus's most controversial sayings. In this conversation, Jesus will not teach against traditions like hand washing and Corban, but He will decree a change in the Law of Moses. He will render an important teaching from the Law obsolete. Jesus will place His authority not only above the Pharisees and scribes, but above Moses and the Law. Jesus will share the seat of God as the true Lawgiver in Israel. It is important to note, however, Jesus does not say, "Moses was wrong, it is actually alright to eat unclean foods," rather He declares, "all foods are now clean." Instead of breaking the Law of Moses, Jesus purifies what Moses called impure. Purity still matters, but Jesus, with authority matched only by God, renders all foods pure.

He teaches a parable, saying, what goes into a man is not what defiles or renders unclean, but what comes out (Mark 7:15). The disciples ask Him more about this confusing riddle in private (remember Mark 4:33–34). It is important that this ensuing conversation is in private. Saying this publicly would have been pandemonium. Only His disciples are ready to hear it. At least He thinks they should be. Sadly, they are still "lacking in understanding" (Mark 7:18).

He says food doesn't impact the heart. It just goes into the stomach and then leaves the body. It has no impact on who you are as a person or your walk with God. Food is irrelevant for discipleship. Mark then adds a parenthetical note to the reader, clarifying the enormity of what Jesus said, "(Thus He declared all foods clean)" (Mark 7:19). This is a radical declaration and Mark does not want us to miss it.

Remember that Jesus already touched a leper (Mark 1:41), a menstruating woman (Mark 5:27), and a dead body (Mark 5:41), and was not rendered unclean. Jesus is not concerned with regulations that render clean or unclean, He is concerned with the heart. He now explicitly teaches that foods cannot defile a person or render someone unclean. Well, Jesus, that's a huge chunk of the Bible you're messing with. That will create controversy. Reading through the Gospel of Mark it becomes clear that leprosy, blood, death, and foods do not have the power to make us unclean.

A Scandalous Teaching

Think about what this means for Jews. Think about what this means for Jewish nationalism. To Jews, these food laws were a matter of their national identity, their devotion to God, and they were literally a matter of life and death. Daniel was determined that he would die rather than defile Himself with the king's food (Dan 1:8). Was Daniel wrong to care about the food laws? Remember, there is no New Testament when Jesus says this. The only Bible is the Old Testament and if you compare what Jesus is saying to what Moses wrote, many will hear them as flatly contradictory. This would be a major problem for the Jews.

In the relatively recent past, the Jews experienced terrible persecution under the reign of Antiochus IV Epiphanes over these exact issues. 1 Maccabees records the details of these persecutions. The lives of those brave, faithful, zealous Jews who stood up for the Law of Moses against the Greek Empire were on the line: "Many in Israel stood firm and were resolved in their hearts not to eat unclean food. They chose to die rather than to be defiled by food or to profane the holy covenant; and they did die" (1 Macc 1:62–63).

These faithful martyrs were honored as heroes for their faith in the time of Jesus. They stood up for their country, they stood up for the Law of Moses, and they stood up for the truth of God. Now Jesus comes along and says, those food laws don't matter. He sounds more like Antiochus than a faithful Israelite. He sounds like the enemy who cares nothing about Israelite identity, history, or religion. This would be shocking and offensive. To say this publicly would be like saying Israel's past soldiers and heroes died for nothing, that Daniel wasn't really a hero, and that Moses was wrong.

This is not just a matter of food; this is their national story, their beliefs about God, and their Law. This is emotional. It's like Jesus just stomped on their Bible, dishonored their soldiers, and burned their flag. When we read this passage, it might not strike us that way because we are so far removed from their time and culture. To really feel it, ask yourself what ideas and symbols are most sacred to you as an American (if you are American)? How do you feel when those are ignored or dishonored? What is sacred to you about your faith and church and Christianity? What if a teacher came along and said those don't matter anymore? This is Israel's sacred history and identity that Jesus is critiquing.

The Jewish Jesus

Jesus is a Jew with the same national story. We need to remember this is Jesus's story too. He's no Greek and He's not a Gentile. Jesus cares about the Law of Moses, He weeps over Jerusalem, and He's serious about honoring God.

To many, these food laws mattered because they made them distinct from the Gentiles who lived around them. They were occupied by Rome, and they had no king in Jerusalem. They had no sovereignty as a nation. Their identity is found in their unique religious practices like circumcision, Sabbath, and food laws. At this bleak moment in their history, they have so little that is uniquely theirs, and they need these laws and practices if they want to remain in any way special, unique, or set apart.

It is offensive when Jesus comes along and tries to take that away. Many would die for these food laws which made Israel the holy, singular people of God. I am curious how this conversation would have gone if Jesus were still among the Pharisees and the crowds, rather than in a private house with His disciples. This type of teaching could start riots.

It's no accident that this story is located right here in Mark's Gospel. The next thing Jesus does after this account is travel to Gentile lands and meet a Gentile woman (Mark 7:24–26). Jesus touched unclean people, has authority over unclean spirits, criticizes sacred Jewish traditions, declares all foods clean, and then goes to Gentile territory and talks to a Gentile woman. This is all strongly suggestive of the larger Gentile mission.

Changes are being made which will prepare the way for everybody to enter God's family. Jesus is preparing His disciples to stop seeing the world in terms of national identity and clean/unclean. Jesus has a mission and a kingdom for the entire world and borders, prejudices, traditions, cultures, laws, washings, and food cannot get in the way. He's breaking down the barriers that keep Jews and Gentiles separate.

What matters is the heart. The heart is something all people share. The heart can unite Jew and Gentile. The heart and the words it spews reveal who we really are (Mark 7:20–23). More than ceremonially cleaning our hands or avoiding pork, the thoughts and words of our heart reveal our true character and our purity. Our heart is a better indicator of our identity than the foods we eat.

Reflection Questions

1. In what ways was declaring all foods clean offensive? Did Jesus break the Law of Moses? What was the purpose of the food regulations? Were they beneficial? What ways might this story apply to American nationalism?
2. How does this story relate to the gospel? How does this story relate to the wider Gentile mission? Why is it more challenging to control what comes out of our hearts and mouths than to limit what goes inside?

REFLECTION 33
JESUS AND THE GENTILES

Mark 7:24–37

Meeting Gentiles

IF YOU'VE PAID attention to His travels, you'll notice that Jesus keeps crossing the sea of Galilee on a boat. When He is on the west of the sea of Galilee, the land is predominantly populated by Jews and when He is on the east of the sea of Galilee, He enters the land of Gentiles. Now, there were some Gentiles in Galilee and there were certainly Jews to the east of Galilee, but crossing the sea probably represents entering the wider Gentile world.

Jesus does miracles on both sides of the sea. In Mark 5:1–20 He cast out Legion on the east side of the sea. In Mark 7:24 Jesus traveled up to "Tyre and Sidon." This is way up north in Gentile territory, and it's no mistake that Jesus meets a woman there who "was a Gentile, a Syrophoenician by birth" (Mark 7:26). Jesus heals her demon possessed daughter.

After Jesus's encounter with this woman, "He returned from the region of Tyre and went through Sidon to the Sea of Galilee, in the region of the Decapolis" (Mark 7:31). Decapolis should sound familiar. It's the ten cities mentioned earlier in Mark 5:20. Jesus was proclaimed there by the man previously possessed by Legion, "and everyone marveled" (Mark 5:20).

This is an extremely long journey from Tyre and Sidon. You should look at a map on Google or the back of your Bible and see that Tyre and Sidon are way up northwest on the Mediterranean coast, and Decapolis is on the east side of the Sea of Galilee to the south. Jesus is taking a long Gentile-focused journey. When He arrives in Decapolis He heals a man who "was deaf and had a speech impediment" (Mark 7:32).

After these two Gentile healing stories, Jesus is surrounded by a crowd which grows hungry, so He miraculously feeds 4,000 (Mark 8:1–9). Where does this happen? The implication of the text is that Jesus is still in Gentile territory. There is no mention of Him coming back to Jewish land until Mark 8:10, when "He got into a boat with His disciples and went to the district of Dalmanutha."[1]

This means Jesus casts out demons for Jews and Gentiles, He heals Jews and Gentiles, and He miraculously feeds large groups of Jews and Gentiles. Mark 7:24–8:9 is a glimpse of the larger Gentile mission that will proceed forth from Jesus and His disciples. Central to the gospel is the unification of Jew and Gentile, and all peoples of the earth, into the one family of God.

It is no accident that these stories immediately follow the arguments about law, tradition, purity, food regulations, cleanliness, and uncleanness in Mark 7:1–23. Jesus "declares all foods clean" (Mark 7:19) and then travels to Gentile territory to show that all people are clean also (see Acts 10:9–23)! The Jesus who touched the leper (Mark 1:41), the menstruant (Mark 5:25), and the dead (Mark 5:41), who declared all foods clean, now goes directly into Gentile land and heals and saves. This is a foretaste of, what Paul calls, "the mystery of the Gospel," that Jews and "Gentiles are fellow heirs, members of the same body, and partakers of the promise in Christ Jesus through the gospel" (Eph 3:6).

The Syrophoenician Woman

When Jesus arrives in Tyre and Sidon, He enters a house. He hoped to do this secretly, as with much of His ministry, but again word got out anyway (Mark 7:24). A Gentile woman comes to Him and "falls down at His feet." This reminds us of Legion (Mark 5:6), Jairus (Mark 5:22), and the woman with the flow of blood (Mark 5:33). Men and women, Jews and Gentiles, from the wealthy synagogue ruler to the maniac living among the tombs, all will reverently fall before the feet of Jesus (Phil 2:10).

This woman has a serious problem. Her daughter is demon possessed and, as a mother, she is powerless to save her own daughter. It is utterly miserable to be unable to save your own child. Saving a child is a common motivation when people come to Jesus. Jairus came to Jesus because his daughter was on the verge of death (Mark 5:23). In a few chapters we'll meet a man whose son is demon possessed (Mark 9:17). Here is a Gentile woman who heard about Jesus and in desperation falls before Him and begs Him to save her daughter.

Jesus's response is perhaps the most un-Jesusy response He gives to any person in the Bible. It's cringy to read and it makes you wonder, "Why?" He says, "Let the children be fed first, for it is not right to take the children's bread and throw it to the dogs" (Mark 7:27). Did Jesus seriously just employ common Jewish nationalist sentiments that Jews are the children of God, but Gentiles are just dogs? Did He really reject a desperate woman calling on Him for help because she was a Gentile? Would He really leave this family in a helpless, miserable state because of her race? Why would Jesus speak this way when He certainly does not share those sentiments and He just declared a new kind of cleanness?

Mark does not clearly answer these questions. Mark often lets us grapple with understanding the words and actions of Jesus.

As I grapple with it, there are four points I think are important to remember: Purpose, Time, Test, and Compassion. First, Jesus's purpose was not to travel to Tyre to heal the masses and start a new ministry there. He went there to get away for a while and perhaps get some rest while tensions died down back home. He didn't even want anyone to know He was there (Mark 7:24), but this woman finds out and comes to Him anyway. Jesus does not owe healing to everyone who wants it, and His mission was not to physically heal as many people as possible. His healings had intentionality and purpose and this wasn't it.

Second, Jesus's statement is more about her timing than her value. He is illustrating the common order of the dinner table where children eat first and then the dogs. The dogs do still get to eat though. This is in line with the common theme that some things happen "immediately" while other things will happen later (Mark 4:22–23; Mark 9:9). The Gentiles will share with the Jews, but that is not Jesus's mission right now. That happens later. He came to prepare Israel and His disciples for this Gentile mission, not to go on it Himself.

Third, this response should probably be understood as a test for the woman. Jesus was tested in the wilderness (Mark 1:12), and He often tested His disciples (Mark 6:37). Perhaps Jesus is testing this woman to see her response. Jewish nationalism was a stumbling block and a hurdle for many Gentiles; Jesus placed it before her to see what she would do. Jesus is playing the role of the nationalistic Jew. She responds, not with offense or insult, but with faith. Rather than walking away, she steps across the Jew/Gentile barrier and joins Jesus where He stands. She becomes an example of unity in a difficult circumstance. She becomes the hero of the story and shows the disciples how to overcome racial/nationalistic tensions. The Gentile woman becomes the example of humility, faith, and unity.

Finally, His compassion and actions speak louder than His words. Jesus does heal her daughter. Even though that was not His mission, it was not the right time, it's not why He was in Tyre, and it was not the purpose of His ministry, He is flexible and out of love and compassion, He saves her daughter. No matter what He has planned, Jesus doesn't get to take vacations. He doesn't ignore or neglect people in need. He removes the uncleanness (an unclean spirit) from the Gentile girl.

Healing the Deaf Man

Leaving Tyre and Sidon, Jesus traveled back to Decapolis, and a deaf man with a speech impediment was brought to Him. Jesus determined to heal this person, but as He so often does, He wanted it to be secretive and quiet. This is surprising because the last time Jesus was in this area, He wanted word to spread about Him (Mark 5:19–20). Now on this return trip, Jesus is back to secrecy. Mark does not tell us why.

Mark does tell us that Jesus took the man away from the crowd so they could be alone. Jesus put His fingers in the man's ears and spat and cried out in Aramaic, "Ephphatha" which means "be opened." Just then, the man could hear and speak.

The Greek word used in Mark 7:35 to describe the man's tongue (which many English translations leave untranslated) is translated as "prison" or "chains" in other texts (Acts 16:26; Phil 1:7, 13, 14, 17; Col 4:18). I'd translate Mark 7:35 this way: "And [immediately][2] his ears were opened, and the chains of his tongue were released, and he spoke properly." Jesus freed the man's tongue from prison!

Jesus then vainly commands this man to tell no one. As always happens, he disobeys and tells everyone (Mark 7:35–37;

Mark 1:44–45). The more Jesus tells people to keep it quiet, the more they go out and spread the news. Isn't it ironic how many Christians do the exact opposite today? When we are told to tell everyone, we often keep it silent; while these characters who are told to keep silent, go and tell everyone.

These people (among the Gentiles) learn that Jesus "has done all things well. He even makes the deaf hear and the mute speak." This sounds a lot like the beautiful wilderness picture of Isaiah 35:5–7. This sounds a lot like a Messiah who has compassion for the lowly and suffering. This sounds like a Messiah who loves Jews and Gentiles alike.

Reflection Questions

1. How would you have felt if Jesus responded to you the way He did to the Syrophoenician woman? Would you have handled it so gracefully? Why do you think Jesus sounded so un-Jesusy in this passage? What can this Gentile focused section in Mark teach us about unity and overcoming racial and cultural boundaries?

2. Why do so many people disobey Jesus's instructions to remain silent? Is it possible they are so thankful and amazed that they cannot help but proclaim the wonders of Jesus? Why is it often so difficult for us?

Endnotes

1. Some manuscripts call this "Magdala" instead of "Dalmanutha," which would be the home of Mary Magdalene.

2. The word "immediately" is bracketed in the 5th edition of the UBS Greek New Testament. It is present in some manuscripts and absent in others.

REFLECTION 34
HEARTS STILL HARD

Mark 8:1-21

Feeding the 4,000

CHAPTER 8 BEGINS with a great crowd gathering again around Jesus. There has been no mention of a trip back across Galilee, so the assumption is that Jesus is still among Gentiles. Jesus, like Moses but even more like God, fed the 5,000 Jews in wilderness (Mark 6:30-34); now, Jesus will feed 4,000 Gentiles. The different setting in these two feeding miracles is significant.

Jesus felt compassion for His Jewish countrymen in Mark 6:34, and He also feels compassion for Gentiles (Mark 8:2). These two feeding miracles share almost the exact same language when read side by side and tell the story in the same arrangement:

1. Large crowd arrives,
2. Jesus has compassion,
3. The disciples don't think they can feed them,
4. Jesus asks, "how many loaves do you have?"

5. They give Him a number (five and seven),
6. Fish are mentioned along with bread,
7. Jesus tells the crowds to sit down,
8. Jesus blesses and breaks the bread,
9. "They ate and were satisfied,"
10. The disciples collect baskets of left-over bread (twelve baskets and seven baskets),
11. The number of people is revealed at the end (5,000 and 4,000),
12. The disciples enter a boat (Jesus joins them the second time).

The similarities in these stories must be intentional. As Jesus cared for the Jews, He also cares for Gentiles. As the Israelites were fed in the wilderness, so the Gentiles will feast as well. Perhaps this illustrates the welcoming of Gentiles into the story of Israel. Jesus has cleansed all foods (Mark 7:19), traveled among and healed Gentiles (Mark 7:29, 35), and now feeds the Gentiles as He fed the Jews. Jesus is treating Gentiles as though they are clean.

The Leaven of the Pharisees and Herod

Jesus and the disciples hop on a boat and head back to the Jewish territory of Dalmanutha (or Magdala depending on the manuscript). They are immediately hit with conflict as the Pharisees start arguing with Jesus. They demand a sign (if only they'd been following or paying attention). Jesus doesn't give them a sign, and He gets back on a boat and leaves, traveling north to Bethsaida.

This boat ride is fraught with confusion. The disciples realize that they didn't pack any bread. They are going on a journey and forgot food! That's kind of important. I wonder whose job it was to make sure they had something to eat. Someone dropped the ball.

As they begin to worry and argue about food, Jesus says, "Beware of the leaven of the Pharisees and the leaven of Herod" (Mark 8:15). The disciples immediately connect the word "leaven" to bread and begin "discussing with one another the fact that they had no bread" (Mark 8:16). Were they pointing fingers? Were they planning to get food once the boat arrived? We're not sure. What we do know is they completely missed what Jesus was saying.

We have seen Herod and the Pharisees several times in Mark already. The Pharisees just argued with Jesus (Mark 8:11) before He got on the boat. Herod, we know, imprisoned and executed John the Baptist. The Herodians and the Pharisees have been scheming together to destroy Jesus since Mark 3:6 (and we'll see what they come up with in Mark 12:13–14).

Mark does not tell us exactly what Jesus means here. Matthew says the "leaven" is the "teaching of the Pharisees and Sadducees"[1] (Matt 16:12), and Luke says it is their "hypocrisy" (Luke 12:1). This is an example, among many, where Mark is intentionally more ambiguous than the other Gospel writers. He often gives the reader material for meditation rather than direct answers, and the ambiguity leaves the disciples arguing about bread.

Deaf, Blind, and Hardened

Back in Mark 4:11–12, the disciples were supposed to understand the parables. They were given insider information. Jesus took them aside and privately explained everything to them, yet somehow, they understand no better than anyone else. They are just as blind and deaf as those on the outside.

Think about where they are and what they are talking about.

The disciples are on a boat with Jesus. They already saw Him do incredible miracles while on a boat in this sea. He calmed the storm in Mark 4:35–41; but the disciples responded with fear and confusion (Mark 4:41). He walked on the water and calmed another storm in Mark 6:47–52; but they responded with fear and hardened hearts and "they had not gained any insight from the incident with the bread" (Mark 6:51–52). They were supposed to learn something when Jesus fed the 5,000 (Mark 6:41–44), but they didn't. Jesus then miraculously feeds 4,000, and they still don't learn anything. We know this because they are on a boat with Jesus, who can multiply bread for thousands and has already done it twice, and they are still worried about bread!

Jesus challenges their lack of faith with a series of questions:

"Why are you discussing the fact that you have no bread? Do you not yet perceive or understand? Are your hearts hardened? Having eyes do you not see, and having ears do you not hear? And do you not remember? When I broke the five loaves for the five thousand, how many baskets full of broken pieces did you take up?" They said to Him, "Twelve." "And the seven for the four thousand, how many baskets full of broken pieces did you take up?" And they said to Him, "Seven." And He said to them, "Do you not yet understand?" (Mark 8:17–21).

If you have ears but do not hear, you are deaf. If you have eyes but do not see, you are blind. The disciples appear to be both. They do not understand because they still have hard hearts (Mark 6:52; 8:17). What will it take to soften their hearts? Apparently, the miracles and the private teachings of Jesus are not working. They saw the miracles, they counted the baskets of bread, they remembered what Jesus did, but it's not impacting how they currently live. They are still concerned about bread. They are still blind, deaf, and hard hearted.

The rest of the Gospel of Mark will be answering the question of how to soften their hearts. Mark is going to take a dramatic turn in the next few verses, and the rest of the book will be focused on bringing Jesus to the cross and preparing the disciples for that reality. Can the cross open their eyes and ears? Will the cross soften their hearts? We need to keep reading to find out.

Reflection Questions

1. What are some ways in which you fail to learn and grow? In what areas can we be blind to the working of God? Are there some messages that are hard to apply and believe no matter how many times you have heard them? What can you do to open your eyes and begin to see?

2. What lessons do you learn from feeding the 5,000 and 4,000? In what ways is this lesson applicable today? What can this teach you about generosity? The provision of God? The identity of Jesus?

Endnotes

1. Matthew says "Sadducees" where Mark says "Herodians," and Luke only mentions the "Pharisees."

REFLECTION 35
TWO BLIND MEN

Mark 8:17–30; 10:46–52

The First Blind Man

THIS UNCOMFORTABLE BOAT ride ends in Bethsaida when Jesus and a thoroughly rebuked group of disciples step on dry land. A blind man is brought to Jesus as soon as He arrives. What takes place next is incredible. This is one of the few incidents that is recorded only in Mark's Gospel.

This miracle is unlike any other and can be confusing if you don't pay attention. This blind man is taken away from the village, so it'll be another private miracle. Jesus spits on his eyes, lays hands on him, and amazingly, the man can see! Kind of.

The man says he can see, but barely: "I see men, for I see them like trees, walking around" (Mark 8:22–26). His eyesight is so bad that people look like trees walking around. That's a cool miracle, I guess, but it really doesn't match the way Jesus normally heals. Jesus only half-way healed the man; it looks a little like a botched miracle, so Jesus tries again.

For attempt number two, Jesus lays His hands on the man's

eyes, and then the miracle is complete. He can see everything clearly and his sight is restored! Jesus tells him to go home and stay out of the village (again, the secrecy).

Granted, it's a better miracle than I can do, but why did it take Jesus two attempts? Was He having an off day? That doesn't seem right. That's why some suggest that Matthew skipped this miracle, instead of placing it in between Matthew 16:12–13. They think this is an embarrassing miracle that the other Gospel writers wanted to ignore. Others think that this man's faith was only halfway there, so Jesus could only halfway do the miracle (like in Mark 6:5–6). If the man had better faith, the miracle would have worked better. There is nothing like that suggested in this passage, and in Mark 9:24–25 Jesus casts out an unclean spirit when a man is clearly struggling with unbelief. I think something else is happening here.

The Second Blind Man

Before we attempt to explain what went wrong in miracle #1, let's skip a few chapters ahead and read about a second blind man Jesus healed (Mark 10:46–52). Jesus calmed two storms (Mark 4:39; 6:51), and multiplied bread for two crowds (Mark 6:41–43; 8:7–9), and Jesus also heals two blind men (Mark 8:22–26; 10:46–52). These stories are doublets that are interesting to compare.

The second blind man's name is Bartimaeus, meaning "Son of honor," but he sat by the road as a blind beggar. Nobody would have ever connected this blind beggar with honor. In fact, when he cries out to Jesus, using the Messianic title "Son of David, have mercy on me!" (Mark 10:47, 48), he was rebuked by the crowd, who basically told him to shut up. It's like they thought Jesus didn't have time for this worthless beggar, but if you know Jesus, you shouldn't be surprised by what happens next.

Jesus tells the crowd to bring Bartimaeus to Him, and they do. Bartimaeus throws off his cloak, jumps up with excitement, and runs over to Jesus. Jesus asks him what he wants, and he says, "Rabboni, I want to regain my sight!" (Mark 10:51). Jesus heals Him immediately, in one attempt, and the man sees clearly. Then he follows Jesus.

There are numerous differences in these two stories. The first blind man is unnamed, but the second one is named Bartimaeus. The first blind man was healed north of the Sea of Galilee in Bethsaida, but Bartimaeus was healed down south in Jericho on the road to Jerusalem. The first blind man was brought to Jesus by others, but Bartimaeus was kept from Him by others. The first blind man did not ask to be healed, but Bartimaeus begged the Son of David for mercy and healing. The first blind man was brought out of the village, but Bartimaeus was healed in front of a crowd on a busy road. The first blind man regained his sight in stages, but Bartimaeus regained his sight instantly. The first blind man went home afterwards, but Bartimaeus started following Jesus.

Seeing Jesus

Healing these two blind men in these radically different ways, bookend, or sandwich, the most intense calls for discipleship in Mark's Gospel. It is between these two healings that Jesus is revealed to be the Christ, explains that He is going to be crucified and raised, and challenges His disciples to carry their own crosses and follow Him. It is between these two healings that Jesus travels from Galilee to Jerusalem for His arrest and crucifixion. It is in this section that we see what following Jesus requires.

So, why would the first healing happen in two stages, with a semi-failure in the middle, while the second healing happens immediately? I believe the best way to read these stories is as though these blind men illustrate the understanding or "sight" of the disciples. Remember, just four verses before we meet the first blind man, Jesus asks His disciples if they have eyes but do not see (Mark 8:18). Jesus calls His disciples blind, and the next thing He does is heal a blind man.

Mark 8–10 is about giving sight to His blind, hard hearted disciples. This sight comes through revealing His identity and destiny and then actually entering Jerusalem for the crucifixion. This is how Jesus will soften their hard hearts.

Immediately after healing the first blind man, Jesus's identity as the Christ is revealed (Mark 8:29). For the first time, the disciples see Jesus as the Messiah. Nothing like this has been said until Mark 8:29. They have asked who He was (Mark 4:41), but they have not declared who He was. They are beginning to see Jesus, but like the blind man, this sight will come in stages.

Jesus then begins to reveal that the Son of Man will suffer, be killed, and raised again (Mark 8:31), and when Peter hears this, he rebukes Jesus. Peter does not think the Son of Man will suffer, and the Christ certainly will not be killed. That's not what Daniel 7 says!

Notice that Peter was blind in Mark 8:18, but now can see clearly enough to identify Jesus as the Christ (Mark 8:29). This is stage one, but men still look like trees. Peter sees Jesus as the Christ but does not know what the Christ looks like. Just as the blind man misidentified the men as trees, so Peter misidentifies the Christ as one who will not face the cross. Peter, and the other disciples, are slowly beginning to see, but it is not yet clear at all.

It's not until that final trip to Jerusalem, the one where Bartimaeus fully receives his sight, that the disciples will see what the cross is all about. It is not until after the resurrection that they will finally see who Jesus is, what the Messiah is destined for, and how the King receives His crown and takes His throne. You cannot see the true Christ without the cross. It is on the cross that finally someone sees, "Truly this man was the Son of God" (Mark 15:39).

Reflection Questions

1. Compare and contrast the healings of these two blind men. In what areas does it feel like you are looking at God's teaching and seeing trees instead of men? What can you do to have clearer sight? How long does clarity take? Can you be faithful without clarity?

2. What do you think the disciples felt when they realized the Man before them was the Christ? What would they have wanted to do with that information? Who might they want to tell? What did their dreams become?

REFLECTION 36
THREE DEADLY PREDICTIONS

Mark 8:27–38; 9:14–29; 10:32–45

Rebuking Jesus

AFTER HEALING the blind man in two stages, Jesus takes His disciples to Caesarea Philippi to complete the first stage of giving them sight. Caesarea Philippi is a long way from home, located about 25 miles north of the sea of Galilee. It housed a temple constructed by Herod the Great to honor Caesar Augustus (the word Caesarea comes from the name Caesar). It was also an important center for pagan mythology and idolatry. Emperor worship and idol worship define Caesarea Philippi.

It is here that Jesus asks His disciples, "Who do people say that I am?" Rumors around the marketplace are that He is John the Baptist (this was Herod's vote), Elijah, or some other prophet. These answers represent a Jewish, rather than pagan or Roman, worldview. In this one scene, Roman emperor worship, pagan idols, and Jewish prophets abound, but they all fall short of the identity of Jesus.

Then Jesus asks, more pointedly, "Who do you say that I am?" Peter steps up and gives the answer, "You are the Christ"

(Mark 8:29). Stage one in giving sight to the disciples is complete. They see that Jesus is the Christ, the Messiah, the Anointed One. Stage two is helping them see that the Christ must suffer and die.

After telling the disciples to keep this information to themselves (Mark 8:30), Jesus begins to describe what will happen to Him, the Son of Man. To understand the significance of this section, you need to have read Reflections 3, 4, and 5. Jesus does not want them telling others that He is the Christ because they do not understand what it means to be the Christ. So, He begins to teach them.

"And He began to teach them that the Son of Man must suffer many things and be rejected by the elders and the chief priests and the scribes, and be killed, and after three days rise again" (Mark 8:31). Jesus clearly and explicitly predicted His coming death and resurrection and Peter rebukes Him for it (Mark 8:32).

Peter has read his Bible and is quite confident in His Messianic expectations. In Daniel 7, the Son of Man is more powerful than the beasts (world empires) and the Son of Man is served by all peoples, nations, and tongues, and His dominion is everlasting and His kingdom is never destroyed (Dan 7:14). The Christ/Messiah receives the nations as an inheritance and breaks them with a rod of iron and shatters them like clay pots (Ps 2:2, 8–9). He certainly is not rejected and killed. Peter rebukes Jesus for getting the story wrong.

Jesus turns around and rebukes Peter right back (this is actually the third rebuke in a row—Mark 8:30, 32, 33. In Greek, Mark 8:30 says Jesus "rebuked them to tell no one"). Peter's problem is that He wants Jesus to carry on the Messianic tradition of victory over Gentiles. David was a mighty king because He killed Goliath and the women even sang that he "killed his ten thousands" (1 Sam 21:11). Moses conquered the Egyptians, Joshua slaughtered the Canaanites,

David killed the Philistines, Judas Maccabeus overthrew the Seleucids, and it's time for Jesus to destroy the Romans. That's what Messiahs do. Because of this, Jesus calls Peter "Satan." Woah.

Peter has set His mind on man's interests, not God's. Peter sees the benefit of Jesus conquering the Romans; he does not see the benefit of the cross. Peter wants to "save his life" and "gain the whole world" (Mark 8:35, 36), but Jesus calls us to lose our lives, to deny ourselves, pick up our crosses, and follow Him (Mark 8:34–36). There is no benefit to gaining the world if you lose yourself in the process.

Jesus's words are hard to stomach. Peter was supposed to get wealth, power, and authority. Instead, he is offered a cross. The Son of Man is not what Peter expected and what Jesus says is shameful. The cross is shameful. Jesus concludes this rebuke by saying, "whoever is ashamed of Me and My words in this adulterous and sinful generation, the Son of Man will also be ashamed of him when He comes in the glory of His Father with the holy angels" (Mark 8:38). Peter, and everyone, will need to rethink the way they view the cross and shame.

Misunderstanding Jesus

Jesus does not give up on Peter or the other disciples. He is patient. He builds them back up with the transfiguration (Mark 9:1–9) and casting out a demon (Mark 9:19–29), before trying to explain His destiny a second time. This second time Jesus explains, "The Son of Man is to be delivered into the hands of men, and they will kill Him; and when He has been killed, He will rise three days later" (Mark 9:31).

The disciples' response is so tragic it's almost laughable. Mark says, "they did not understand this statement, and they were afraid to ask Him" (Mark 9:32). The disciples still do not understand (see Mark 8:21; 9:9–10), and after the rebuke Peter received last time, they aren't about to ask. Fear again motivates their response to Jesus.

They decide to talk about something else instead. They begin discussing which of them is the greatest (Mark 9:34). This may seem unbelievable, but imagine you just met the Messiah, you know the kingdom is coming, and you are in His inner circle. This Messiah can feed an army, heal the wounded, and raise the dead. He can do greater things than Moses, Joshua, and David combined. This means a new world is bursting onto the scene and you get to design it. It's time to start discussing leadership opportunities.

Who will be the Vice-Messiah? Who gets Secretary of State? Who has the most impressive resume? Who has been the most loyal? Which man proved his worth? Who should be paid the most? Like when America defeated the British, they needed to start discussing and forming a new government. Who is going to get the most important positions? These are important conversations, right?

In the same way that they are blind to the Messiah, they are blind to His kingdom. To help them see a little more clearly, Jesus takes a child, who has no greatness or authority, and say, "Whoever receives one child like this in My name, receives Me; and whoever receives Me does not receive Me, but Him who sent Me" (Mark 9:37). This is not the same thing He says in 10:15 about receiving the kingdom like a child. Here He tells them to receive the child. The kingdom is not about personal greatness, it's about receiving even the small, fragile, and powerless.

"If anyone wants to be first, he shall be last of all and servant of all" (Mark 9:35).

Ignoring Jesus

After an interval of intense calls to radical discipleship, Jesus tries a third time to explain the Messiah's destiny (Mark 10:32–

34). This time He is on the road to Jerusalem where His death will take place. On the road He takes His twelve aside and explains again:

> Behold, we are going up to Jerusalem, and the Son of Man will be delivered to the chief priests and the scribes; and they will condemn Him to death and will hand Him over to the Gentiles. They will mock Him and spit on Him, and scourge Him and kill Him, and three days later He will rise again (Mark 10:33–34).

In the clearest words possible, Jesus explains what is about to happen, and the disciples completely ignore Him. They say nothing about it. Are they so deaf that they cannot hear that their friend is going to die? Do they care?

James and John, instead of responding to Jesus, ask Him for a favor. How selfless and thoughtless! I can't read Jesus's response without assuming a despondent sigh when He says, "What do you want me to do for you?" (Mark 10:36).

They ask to sit on His right and His left in glory. They are thinking about their seats, their positions near the Messiah in the coming kingdom. They have not been listening and Jesus tells them, "You do not know what you are asking" (Mark 10:38). They think the seats to the right and left will be nice cushy elevated thrones, but they have no idea what is really to the right and left of Jesus.

In the context of the crucifixion, which He just explained, those on His right and left are dying with Him on crosses (Mark 15:27 is the moment to which Jesus is cryptically hinting). To be on His right and left is to "drink the cup" He drinks and "be baptized" with the baptism He is facing. To "drink the cup" is further elaborated in His prayer in Gethsemane when He prays for the cup to be removed (Mark 14:36). God is the One to grant who sits on Jesus's right and left, who drinks His cup, and receives His baptism of suffering.

The ten other disciples become furious with James and John after this conversation. James and John, after discussing who would be the greatest (Mark 9:34) decide to cut out the other ten and take the place of prominence for themselves. They go above everyone's head to Jesus.

Jesus again calls them all to Him and explains how they are misunderstanding the kingdom. They are still blind to what Jesus is doing. Jesus says,

> You know that those who are recognized as rulers of the Gentiles lord it over them; and their great men exercise authority over them. But it is not this way among you, but whoever wishes to become great among you shall be your servant; and whoever wishes to be first among you shall be salve of all. For even the Son of Man did not come to be served, but to serve, and to give His life a ransom for many (Mark 10:42–45).

Jesus explicitly contrasts the politics of His kingdom from the politics of the beasts. When power and authority act with aggression, force, and intimidation, the beasts are roaming. When you see service, humility, and love, you see the kingdom of God.

In Mark 10:45, Jesus connects two passages that had never been connected in this way before. Jesus speaks of a servant who gives His life as a ransom for others. That is an allusion to the Suffering Servant of Isaiah 53. Jesus connects the Suffering Servant to the Son of Man who receives glory and a kingdom in Daniel 7. Jesus breaks new interpretive ground by claiming that the Suffering Servant and the Son of Man are in fact, the same. Jesus inaugurates the Son of Man's kingdom through the Servant's suffering. This is the model of the kingdom of God that we are called to embrace. Soon, hopefully, His disciples will complete stage two, and be able to clearly see this as well.

Reflection Questions

1. Why did Jesus wait until they identified Him as the Christ to reveal His death and resurrection? How would the rejection and death of the Messiah change their views about Him? Why did Peter rebuke Jesus? In what way was Peter wanting to "gain the whole world"?
2. Why were the disciples discussing who was the greatest? Do we do that in churches today? Why is there a temptation to turn our place in the kingdom into a competition? How might 1 Corinthians 12:12–26 connect to this passage?

REFLECTION 37
THE. TRANSFIGURATION

Mark 9:1–13

The Kingdom Coming with Power

MARK 9:1 is an interesting verse with many diverse interpretations. Jesus tells His disciples, "Truly, I say to you, there are some standing here who will not taste death until they see the kingdom of God after it has come with power" (Mark 9:1). This word of encouragement is no doubt exciting news for the disciples. The long-awaited kingdom is finally coming (as Jesus preached in Mark 1:14–15). After the rebuke of Mark 8:33, and the unsettling challenge of 34–38, this message is exactly what they need to hear. So, what does it mean?

The kingdom is coming soon and will be seen during the lifetime of some of Jesus's contemporaries. The disciples, who have been called blind, will eventually *see* the kingdom of God. As Jesus heals the blind men, sight is coming for the disciples.

Jesus does not specify the exact moment He has in mind. This is another ambiguous passage that requires some contemplation and reflection. Mark loves doing that. Many interpretations have been offered. Some suggest that Jesus is predicting His ultimate second coming (which was referenced in the previous verse, Mark 8:38). This suggestion implies Jesus was wrong, and He expected the end to come sooner than it did. After all, Jesus admitted that He didn't even know when "that day" would be (Mark 13:32). Obviously, this view is problematic.

Another interpretation is that Jesus spoke about the destruction of Jerusalem when "they will see the Son of Man coming in clouds with great power and glory" (Mark 13:26). The destruction of Jerusalem could potentially be what Jesus is referring to in Mark 8:38 (the language matches Mark 13:26 almost perfectly), and "some standing" there would live to see it. Mark 9:1 and Mark 13:26 share the language of "coming with power."

Another interpretation is that Jesus spoke of the beginning of the church on Pentecost, which you can read about in Acts 2. This is a hard connection to make contextually, but it's within the realm of possibility. In Acts 1:8 the disciples are promised "power" when the Holy Spirit comes.

Another interpretation is that Jesus spoke of His own death and resurrection. This would fit nicely in the context of Mark 8:31, where Jesus initially predicts His death and resurrection. Mark 9:1 (if you ignore the chapter break) is the end of the conversation about death and discipleship started in Mark 8:31. Kingdom language saturates the crucifixion narrative. Jesus is given purple robes and a crown and hailed as King (Mark 15:17–18). A plaque is placed above His head that calls Him, "The King of the Jews" (Mark 15:26), and He is mocked as the King of Israel (Mark 15:32). At His death He is called "The Son of God" (Mark 15:39). Mark ends with an empty tomb, and the King they once mocked is now risen to reign in the kingdom. I tend to lean towards this interpretation, and Mark ends his Gospel with the in-breaking of God's kingdom.

A final interpretation, that reads smoothly, is that Jesus referenced the transfiguration. Six days after this statement, Jesus takes Peter, James, and John up a mountain and gives them a brief glimpse of the ultimate eschatological kingdom of God. These three are the "some standing here" who will see the kingdom before they taste death. When Peter reflects on the transfiguration, he connects it with "the power and coming of our Lord Jesus Christ" of which He was an eyewitness (2 Pet 1:16–18).

The Transfiguration

Whichever interpretation you find most compelling, no reader should disconnect Mark 9:1 from the transfiguration. Contextually, they should be read together. The transfiguration certainly is a glimpse of what the kingdom of God ultimately has in store, and some standing there were able to see it.

The transfiguration should also be read with the whole story of Israel in mind. Israel's greatest leaders appear together in a glorious moment that connects the past, present, and future of God's people. Jesus's clothes shine a more radiant and pristine white than anything else that's ever been worn. Elijah and Moses appear together with the Lord, and they begin talking to each other.

Peter suggests making three tents to commemorate the occasion because he has no idea what to say, and being quiet and observing isn't usually his choice (Mark 9:5–6). Like so many other amazing moments in the ministry of Jesus, the disciples respond with confusion and fear.

Then a cloud overshadows them, and a voice booms forth, "This is My beloved Son, listen to Him" (Mark 9:7). Following this declaration, the transfiguration concludes. Moses and Elijah disappear, and everything returns to normal.

What Does it All Mean?

The first thing you should notice is that Jesus went on a mountain, spoke with Moses, and a cloud with the presence of God appeared. This imagery all comes from the book of Exodus. Moses has seen that cloud before. When Moses met God in the cloud on the mountain and was given the Law, all Israel knew they should listen to him. Now that Jesus goes up on the mountain and meets God in the cloud, we are told to listen to Him. Jesus, in the presence of Moses, takes the role of the leader of Israel.

Additionally, Elijah was there also. This piques the disciples' interest, and they ask Jesus about it on the way down afterwards. They know that the prophets predicted the return of Elijah (Mark 9:11; Mal 4:5–6, see also Mark 6:15 and Mark 8:28). They may be wondering if that was it; they literally just saw Elijah return.

Jesus cryptically and ambiguously suggests something else. He says that Elijah will "restore all things," which seems to be a summary of the mission described in Malachi 4:5–6, and that Elijah already came, and men did to him as they pleased. While Jesus does not say here that Elijah is John the Baptist, if you remember how John was dressed like Elijah in Mark 1:6 and preached a message of repentance and restoration, and was mistreated, arrested, and executed by godless men, the connection becomes apparent. Elijah suffered tremendously at the hands of kings during his ministry and John the Baptist shared in the same afflictions.

One further point needs to be made about this section, and it relates to Jesus's identity as the dying and rising Messiah. Jesus tells His disciples to be quiet about the transfiguration "until the Son of Man had risen from the dead" (Mark 9:9). This timeline is probably the same for all His secrecy (Mark 8:30).

Jesus wants His blind disciples to be quiet until they can see, and they clearly are not seeing yet. They don't understand "what this rising from the dead might mean" (Mark 9:10).

The disciples do not understand the Son of Man's resurrection because they do not understand His suffering. The disciples must be wondering, "Might Jesus be talking about the general resurrection at the end of time? Is He using "resurrection" in some symbolic or metaphorical way?" They don't know what He means because they didn't understand Mark 8:31. They don't understand that the Messiah will suffer and die.

Jesus ends this post-transfiguration conversation by again reminding them that "the Son of Man ... should suffer many things and be treated with contempt" (Mark 9:12).

The transfiguration offers a glimpse of the glorious kingdom of God. It looks to past prophets like Moses and Elijah and shows that the present Lord Jesus is the greatest of all. It offers hope for the future God has in store for all His people. It hints towards the resurrection of Jesus and the suffering that will precede it. The transfiguration is a gospel moment where Jesus is proclaimed to be God's Son from a voice on high (like Mark 1:11). We should believe it and listen to Jesus.

Reflection Questions

1. Why is it encouraging to hear that the kingdom is coming? What do you think it means that the kingdom is coming with power? When do you think Jesus has in mind? Has the kingdom come? Is there a sense in which we are still awaiting the kingdom of God?

2. What was the purpose of Jesus's transfiguration? Why did it matter that His clothes changed colors?

Why did Moses and Elijah appear? Why did God command us to listen to Jesus instead of Moses and Elijah? Why did God appear as a cloud? What can the transfiguration teach us about the resurrection?

REFLECTION 38

"HELP MY UNBELIEF"

Mark 9:1–29

A Distraught Father

THERE IS NO MORE helpless or miserable feeling than watching your child suffer and being powerless to stop it (remember Jairus in Mark 5:23 and the Gentile woman in Mark 7:26). Immediately following the transfiguration, we meet a man whose world has been turned upside down because of the powers of Satan. His own son has an unclean spirit and has epileptic seizures. The spirit has intentionally tried to kill him from childhood by burning and drowning him. I cannot imagine what this father and son have endured.

While Jesus was on the mountain with Peter, James, John, Moses, and Elijah, the other disciples were down below meeting this man. He asked them to cast the demon out of his son. They agreed to do it, but soon realized they were outmatched. Even though Jesus gave them authority over unclean spirits (Mark 6:7), they somehow could not cast him away. They lost.

When the scribes heard about it, they just had to find the

disciples and gloat. The disciples act like they can cast out demons, but in front of everyone they fail to do it. The scribes no doubt see this failure as evidence against Jesus and His movement. They will no doubt use this to drive people away from Jesus and His charlatan disciples.

When Jesus comes down, this is the scene He finds. There is an argument between His disciples and the scribes, a helpless father, a demon possessed son, and a crowd of people watching. What will Jesus do?

A lot has been building up to this moment. Jesus met with Satan in the wilderness and overpowered him (Mark 1:13). With a vengeance, Jesus silenced and cast out demons throughout Galilee (Mark 1:25, 34). The scribes from Jerusalem accused Jesus of getting his authority over demons from the ruler of demons (Mark 3:22). They think Jesus has some alliance with Satan himself. Jesus demonstrated how foolish this thinking was and continued to cleanse the land from the demonic forces of darkness.

For God's kingdom to take over, Satan must be bound, plundered, and finished (Mark 3:26–27). Even leaving Galilee, in the unclean Gentile region, among the tombs, thousands of unclean spirits, a whole Legion, took residence in one man. Jesus cast those demons into pigs who ran into the sea and drowned (Mark 5:1–20). No power of Satan in any place on earth can stand before Jesus.

Jesus then gave this authority over demons to His disciples and sent them out (Mark 6:7). The disciples went out and had some success, but here in this moment, they failed publicly, and the scribes are reveling in it.

All Things Are Possible

When Jesus hears all that is happening, He cannot help but feel frustration at the "unbelieving" generation (Mark 9:19).

"Unbelieving" is an important description for the story that follows.

The boy is brought to Jesus and immediately begins convulsing, foaming at the mouth, rolling around, and seizing across the floor (Mark 9:20). The father, after giving Jesus information about his son's condition, finally says, "But if You can do anything, take pity on us and help us!" (Mark 9:22).

This father is struggling. He is helpless to save his own son. Nobody can help. He heard about Jesus and His disciples, as word about them has spread throughout the region, and he brings his son to them for help. Jesus isn't even there when he arrives, and the disciples try and fail. Their failure must have been crushing for him to see. He knows the disciples failed, and he is now doubting if Jesus can do anything.

Jesus notices this father's struggle and responds, "'If you can?' All things are possible to him who believes" (Mark 9:23). This is a key message in the Gospel of Mark. It's a message Jesus's disciples need to hear. Jesus challenged them to feed the crowds, but twice they didn't believe it was possible. Jesus gave them the authority over unclean spirits, but when it got hard, they were unable. Jesus is preparing them for His suffering and death (and their own), and they refuse to believe. They refuse to see it. Jesus's disciples need this lesson just as much as the father does.

Jesus soon tells His disciples,

> Have faith in God. Truly I say to you, whoever say to this mountain, "Be taken up and cast into the sea," and does not doubt, but believes that what he says is going to happen, it will be granted him. Therefore I say to you, all things for which you pray and ask, believing that you have received them, and they will be granted you (Mark 11:22–24).

When I read these grand statements, I get how the father

responds to Jesus. I want to believe that, but sometimes it's unbelievably hard.

The father answers Jesus, saying, "I do believe; help my unbelief" (Mark 9:24). What a real, powerful, and authentic statement to make. This is one of the most relatable passages in the Bible. There are so many times I find myself burdened by the tension between belief and unbelief. When you find yourself struggling between the two, offer this man's prayer: "I do believe; help my unbelief."

In the same way that the blind men should be seen as pictures of Jesus's disciples, I wonder if this father should also. This man, who is struggling to believe, is part of the "unbelieving generation" Jesus decried moments earlier. So are the disciples. As this man needs to trust and believe the unbelievable, so do Jesus's disciples.

As a large crowd begins to rapidly gather, Jesus rebukes the unclean spirit and in a final effort to destroy the boy, the spirit convulses him terribly. The spirit flees at the authority of Jesus and leaves the boy's body motionless on the ground. They think he is dead until Jesus grabs his hand and raises him back up.

I like to smile and imagine the celebration that took place for that family later that night.

Prayer

Belief and prayer are often linked together. There are times we might believe something can happen, but we don't ever pray about it. Or we may pray for something, but we don't truly believe. Jesus says "all things are possible to him who believes" but, like in Mark 11:22–24, He will soon add prayer to that recipe.

After Jesus saved the day, they all return to a house and the disciples, embarrassed and downtrodden, ask Jesus, "Why could we not drive it out?" (Mark 9:28). I mean, Jesus gave them the authority to do so back in Mark 6:7. Why didn't it work?

Jesus gives a simple answer. He doesn't usually make things this simple. Jesus says, "This kind cannot come out by anything but prayer" (Mark 9:29). It's interesting that Jesus says, "this kind." Are there some kinds of demons that come out without prayer? When the disciples cast out demons in the past, were they different kinds of demons? When Jesus cast out the demon, the text reads, "You deaf and mute spirit, I command you, come out of him and do not enter him again" (Mark 9:25). The text doesn't say that Jesus prayed about it, just that He commanded it.

Herein lies two important points. First, by saying "this kind" can only come out by prayer, Jesus implies that only God can cast out this kind of spirit. The disciples cannot do it on their own, but God can, so pray to God. Second, Jesus casts out the demon, not by praying to God, but by acting with the authority of God. God doesn't pray to cast out demons, He does it by His own authority. God's authority is shared by the Son of Man. Jesus casts out demons with the authority of God because He is the Son of Man who shares the throne room with God, exercises the authority of God, and enjoys equality with God.

Reflection Questions

1. Do you ever struggle with unbelief? In what ways do we live in an unbelieving generation? Who can you go to for help with unbelief? What can you do to face your doubts? Can you be faithful even with doubts?

2. Do you truly believe all things are possible with faith? Do you think God can move mountains? How bold are you in your prayer life?

REFLECTION 39
PRIDE AND SELF-SACRIFICE

Mark 9:38–50

Looking Out for #1

MARK 9:38–50 contains the most difficult verses to contextually read together as a single flowing unit. It feels like a collection of sayings has been compiled, rather than a single conversation. Even if that was the case, they would have been compiled because in some way all these verses fit together.

I think the key to unifying these verses is to remember they are introduced by a conversation about "who is the greatest" (Mark 9:33–37). Without that conversation, these verses seem disjointed, but with that conversation in mind, they begin to make more sense. These passages center around the folly of "looking out for #1."

For example, John (and all the apostles) wants to prevent a man from casting out demons in the name of Jesus. This unnamed exorcist was legitimately casting out real demons and was truly doing it in Jesus's name. There was no deception involved. The problem is he wasn't following Jesus or the disciples. He was doing wonderful kingdom works, but with the "wrong" group. Earlier in Mark, the scribes saw Jesus casting out demons and instead of appreciating Him, they tried to discredit Him (Mark 3:22). Now the disciples are walking a similar path.

Jesus immediately corrects this way of thinking. All around Jesus, people are taking sides either for or against Him. You see this happening on nearly every page of Mark's gospel. The last thing Jesus wants is bickering and infighting on His own side. This man might not have "officially" been one of Jesus's followers and he may not have been there for Mark 6:7, but God was working through Him in the name of Jesus. He is on Jesus's side. He's not going around speaking evil of Jesus.

Those who act in kindness towards the disciples, like giving a cup of water for the sake of Christ, are on the side of Jesus (Mark 9:41). They will not lose their reward. So, rejoice when people speak well of Jesus and serve in His name. If Christ is proclaimed, we have reason to celebrate (Phil 1:15–18). Do not stop others from doing a good thing in the name of Jesus because they are not "with us."

Little Ones and Stumbling Blocks

Three times in the surrounding context Jesus refers to little children/little ones: Mark 9:37, 42; 10:13–16. The first passage tells us to receive little children. The last passage tells us to receive the kingdom as little children, but this middle passage speaks to the importance of building up little children rather than tearing them down or causing them to sin. In this context the "little ones who believe in me" may well include the man who was casting out demons in the name of Jesus. In these three passages, "little children" seem to sometimes be literal children, but also metaphorically represent those deemed insignificant or inferior. By stopping that man's ministry and exorcisms, they are putting a stumbling block before him.

Speaking of stumbling, we shouldn't cause others to stumble, but we should also do everything possible to make sure we do not stumble. The ESV translates the word σκανδαλίζω as "cause to stumble". This word is repeated in 9:42, 43, 45, 47 where Jesus challenges us to rid ourselves of anything that might cause us to stumble.

Jesus, hyperbolically, begins listing the most extreme acts of self-denial imaginable. Jesus says amputation is worth it for the kingdom of God; even plucking eyeballs and cutting off hands and feet. Sometimes we can overcome temptation, but most of the time we should try to sever ourselves from it (see Matt 5:27–30). The pain caused by self-denial doesn't compare with the misery of hell (γέεννα, gehenna) "where their worm does not die and the fire is not quenched" (Mark 9:48; Isa 66:24).

Have Salt in Yourselves

This chapter concludes with three quick ambiguous "salt" statements: 1. "For everyone will be salted with fire." 2. "Salt is good, but if the salt has lost its saltiness, how will you make it salty again?" 3. "Have salt in yourselves, and be at peace with one another."

The best way to think of the "fire" seems to be as trials/persecution. "Salt" is probably best interpreted as a kingdom disposition, an attitude and mindset consistent with the kingdom of God. More specifically, perhaps, we can say salt is seen in humility/self denial. Read this way, these verses teach that trials and persecution can help you develop a humble/selfless kingdom mindset, which is good. If you lose it, it's extremely difficult to get it back. So have a humble/self-denying kingdom attitude within yourselves and be at peace with each other.

The thread that ties all these seemingly disconnected verses together is humility/self-denial. It is rejecting a "me first" attitude that argues for who is the greatest (Mark 9:34). The disciples tried to stop the unnamed exorcist, thinking that they were worthy, and he was not. They thought they were greater than him. A "me first" attitude competes in the kingdom and looks down on the ministry of others. A "me first" attitude places stumbling blocks before others. A "me first" attitude does not make sacrifices for the kingdom and does not practice self-denial. A "me first" attitude is not the salt of the kingdom of God. A "me first" attitude dives headlong into Gehenna.

"When Christ Calls a Man ..."

A "me first" attitude is going to struggle with wealth and marriage commitments. It's no coincidence that Jesus's teaching on marriage and divorce and His dramatic offer to the rich young ruler come after His words to pluck out eyes, and cut off hands and feet. Only through self-denial and sacrifice can disciples of Christ enter marriage and finances. Mark is now laying before us the most radical and intense calls of the kingdom of God. After telling us to cut off anything that causes us to stumble, Mark details Jesus's challenging words about marriage and wealth.

In this section, Mark has already challenged us to deny ourselves, carry our cross, and lose our lives (Mark 8:34–37). He has challenged us to be "last and servant of all" (Mark 9:35). He challenged us to amputate anything that causes us to stumble on our path to the kingdom (Mark 9:43–48). He will soon tell us to leave homes, families, and possessions for the sake of Jesus and the gospel (Mark 10:29). He'll tell us that even the Son of Man came "to serve, and to give His life a ransom for many" (Mark 10:45). At the beginning, middle, and end of these challenges are three descriptions of the rejection, humiliation, suffering, and death of Jesus Christ (Mark 8:31; 9:31; 10:33–34). Jesus is calling us to follow Him by giving up everything.

Dietrich Bonhoeffer famously wrote,

> The cross is laid on every Christian. The first Christ-suffering which every man must experience is the call to abandon the attachments of this world. It is that dying of the old man which is the result of his encounter with Christ. As we embark upon discipleship we surrender ourselves to Christ in union with his death—we give over our lives to death. Thus it begins; the cross is not the terrible end to an otherwise god-fearing and happy life, but it meets us at the beginning of our communion with Christ. When Christ calls a man, he bids him come and die.[1]

For marriage to work, we must die to ourselves. To practice the radical generosity of the kingdom (Mark 12:43–44), we must die to ourselves. Some will put marriage above the kingdom, and some will put wealth above the kingdom; both are examples of the "me first" attitude that cannot embrace the kingdom of God. The following stories can only be embraced by those carrying a cross, prepared to die.

Reflection Questions

1. In what ways is exclusivity dangerous to the church? In what ways is exclusivity rooted in arrogance? Or fear? What is meant by "little children?" How should the church open its arms to little children?
2. What are some things you may need to amputate in your service to God? What might the church need to

amputate for the kingdom? Is it better to overcome temptation or avoid temptation? Is there a time for both? Why?

Endnotes

1. Dietrich Bonhoeffer, *The Cost of Discipleship* (United Kingdom: Touchstone, 1995), 89.

REFLECTION 40
MARRIAGE AND THE KINGDOM

Mark 10:1–12

The Hot Topic

As JESUS TRAVELS south towards His scandalous destiny (He is
in Capernaum in Mark 9:33 and travels south, arriving in Judea
in 10:1), He ramps up His radical calls for discipleship. We are
entering the most challenging calls for self-sacrifice in the
Gospel of Mark. Immediately following Jesus's vivid summons
to amputate hands and feet and pluck out eyes (Mark 9:43–48),
Mark now shows us how that mindset manifests itself with two
real-world subjects: marriage and money. Mark 10:1–31 is how
you carry a cross with your family and finances.

In Mark 10:2, the Pharisees approach Jesus with a disingen-
uous question, intentionally testing Him, asking, "Is it lawful
for a man to divorce his wife?" (Mark 10:2). This was a hotly
contested topic in Jesus's day (and still is in ours), and His
answer will no doubt outrage a portion of His followers. The
Pharisees hope to divide Jesus's movement from within. As
usual, Jesus refuses to give a simple "yes" or "no." He throws the
ball back in their court and asks them what Moses said about it.

The Pharisees answer with Deuteronomy 24:1–4, basically saying, "Yes, as long as you give her a certificate of divorce."

There is important historical background to this controversy that we should recognize as we begin this discussion. Deuteronomy 24:1 mentions divorce after a wife "finds no favor" in her husband's eyes because he found "some indecency" in her. In Jesus's day, debate raged between two famous Rabbis, Hillel and Shammai, about this text and the interpretation of "indecency." Hillel argued that the "indecency" was anything at all that the husband didn't like (even burning the toast). Shammai argued that the "indecency" was only fornication.[1] Surprise, surprise, Rabbi Hillel's view was the most popular in Jesus's day. I wonder why men would prefer that view so much?

The Pharisees' answer, and most of the controversy surrounding Deuteronomy 24, misses the point of what Moses actually wrote. Read Deuteronomy 24 and you'll see that Moses is answering a different question altogether. The first three verses of Deuteronomy 24 provide a scenario and verse four gives the law. Here is the scenario: A man marries a woman, he sees "some indecency" in her and divorces her, sending her away with a certificate of divorce, so she marries someone else who eventually also sends her away with a certificate of divorce (or he dies). Here is the law: that first husband, in that scenario, cannot remarry the wife he originally sent away (which is interesting considering what Paul says in 1 Cor 7:11).

Deuteronomy 24 was not written to justify divorce, enumerate acceptable reasons for divorce, or to command a certificate of divorce be given to the wife. The text assumes such was already happening. The law was that once all that happens, you cannot ever remarry her after she has married someone else. To the first husband, this woman becomes defiled by marrying someone else. Others can marry her, but that first husband cannot.

The certificate of divorce protected the wife from any future claims of her first husband by legitimizing the divorce, but the certificate of divorce is not the main thrust of Deuteronomy 24. This law says, once you let her go and give her that certificate and she marries another, she's gone for good. She is free of you and you can never take her for yourself again. This law should generate some apprehension on the part of the husband before hastily casting aside his wife. He may regret that decision for the rest of his life. Deuteronomy 24 honors the finality of divorce and the legitimacy of remarriage. It completely ended the first husband's right to his wife.

Now, to Jesus's point, a law like this is only needed if men are hard hearted and neglect their responsibilities as husbands. A wife is a human being, created in God's image, who has greater worth than simply pleasing her husband. Marriage is about much more than a man's happiness. The idea that marriage exists to please man is a hard-hearted idea, completely contrary to the sacrificial cross-bearing call of Christ. Jesus's answer is to stop selfishly looking for ways to divorce your wife!

In Mark, Jesus ignores the "indecency" controversy of Deuteronomy 24. Jesus thinks they are fighting over the wrong passage to justify a wrong practice. God's desires for the marriage covenant are not found in the fallen, hard-hearted world of Deuteronomy 24, but in the first pages of your Bible. Read Genesis 1 and 2 if you want to see God's view of marriage.

God created humanity in His image, both male and female (Gen 1:26), and in the Garden of Eden He joined them together (Gen 2:24). In the garden, Adam was one. From Adam's side, God made another, so humanity became two. Then in marriage, God reunified humanity back into one. God joined Adam and Eve together into one flesh and to tear them apart is to rip the flesh. It is an act of violence in God's world. Humans should not forcibly tear asunder what God has lovingly joined together.

Jesus's Summary Statement

Jesus answered the Pharisees question in an unexpected way. He avoided their trap by reframing the controversy in light of Genesis 1 and 2 and honoring God's original intentions in marriage. Jesus's conversation with the Pharisees ended in Mark 10:9 and, as He often did (Mark 4:34; 7:17; 13:3), He privately explained more to His disciples.

Keeping with the narrative of Genesis 1 and 2, and the spirit of Deuteronomy 24, Jesus offers a teaching to protect women from being indiscriminately tossed aside at the whim of their husbands. Hillel's popular teaching depended on the idea that marriage existed to please men. If the man wasn't pleased, he could go find a better wife. The woman was basically his property. If you don't like your current lawnmower, just go get a better one. Jesus doesn't think we ought to treat wives the same way.

Jesus seeks to honor God's original Eden intentions and the covenant responsibilities associated with marriage. While alone with His disciples, He explains, "Whoever divorces his wife and marries another commits adultery against her, and if she divorces her husband and marries another, she commits adultery" (Mark 10:11–12).

Notice this verse is a bit different than Matthew's parallel (Matt 19:9). First, in Mark's account the husband who divorces his wife and marries another commits adultery specifically "against her." This is a fascinating and revolutionary idea. This means that the wife has rights and is not the husband's property. He owes her life-long faithfulness and monogamy. She is no object to be discarded or replaced. Second, Mark also applies the same responsibilities to the wife. Wives could scarcely initiate divorce in Judaism (Matthew doesn't even mention the possibility). Mark applies these duties equally to both genders (writing to a Roman audience, this may have been necessary since Roman women could initiate divorce more freely). Finally, Mark does not include the "exception clause" that generates so much discussion in Matthew 19:9. Mark does not say, "except for fornication." If we were the first century church that initially received the Gospel of Mark, we wouldn't know that Jesus' teaching had any exceptions. Mark presents a more strict and egalitarian account of this teaching.

Taking Marriage Seriously

This is not even close to a comprehensive study on the topic of divorce and remarriage, but some important truths emerge from this passage.

1. God desires for us to honor our marriage commitments and not get divorced.
2. To divorce and remarry another person is to commit adultery.
3. Unlike Deuteronomy 24, Jesus does not legitimize the certificate of divorce or the second marriage.
4. Jesus issued this teaching for the benefit and protection of people, particularly women. This may seem counterintuitive in our divorce-happy culture where we equate divorce with freedom, but making marriage work, even through difficulties, is good for human flourishing. This teaching makes life better, not worse (keep in mind, this discussion is not in the context of abusive or dehumanizing relationships).
5. Husbands must faithfully practice love towards their wives, instead of looking for ways out. Wives must exercise that same loyalty to their husbands. Marriage is about service and self-denial for the sake of another. Discipleship isn't seen solely in "not divorcing" but in embodying sacrificial love for your

spouse during the marriage. Abuse in any form is the antithesis of discipleship.

6. Marriage is not about personal happiness but covenantal, God-like love. God does not abandon us, and we should not abandon our spouses.
7. The ethics of Jesus often critique our cultural norms.

Let's conclude this discussion with a helpful reminder from Richard Hays:

> The church must recognize and teach that marriage is grounded not in feelings of love but in the practice of love. Nor is the marriage bond contingent upon self-gratification or personal fulfillment. The church has swallowed a great quantity of pop psychology that has no foundation in the biblical depiction of marriage; consequently, critical discrimination is necessary in order to restore an understanding of marriage based on the New Testament. When a marital union is rightly understood as a covenant, the question of divorce assumes a very different aspect. Those who have made promises before God should trust in God for grace sufficient to keep those promises, and they should expect the community of faith to help them keep faith, by supporting them and holding them accountable.

Reflection Questions

1. If you are married, what can you do today to strengthen your marriage? What makes your spouse happy? Stop reading for a moment and go do something kind for your spouse. What can you do to show your spouse how much you value, love, and

respect him or her? How can you make sure you
never face the questions asked in this chapter?

2. How can you help someone who is struggling
through a divorce? How can the church reach out to
the divorced? How can the church as a community
help prevent divorces, strengthen marriages, and be
a source of healing?

Endnotes

1. Shamai also factored in the marital expectations of Exodus
23:10–11. If those were not met, divorce was lawful.

2. Hays, *Moral Vision*, 372.

REFLECTION 41
WEALTH AND THE KINGDOM

Mark 10:13–31

Receiving Children

JESUS LIKES KIDS. As a father of two small children, that makes me smile. It's important to remember Jesus, during His turbulent ministry, heading towards Jerusalem to meet His violent end, stopping to pick up children and teaching His disciples to do the same. As disciples of Jesus, never be too busy for kids. Make time for them. Receive them. Learn from them. Imitate them. In this brief but powerful scene that bridges Jesus's teachings on marriage and wealth, Jesus welcomes, holds, and blesses children (remember Mark 9:37 and 42).

The disciples, seemingly learning nothing from Jesus (Mark 9:37), try to keep the kids away from Him. Jesus is indignant with His disciples and reminds them that the kingdom belongs to the children (Mark 10:14). Children, the least of all and servants of all, are our spiritual mentors in God's kingdom. Do not keep them away.

Jesus keeps correcting His disciples about pushing people away. Do not keep the blind man away (Mark 10:47–48). Do not stop the unnamed exorcist (Mark 9:38–39). Do not forbid the children from coming to Jesus (Mark 10:14). An important theme is emerging that the ignored, neglected, infirmed, young, and weak are welcomed by Jesus, while others try to stop them and push them away.

Notice the contrast between these children who are welcomed by Jesus and the rich man (often called the rich young ruler) who sorrowfully walked away from Him. It wasn't because Jesus wouldn't accept him. Jesus "loved him" and called him to be a follower (Mark 10:21), but something stood in the way. It wasn't the commands of God found in Torah, which the wealthy man took seriously and obeyed (Mark 10:20). It was his wealth.

Children have no money, power, or prestige. The disciples saw them as a nuisance and hindrance to the important ministry of Jesus. Conversely, this rich man has money, power, and prestige. This is the type of guy that churches often bend over backwards to get. He can fund the ministries, bring respectability to the congregation, and open the door to the higher echelon of society. But the kids Jesus welcomes, while this man walks away. Jesus does not beg him to stay. Jesus didn't dull His call to discipleship hoping to win the man, instead He intensified it. Jesus challenges him to do something He never tells anyone else to do: "sell all that you have and give to the poor" (Mark 10:21). That's not what you would call a brilliant church growth strategy.

Wealth and Allegiance

In a few chapters we meet an impoverished widow who gives all she has for others (Mark 12:41–44). This man is being asked to do what this widow does freely. He should follow her example. He would end up with the same amount as her, but it would cost him more to get there. He can find eternal life and become a follower of Jesus, who loves him, but money gets in the way. Like Judas, who chose to betray Jesus for money (Mark 14:10–11), this man's allegiance was to his wealth.

Money (sometimes) provides freedom, peace of mind, and opportunity. Money gives us a (false) sense of security and self-importance. Making a lot of money can deceive us into thinking we can take care of ourselves. Why thank God for the food when I provided it for myself with my own money and hard work? That's one reason God kept the children of Israel living day to day on manna in the wilderness for 40 years. Every night they went to bed with nothing, trusting in God alone to provide the next day's portion. Poverty can cause us to rely on God every minute of every day; wealth can cause us to forget Him. This makes it hard to trust God and be rich.

Jesus, after the rich man walks away from Him, tells His disciples how hard it is for the rich to enter the kingdom. It's like fitting a camel through the tiny hole of a needle.[1] Jesus gave this rich man a path for eternal life, but wealth was too big of a hurdle.

This is not at all what the disciples expected to hear. When Jesus says it is difficult for the rich to enter the kingdom, they "were amazed at his words" (Mark 10:24). When Jesus says it is easier for a camel to fit through the eye of a needle than for a rich man to enter the kingdom of God, they ask, "Then who can be saved?" (Mark 10:26). These responses convey two important points about the disciples' mindset.

First, perhaps like Job's friends, they view wealth as a sign of God's blessing and approval. If anyone is pleasing to God, surely, it's the person God has blessed with riches. When Jesus says the opposite, it bewilders them.

This should remind us that God makes no promise to reward our faithfulness with riches. We should not expect that at all. The so-called "health and wealth" gospel is advanced by charlatans. Your personal wealth, or the wealth of your nation, or church, is not a sign of God's approval. In fact, very often, it can be the opposite. If that seems counterintuitive, welcome to the kingdom of God where the first is last and the last is first.

Second, the disciples are still struggling to grasp the reality of the kingdom of God. If it really is a second coming of the reign of David, wealth is expected to be a sign of the kingdom. Jesus's crown is made of thorns and not gold. The poor, the weak, the blind, and the children find their place in God's kingdom before the wealthy, the strong, the healthy, and powerful.

Jesus's words don't give the rich much hope. If it really is easier for a camel to fit through a needle's eye than for a rich man to enter the kingdom, is it not impossible? As citizens of a wealthy nation, we should be concerned. I know that compared to many throughout this world, I am rich. I also know that I have not done what this rich young man was charged to do. I haven't sold all that I have and given it to the poor. I don't know anyone who has. If this makes you uncomfortable, good. We should be uncomfortable with our wealth. Jesus isn't trying to make us comfortable. This discomfort should motivate generosity.

I've heard it said many times that it's not a sin to be rich. It's a sin to love money and be greedy, but not to be rich. I'd rephrase that. I think perhaps it is a sin to be rich. It's a sin to be rich if you are not sacrificial, generous, and hospitable. Wealth comes with obligations attached to it. Collecting wealth, craving excess, building bigger barns, and storing away our treasures on earth are all contrary to the message of Jesus. These are ways we serve wealth rather than God. These kept this rich young man away from the kingdom.

Jesus actually says it is impossible "with man" for the rich to be saved, "but not with God. For all things are possible with God (Mark 10:27; see Mark 9:23). There is some hope. The generosity and grace of God always provides hope. With God the door is not entirely closed, but it will be a challenge. We cannot fit through the narrow gate carrying all this world's goods. To pick up the cross, we may have to lay down our treasures.

Dietrich Bonhoeffer reminds us:

> Earthly goods are given to be used, not to be collected. In the wilderness God gave Israel the manna every day, and they had no need to worry about food and drink. Indeed, if they kept any of the manna over until the next day, it went bad. In the same way, the disciple must receive his portion from God every day. If he stores it up as a permanent possession, he spoils not only the gift, but himself as well, for he sets his heart on accumulated wealth, and makes it a barrier between himself and God. Where our treasure is, there is our trust, our security, our consolation and our God. Hoarding is idolatry.[2]

Kingdom Wealth

Having written that, we can rest assured that God does not leave us with nothing. We are not destitute in the kingdom of God. While this rich young man wouldn't give up his possessions for the kingdom, the other disciples did (Mark 10:28). Jesus reminds them that, "there is no one who has left house or brothers or sisters or mother or father or children or lands, for my sake and for the gospel, who will not receive a hundredfold now in this time, houses and brothers and sisters and mothers and children and lands, with persecutions, and in the age to come eternal life. But many who are first will be last and the last first" (Mark 10:29–31).

In 2016 a flood hit Monroe, LA. My wife, pregnant with our first child, and I helplessly watched the waters fill up our street, cover our yard, and enter our living room. Our first home was being destroyed before our eyes. We had no flood insurance (we did not live in a flood zone); this flood was historic and unprecedented. Eventually, we left our house behind, wading through waist deep water with our dog in a laundry basket until we reached high enough ground that we could get a ride to someone's house.

You know who waded through water with us and gave us a ride in his vehicle to his house? A wonderful friend with a generous family from church. In fact, until the flood waters subsided and the work on our house was finished, we stayed in the homes of our church family. When parts of our house needed to be repaired, it was our church family who helped with both time and finances (we even received financial help from a church we had never met before).

Ultimately, our house was not hit nearly as hard as many others (the rain stopped shortly after we left). For countless others, though, the church offered housing, furniture, work crews, food, and support within our fellowship and community. The church offered family. My wife and I did not live near parents or siblings, but we were surrounded with brothers, sisters, mothers, and fathers who shared homes, food, and money with us. We received a hundredfold what we lost, and we were not unique.

If our churches practiced generosity, hospitality, and sharing in the sacrificial example of Jesus, the One who was rich, yet became poor for our sake (2 Cor 8:9), there would be no poverty among God's people (Acts 4:32–37). If we really accepted one another as brothers and sisters and mothers and fathers (remember Mark 3:34–35), then no follower of Jesus should ever be without family. The price of discipleship is self-denial, persecution, and a cross, but the reward is family, shared possessions, and divine favor, now and forever.

Reflection Questions

1. Why is it hard for the wealthy to enter the kingdom?
   How can wealth take the role of God in your life? Do
   you want to be wealthy? In what ways do you put the
   kingdom above wealth?
2. How does one receive more family, houses, and land
   in the kingdom? How can the church exercise
   generosity? In what ways are you practicing
   hospitality? How do you become family with your
   fellow Christians?

Endnotes

1. At this time there was no gate into Jerusalem called the "eye
of a needle." That myth has been repeated and it makes Jesus's
words easier to swallow, but there is no evidence for it.

2. Bonhoeffer, *Discipleship*, 175.

REFLECTION 42

SON OF DAVID ENTERS JERUSALEM

Mark 10:46–11:10

Son of David

AS WE MOVE ALONG, let's take a moment to recap where we are in the story. Jesus is nearing Jerusalem where He will be rejected and crucified (Mark 10:32–34). He already told us that. Mark just recorded Jesus's third declaration of His impending death and resurrection (Mark 10:33–34; see Mark 8:31; 9:31 and Reflection 36), and as He travels through Jericho (Mark 10:46), a blind man named Bartimaeus begins calling out to Him (see Reflection 35).

The three predictions of His death and resurrection are sandwiched between two stories of giving sight to the blind (Mark 8:22–26; 10:46–52). This structure is intentional. Between these healings, Jesus travels towards Jerusalem (Mark 10:46, 11:1), and along the way, predicts His own fate on the cross and challenges His disciples to pick up their crosses as well (Mark 8:34).

Jesus is preparing His disciples for the fact of His death and challenging them to live the lives of discipleship thereafter. As

Jesus geographically moves closer to His sacrifice, He calls His disciples to make their own sacrifices. Placing these events between the two healings of the blind men illustrate the blindness of the disciples (Mark 8:18) as they slowly begin the process of seeing Jesus for who He truly is. These chapters bring blindness and blurred vision to sight and clarity.

This second blind man, Bartimaeus, calls out to Jesus, "Son of David, have mercy on me" (Mark 10:47–48). Several themes converge at this moment. First, the title "Son of David" is an important Messianic descriptor that will become increasingly important as the story continues. It has its roots in passages like 2 Samuel 7:14 where God promises to "establish the throne of his kingdom forever." This promise is made concerning David's son and was seemingly unfulfilled in Solomon. I mean, where is Solomon's throne now? After Babylon destroyed Jerusalem and their temple and ended the monarchy, Jews longed for a new Son of David who would fulfill God's long-awaited promise. Bartimaeus, though blind, sees Jesus as the culmination of God's promises and the hope of Israel.

A second theme in this passage is that secrecy motif pops up again. When Bartimaeus calls out to Jesus, the crowds try to silence him. Why? It may be that the crowds have heard how often Jesus told people/demons to keep silent about Him (Mark 9:9; 8:30; 7:36; 5:43; 3:11–12; 1:43–44, 34, 25, etc.), and they are following His pattern. Jesus breaks the pattern here (as He did in 5:19) and allows Bartimaeus to speak.

It may also be that they try to silence him because he is blind and insignificant and Jesus is on an important mission. Maybe they are trying to save Jesus from distractions and interruptions. The disciples tried to silence the unnamed exorcist (Mark 9:38) and the children (Mark 10:13) and in both instances Jesus corrected them. The major point here is to never hinder anyone's path to Jesus or the kingdom.

Jesus asks, "What do you want Me to do for you?" This

question should sound familiar. This is the same question Jesus asked James and John a few verses earlier (Mark 10:36–37). James and John answered that they may sit at the right and left of Jesus in glory, but they did not really understand their request (Mark 10:38). They were blind to what they were asking. Perhaps they should have asked what Bartimaeus does, "Rabboni, I want to regain my sight!" (Mark 10:51). True sight is the most dire need for the disciples right now, but they do not ask for it. Bartimaeus does. He regained his sight and began following Jesus (Mark 10:52).

Zechariah 9:9

Passing through Jericho, Jesus arrived at Bethphage and Bethany, neighboring towns to Jerusalem. He sent two disciples ahead of Him with a mission. He told them, with prophetic insight, that up ahead in the village opposite you is a colt, which no one has ever sat on before, tied up. Jesus wants them to untie it and bring it to Him. Jesus also gives them an answer in case anyone asks why they are taking the colt, "You say, 'The Lord has need of it and will send it back here immediately'" (Mark 11:3)

It's possible Jesus prearranged these plans and nothing out of the ordinary occurs here, but those arrangements are not presented in the text. It's presented as though Jesus mysteriously knows what lies ahead: He knows the history of this colt (no one has ever sat on it), He knows what questions may be asked, and how His disciples should respond. This knowledge is remarkable in and of itself, but as Jesus gives these instructions, He notably refers to Himself as "the Lord," or more literally (ὁ κύριος αὐτοῦ) "his Lord" (Mark 11:3). This reminds us again of Mark 1:3 and again hints towards the divine identity of Jesus.

A helpful case study for understanding Mark's literary style is to compare Mark 11:1–7 with Matthew 21:1–7. Except for a few minor details, these stories are told in the same order, sharing the same nuances, and almost verbatim the same language. This happens regularly with Mark and Matthew, but a few obvious differences emerge in these passages. Matthew clarifies what animal the colt is, a donkey, and also informs his readers that these events "took place to fulfill what was spoken through the prophet: 'Say to the daughter of Zion, "Behold, your King is coming to you, gentle, and mounted on a donkey, even on a colt, the foal of a beast of burden"'" (Matt 21:4–5; Zech 9:9; see Gen 49:10–11 also).

Jesus's actions are the same in both parallel passages, but Matthew makes explicit what Mark only implies. Zechariah 9:9 is fulfilled by Jesus in both passages, but Matthew gives you the citation while Mark leaves the reader with the responsibility to dig and see it. Matthew and Mark both have Zechariah 9:9 in mind, but only Matthew quotes it. Mark expects more of his readers than Matthew does. As we have made our way through Mark, we've made regular connections to the Old Testament which Mark merely hints towards. If you want to see how Mark uses the Old Testament, you must do more than note his direct citations and obvious quotes. He often weaves Old Testament details into his story and leaves the reader to meditate on them to see the big picture.

When one stands back and looks at Mark's subtle allusion to Zechariah 9:9, we see the unexpected arrival of a humble king. Jesus enters Jerusalem as a king seated atop a humble beast of burden. Here is a quick tip for Bible study that will prove beneficial to you: if you see an allusion or quotation from an Old Testament passage, go back and read the content and context of that passage. Doing so will help illuminate the New Testament passage as you see how that old phrase or word is now adopted into a new context. The technical term for this practice is "metalepsis."

The humble king of Zechariah 9:9 is now read in light of Jesus. This king, in Zechariah 9:10, will "cut off the chariot from Ephraim and the horse from Jerusalem; and the bow of war will be cut off. And He will speak peace to the nations; and His dominion will be from sea to sea." Jesus enters Jerusalem in Mark 11, intentionally seated on a colt, as a message to all who are familiar with their Old Testaments, that He is coming as a humble king, not bringing war and destruction, but ending war and bringing peace. This is a prophetic demonstration that teaches through actions. Jesus enters Jerusalem this way to provide a lens through which to see His peaceful kingdom.

A King's Welcome

The image Jesus portrays is not missed. The crowds clearly recognize that this is a king's entry into a city. Specifically, this is the Son of David's entry into Jerusalem, the city of David. This account is quite the contrast from when David entered Jerusalem as king. Jesus entered Jerusalem, after healing a blind man, humbly seated on a colt to end war and bring peace. David entered Jerusalem by defeating the Jebusites, collecting wives and concubines, and taunting his enemies saying he hated the lame and blind (probably tongue-in-cheek) (2 Sam 5:6–13).

Jesus rides the colt into Jerusalem as the crowds celebrate, spread coats and leafy branches on the ground before Him, and shout, "Hosanna! Blessed is He who comes in the name of the Lord; Blessed is the coming kingdom of our father David; Hosanna in the highest!" (Mark 11:9–10). These words of celebration combine a quotation of Psalm 118:26 and a word of praise about the kingdom of David. This final word about the kingdom of David is a dangerous thing to shout in a Roman occupied city.

Calling it the "kingdom of David" is unique. Jesus has

referred to the kingdom of God, but the crowds celebrate the kingdom of David. Are these terms being used synonymously? Or is this yet another indication that the crowds fail to recognize that Jesus is doing something different than David? His kingdom is not a mere restoration of the Davidic monarchy and calling Him the "Son of David" does not mean He will act like David. Something new is taking place and, even as they celebrate, the crowds might be missing it.

This public celebration is out of step with the secrecy with which Jesus had been conducting Himself, but as the story continues from here, Jesus's actions become far more public and controversial. From His public entrance into Jerusalem as a king, to flipping tables in the temple, to the public crucifixion, Jesus is now demonstrating the nature of His kingdom before everyone. It's time to open the eyes of the blind.

Reflection Questions

1. How is Jesus's entry into Jerusalem similar to a king entering a city? How is it different? How is Jesus's entry into Jerusalem similar to David's entry into Jerusalem? How is it different?
2. What does Jesus's entry into Jerusalem teach you about His kingship? What does Zechariah 9:9, 10 teach you about Jesus's kingship? How does this passage relate to the mockery Jesus experienced during His trial and crucifixion?

REFLECTION 43
THE FRUITLESS TEMPLE

Mark 11:11–26

Cursing the Fig Tree

UPON ENTERING JERUSALEM, Jesus goes straight for the heart of
the city. He enters the temple. This is Jesus's first time at the
temple in Mark. He enters, looks around at everything, then
turns and leaves (Mark 11:11). He doesn't do anything. This first
trip to the temple was not an accident. Jesus was taking it all in
and planning something. He was "casing the joint." He plans on
returning and His actions on that second trip will be instrumental in getting Him arrested and crucified.

Jesus turns back, leaving the temple behind, and returns
with the twelve to Bethany for the night. The next morning, He
treks back up to the temple in Jerusalem. Along the way, He
becomes hungry and sees a fig tree. We are now beginning
another one of those Markan Sandwich stories. This fig tree is
the first part of a multifaceted story.

The fig tree was covered in leaves, but it had no figs on it.
Mark tells us, "for it was not the season for figs" (Mark 11:13).
The fig tree had a purpose, but it was no longer a useful

purpose. That season had passed. All that was left on the fig tree was leaves. It looked like a useful and productive tree, but upon closer inspection, it was serving no useful purpose. The tree bore no fruit.

Jesus shocks everyone by cursing the fig tree, saying, "May no one ever eat fruit from you again!" The disciples heard Him. Mark wants the reader to know that they were listening (Mark 11:14). By this point, we should know that Jesus isn't a petulant child who throws temper tantrums. He does not lose His cool and curse fig trees for no purpose, but He does like to teach in mysterious ways. We should read this passage, scratch our heads for a moment, and then dig deeper to find the meaning that must be there. The clues will come as the story unfolds.

Cleansing the Temple

Jesus then enters the Jerusalem temple and drives out those who were buying and selling. He flips over tables and chairs and "would not permit anyone to carry merchandise through the temple" (Mark 11:15–16). Walking directly into the temple, flipping tables, creating a massive public disturbance in the most important building in the most important city of Israel, is beyond dangerous. That will get you killed. This event takes the Jesus controversies to a whole new level.

In teaching this passage over the years I have often described this event like "storming into the capitol building in DC and flipping tables and causing a major disturbance." I am writing this in 2021, about 7 months after that very thing took place. Following the results of the most recent presidential election, a violent mob of angry protestors stormed the capitol building, vandalized it, and beat and injured many with weapons and pepper spray.

I remember the shock I felt when seeing those events. It has been described as insurrection, an attempt to overturn the election results. When the leaders of Jerusalem saw Jesus enter the temple and boldly throw tables and stop all the normal temple procedures, I wonder if they saw it the same way? Granted, Jesus did not harm the people working there and nobody was injured or left dead in the wake of His actions, but it would have been a frightening moment. People would have been enraged at His behavior.

Jesus's actions in this story are best understood in concert with the prophetic tradition of Israel. Prophets often acted in bizarre and controversial ways to demonstrate divine truth. Isaiah walked around naked for three years, Hosea married a prostitute, Ezekiel built a mini-city and laid on his left side for three hundred and ninety days before laying on his right side for forty days before eating bread cooked over cow dung. Basically, you don't want to be a prophet in Israel.

When Jesus arrived at the temple, He did not throw a tantrum or lose His temper. Jesus knew how to exercise self-control. He spent the previous evening at the temple, investigating everything and planning what He would do. This was a carefully planned and strategic demonstration, not a momentary fit of rage.

This is Jesus's third prophetic demonstration in a row.

1. Entering Jerusalem on a colt was a symbolic demonstration of the king's arrival.
2. Cursing the fig tree and
3. Cleansing the temple are also symbolic prophetic demonstrations of divine truth.

Jesus uses this disruption as a teaching opportunity, saying to them, "My house shall be called a house of prayer for all the nations ... but you have made it a robber's den" (Mark 11:17). We need to keep those words in mind as we begin interpreting what Jesus did at the temple that day. The chief priests care nothing about the message Jesus is teaching. Instead of listening to Him, they begin working on killing Him (Mark 11:18; see Mark 3:6).

If they had listened to Jesus, they would have heard two Old Testament references come from His mouth. The first is Isaiah 56:7, which is part of an invitation to all, even the foreigners and eunuchs (Isa 56:3–7), to join with the people of God on God's holy mountain, praying and rejoicing in His temple. The glorious purpose of the temple was ultimately to unite all the world together, Jew and Gentile alike, into a house of prayer. As Jesus sees it, the temple has become exclusive, nationalistic, and prideful. It has become a den of robbers.

Jesus says instead of fulfilling the beautiful image of Isaiah 56, the temple has fallen back to the state of Jeremiah 7. When Jesus calls the temple a "robbers' den" He is borrowing a line from a sermon in Jeremiah shortly before the temple was destroyed by Babylon. In Jeremiah 7, the prophet stands at the gate of the temple and announces God's judgment because of Jerusalem's sinful actions (Jer 7:1ff). The Lord cries out through Jeremiah, "Has this house, which is called by My name, become a den of robbers in your sight?" (Jer 7:11).

As the temple was destroyed by Babylon, so it will be destroyed by Rome. The fig tree is a mirror image of the temple. The temple had a purpose, but Jesus now sees it as unfruitful and unproductive. Analogous to the fig tree, the temple is out of season and is going to wither away. Cursing the fig tree and cleansing the temple together represent the temple's unfruitfulness and coming destruction.

This begins a major theme about the destruction of the temple that will become prevalent in Jesus's teaching from this point forward (Mark 13:1, 2). Jesus prophetically demonstrated the destruction of the temple by halting all temple service, not letting people pass through, and creating chaos inside (by the way, this story has nothing to do with kids selling candy at church for their little league team). It was a small picture of what the Romans will do in AD 70. It is first seen in the unproductive fig tree then demonstrated in the unproductive temple. And like the fig tree, that temple will never bear fruit again.

It's no surprise then that only a few verses later in Jeremiah, in chapter 8:13, describing the punishment of Jerusalem, the Lord says, "There will be no grapes on the vine, And no figs on the fig tree, and the leaf will wither." Jesus curses the fig tree for producing no figs and the leaves then wither. What happened in the days of Jeremiah was happening again. Instead of Babylon, now it is Rome, and instead of Jeremiah, now it is Jesus standing at the temple issuing the warning.

Faith, Prayer, and Forgiveness

After all the chaos of that day, Jesus leaves the city until the morning. Walking with his disciples in the early hours of the next day, Peter sees that fig tree again. He notes that the fig tree is now withered and dead. The leaves have rotted. It no longer looks leafy and productive, but it is seen for the unfruitful tree it has become.

When Peter points out the withered tree, Jesus responds with a series of statements about faith and prayer and forgiveness. It is difficult to smoothly connect this answer to the events that have just taken place, but several links can be made. Jesus's "curse" could be read as a prayer. As Jesus's words had a profound impact on the fig tree, so our words can have a profound impact in prayer. To the extent that, in trusting prayer, a mountain can be taken up and hurled into the sea. Given the context of the previous day, this may well be a reference to the temple mount (or the mount of Olives the disciples were passing on the way to Jerusalem). Trusting prayer is powerful (11:23), effective (11:24), and forgiving (11:25).

This paragraph, which immediately follows two prophetic

demonstrations symbolizing the destruction of the temple, becomes a message of hope in turbulent times. Warfare and death are on the way to Jerusalem and the disciples need to trust, hope, pray, and forgive. As Jerusalem falls, and the events described in Mark 13 take place, the disciples need to remember to have faith in God, pray for the unimaginable, and forgive graciously.

Reflection Questions

1. What are some things that may look righteous and holy but are not actually bearing fruit? Do you ever put on the appearance of holiness but bear no fruit? Why did Jesus curse the fig tree? What is Jesus teaching in this section of Mark?

2. Why does Jesus quote Jeremiah when he cleanses the temple? How is Jesus's message like Jeremiah's? Is Jesus angry when He cleanses the temple? What is Jesus's prophetic intention in cleansing the temple?

REFLECTION 44

JOHN'S BAPTISM AND A VINEYARD

Mark 11:27–12:12

The Interrogation Scene

JESUS MUST NOW ANSWER for His crimes. The chief priests and the scribes, while plotting behind the scenes to have Jesus killed (Mark 11:18), confront Him face to face (Mark 11:27–28) on His third trip back to the temple (Mark 11:11, 15, 27). This is the beginning of another series of confrontations and conflicts (Mark 11:28; 12:14, 19–23, 28, 35). The day after He disturbed the peace and flipped the tables, they asked, "By what authority are You doing these things, or who gave you this authority to do these things?" (Mark 11:28).

This is a fair and important question. It's a question people should have been asking throughout Mark's Gospel and, to those who paid attention, the answer has been clear: Jesus's authority comes from God Himself. At Jesus's transfiguration and baptism, a voice from above declares that Jesus is God's Son. That is a pretty good answer to the question.

Jesus has authority to walk into the temple, teach, or even halt the temple services because He is Lord of the temple. He acts like He owns the place because, well, He does. Jesus can forgive sins (Mark 2:7) and is Lord of Sabbath (Mark 2:28). He can calm storms (Mark 4:41), cast out demons (Mark 5:12–13), heal the afflicted (Mark 5:34), and raise the dead (Mark 5:43). Jesus can miraculously feed thousands (Mark 6:41), walk on water (Mark 6:48), challenge the traditions of Israel (Mark 7:9), declare all foods clean (Mark 7:19), exorcise demons in Gentile lands, and heal Gentiles (Mark 7:29, 35). Jesus has been demonstrating His divine authority since His baptism and this authority is what led Him to take charge of the temple. The temple is His Father's house.

The Baptism of John

Instead of answering their question directly, Jesus answers their question with a question about John's baptism. Was John's baptism legitimately divinely authorized, or was it some human innovation? This question might at first seem unrelated, but it's actually central to the controversy. The answer to Jesus's question provides a solid foundation to answer to the chief priests' question about His authority. When Jesus was baptized by John, the Holy Spirit came upon Him, and He was pronounced God's Son from the heavens. The Gospel of Mark and the authoritative ministry of Jesus begin with John's baptism. So, was it legitimate?

The chief priests and scribes and elders are good at asking questions, but when it is their turn to answer, they flounder. Here's the problem with the question. If they say the baptism of John is from God, they will be judged as hypocrites for not adhering to it. They'll also be validating Jesus and John, which they really do not want to do.

They could state what they truly believe, that John's baptism was a man-made innovation and should be rejected. After all, the Law of Moses did not command John's baptism.

John's baptism even challenged the sacrificial system within the Law of Moses and the authority of the temple itself. The priests could make a solid biblical argument for rejecting John's baptism. But if they do, they run into another problem. All the people believed that John was a legitimate prophet of God. If the priests dismiss John's baptism, they fear the people will dismiss them. They would essentially be calling John a false prophet and that would anger the crowds.

Instead of answering sincerely, they say "We do not know." They hide their beliefs. Since they won't answer Jesus's question, He doesn't answer theirs (Mark 11:33).

Notice three points about this exchange. First, the chief priests and scribes and elders know how to answer this question. They believe John's baptism is from man, but instead of answering what they truly believed, they played the role of the hypocrite. They did not care about truth; they cared about the opinion of others.

Secondly, if they had accepted John's baptism as legitimate, they would have lost authority in the temple. If they said, "Instead of going to the temple, go to the wilderness and find John and he will baptize you for the forgiveness of your sins" (John 1:4), then the temple loses one of its primary functions. If John's baptism is from God, the temple is growing out of season and becoming irrelevant. The fruit that the temple once bore is now produced in faith, repentance, and baptism. It would legitimizes Jesus's actions in the temple and the chief priests do not want to do that.

Thirdly, if they had accepted the truth about John's baptism, they would have known the source of Jesus's authority. Jesus's authority, like John's baptism, came from heaven. To answer one question is to answer the other. Jesus and John's authority came from the same source. If the chief priests and scribes reject John's authority, they will reject Jesus's also. In this short little exchange, Jesus demonstrates that the leaders of the people are dishonest, disobedient, and hypocritical.

Unfaithful Leaders in Israel

Jesus then illustrates this uncomfortable fact with a parable (Mark 12:1). Way back about 750 years before Jesus, there was a prophet named Isaiah. Isaiah records a parable about a vineyard (Isa 5:1–7). In that parable, God planted a vineyard, dug all around it, removed the stones, planted the best vines, built a tower in the middle, and cut out a wine vat for the juices to flow. In Isaiah's parable, this vineyard represented the house of Israel (Isa 5:7). God planted Israel and expected them to produce good fruit. Instead, they produced only worthless grapes (Isa 5:2, 4, 7). The "good grapes" God looked for were "justice" and "righteousness," but the worthless grapes He found were "bloodshed" and "a cry of distress" (Isa 5:7). After putting so much work into the vineyard, nothing useful came from it. So, God promises to deconstruct and remove the vineyard (Isa 5:5–6).

When Jesus begins His parable in Mark 12, He describes a vineyard in almost the exact same language as the LXX translation of Isaiah 5. While the priests are probably expecting a parable like Isaiah's, Jesus's parable takes an unexpected twist. Jesus does not see Israel as a worthless vineyard. He sees Israel as a productive vineyard that yields wonderful grapes, but the leaders of Israel keep the grapes for themselves. They are disobedient and violent men who kill those sent to them and steal God's produce.

In Jesus's parable, God plants Israel and leaves it to vinegrowers (like the priests) to watch after her while He is away. At harvest, God sends servants to the vineyard to bring back some of the produce, but His servants are rejected and beaten. As things escalate, eventually these servants are killed. This probably represents the history of prophets sent to Israel who were rejected and killed.

Throughout this parable, Israel is producing fruit, but the leaders are standing in the way of God's harvest. Eventually God sends His "beloved Son" (Mark 12:6), and they take the Son and beat and kill Him and throw Him out of the vineyard. This is the third and final "beloved Son" passage in Mark. The first two are when Jesus is baptized by John (Mark 1:11) and the transfiguration (Mark 9:7). In those passages we learned that Jesus is God's beloved Son, now we see the beloved Son will be killed and discarded.

Jesus concludes the parable, not with the vineyard being destroyed, but with the leaders being destroyed and the vineyard given to others. This is likely another reference to the destruction of the temple (and her priests and leaders and the whole temple system). The priests and leaders of the temple will lose control of Israel when the temple is destroyed but Israel will continue under new leadership.

Jesus ends the parable with a citation from Psalm 118 (a psalm which was cheered by the crowds as He entered Jerusalem a few days earlier, Mark 11:9), about the builders rejecting the stone which was the chief cornerstone. Jesus uses' temple imagery to say that those leading the temple rejected what the temple should have been founded upon. They rejected the temple's chief stone.

This parable is an obvious challenge and direct condemnation of the leaders of the temple. They knew "He spoke this parable against them" (Mark 12:12). They are so offended, they want to seize Jesus, but don't because they fear the people (Mark 12:12). The crowds keep them from openly killing Jesus in Mark 11:18, from answering His question honestly in Mark 11:32, and from arresting Jesus in Mark 12:12. But the time is coming when the crowds will turn against Jesus and each verse from this point forward moves us closer to His arrest and crucifixion.

Reflection Questions

1. Why does Jesus often answer questions with questions? How is John's baptism relevant to the cleansing of the temple? What does the answer of the chief priests and scribes reveal about their integrity?

2. How does Jesus adapt the parable in Isaiah 5 to His setting? Who is Jesus critiquing? In what ways do church leaders sometimes steal the fruit of the church for themselves? How can we make sure this does not happen?

REFLECTION 45

TAXES AND RESURRECTION

Mark 12:13–27

Pharisees and Herodians

JESUS NEVER GIVES the answers people want. If He is asked a "Yes" or "No" question, you can virtually guarantee His answer will not be "Yes" or "No." Whether it's a question about divorce (Mark 10:1–9) or the source of His authority (Mark 11:28), He usually answers a question with a question to show the folly of the question.

Mark 12 contains a series of debates Jesus has with different factions of Jews in Jerusalem. Jesus just finished arguing with the chief priests, scribes, and elders (Mark 11:27–12:12), and now will tangle with Pharisees and Herodians (Mark 12:13), Sadducees (Mark 12:18), and scribes (Mark 12:28). It is like everyone is taking their final shot to trap Him or catch Him in some inconsistency.

The Pharisees and Herodians team up to ask a question about taxes. They began conspiring together to destroy Jesus in Mark 3:6 (also see Mark 8:15), and now we see their plan. They attempt to snare Jesus into a political trap. Their first step is to butter Him up by paying Him insincere and duplicitous compliments: "We know that You are truthful and defer to no one; for You are not partial to any, but teach the way of God in truth" (Mark 12:14).

The expression "You are not partial to any" (οὐ γὰρ βλέπεις εἰς πρόσωπον ἀνθρώπων) in Greek could be translated, "For you do not see into the face of men." They surround Jesus and ask a controversial and dangerous question. He is surrounded by faces who will pounce on Him the second He says the wrong thing, and He must answer. The chief priests answer questions based on what the crowds think (Mark 11:32). Jesus does not. Justice is blind to the faces of men and so is Jesus.

This "compliment" is an essential part of setting up their trap. The Herodians and Pharisees do not ordinarily get along. They are political enemies. The Herodians are loyal to the house of Herod, the Roman appointed king of the Jews. The Pharisees tend to dislike all things Roman. They hate that Rome has occupied Israel and they want to kick Rome out. These two hostile groups find unity only in their hatred of Jesus.

They ask Jesus about paying the poll-tax to Caesar. This is a question to which the Herodians would answer "Yes" and the Pharisees would answer "No." So, which face is Jesus going to see? The Herodian political platform is to show your loyalty and get along with Rome. Rome has improved the temple, built roads, given good leadership, and is a military ally (see 1 Macc 8). Pay your taxes, be thankful, and stop complaining.

The Pharisees, however, do not think Jews should pay tribute to pagan foreign powers (they still reluctantly do, but they hate the taxes and the tax-collectors). They have read books like Isaiah and Hosea which strongly condemn making foreign alliances and paying tribute to pagan kings. They have read Daniel and know that the empires of this earth are beasts that must be slayed. Pharisees believe one should trust in God for deliverance rather than making alliances with Rome and giving them money for friendship.

Will Jesus advocate rebellion against Rome? Or will He accept pagan rule of Israel? Will He stand up against the beasts (Dan 7) or financially support them? Will Jesus take up the reins as the true ruler of this world or passively bow down to Caesar? Will He support Rome or the kingdom of God?

Icons and Idols

They say Jesus doesn't see men's faces, but He does see at least one. Roman coins, much like our modern American coinage, depict men's faces. Jesus sees Caesar's face on a coin and asks, "Whose likeness (εἰκών) and inscription is this?" (Mark 12:16). The Greek word, translated as "likeness" is eikōn (we get the word *icon* from it), a word often associated with idolatry (Deut 4:16; 2 Kigs 11:18; 2 Chr 33:7; Isa 40:19-20; Rev 13:14; 14:9; 15:2; 16:2; 19:20; 20:4). It is regularly translated as "image" (Col 1:15; Gen 1:26).

The image on the coin is Caesar's. This particular coin also has an "inscription" (ἐπιγραφή). This coin pictures

> Tiberius' laurel-crowned head ... surrounded by the inscrip-
> tion, TI[BERIVS] CAESR DIVI AVG[VSTI] F[ILIUS] AVGC-
> STVS ("Tiberius Caesar, son of the deified Augustus,
> [himself] Augustus"). This inscription continues on the
> reverse side of the coin, where it reads Pontif[ex] Maxim[us] =
> "High Priest" and is accompanied by a picture of a seated lady
> who probably represents Pax, the embodiment of the peace of
> the empire.[1]

Roman coins are different in this regard to Jewish coins. Jewish coins did not inscribe images of men with decrees of deification. Jews have a word for images of a men engraved on metal with inscriptions about their divinity. It's called an idol.

> There would be good reason for the Jews to be outraged at the requirement that they pay their taxes with this sort of coin ... The coin, then, is not only an economic instrument and a symbol of the Jew's political subjection to Rome but also a part of the developing ruler cult of the first century.[2]

Jesus does not answer by saying, "Yes, pay your taxes." That would have fallen into the trap by siding with the Herodians. He also does not say, "Refuse to pay your taxes," siding with the Pharisees. Instead, Jesus says take the idolatrous coins and return to sender. "Render to Caesar the things that are Caesar's, and to God the things that are God's (Mark 12:17). Because the coin has Caesar's icon, give it back to Caesar, and whatever has God's icon, must be given back to God. This riddle leaves people "amazed" (Mark 12:17) in a way that answering "Yes" or "No" would not.

The riddle leaves the listeners (and us readers) with one big question. What belongs to God? What has God's icon/image? The answer to the riddle is found in Genesis 1:26, where God says, "Let us make man in our *image (icon/εἰκὼν)*, according to our likeness." Your money may be Caesar's, but you are not. So, sure, give your coin back to Caesar, but give your life, your body, your loyalty and allegiance, your soul, and your whole self to God.

Sadducees and the Resurrection

Up next to challenge Jesus are the Sadducees. These were the ruling class in ancient Israel; most of the priests, Sanhedrin, and men of status were Sadducees. This group denied the resurrection at the end of the age and the existence of angels and spirits (Acts 23:8). There is also some evidence that the Sadducees only accepted the five books of Moses, the Torah, as authoritative.

They come challenging Jesus on the topic of resurrection. The levirate marriage instructions of Deuteronomy 25:5–10 stand in the background of this question. Basically, if two brothers live together, and one of them has a wife but dies, the brother of the deceased could marry the widowed bride and be her husband. Their first son would belong to the departed brother. While this sounds odd in our culture, this law ensured protection and provision for the widow and that the family line and name of the deceased brother could continue. Of course, this was voluntary. The brother may refuse to marry her. If he did, she could take his sandal, spit in his face, and he'd always be known as the jerk who lost a sandal. I love that law.

The Sadducees ask a question about this instruction and the resurrection. Here's the scenario, (which comes from Tobit 3:8; 7:11): a woman has married seven brothers, all of them die, and she has a child with none of them (by the way, if I was that seventh brother, I'd be a little suspicious). When they all reunite in the resurrection, it will be a bit awkward, right? Whose wife will she be?

This question is supposed to show the absurdity of the resurrection, and it presents an interesting conundrum. Jesus initially retorts that the Sadducees do not know the Scriptures nor the power of God, which is an accusation that they are unqualified to be leaders of God's people. He answers their question by saying there is no marriage in the resurrection. The question is based on a false assumption.

Side Note: If you are in a happy marriage, the idea that your marriage will not continue into the resurrection can be pretty depressing. I feel like I won't like that. I must remember, though, one of the purposes of marriage in the Bible is procreation and the preservation of the family, but since there is no death, there is no longer the need for procreation. So, marriage begins to lose some of its purpose and meaning in the resurrection. A second purpose of marriage is love and companionship and shared experiences, but there is no reason to think those will not be part of the resurrection life. In fact, the love and companionship we will share in the resurrection, I believe, will be even more meaningful and intimate and true and sincere than what we experience now. I don't think marriage ceases in the resurrection because our relationships will be worse, but marriage cannot keep up with how beautiful and fulfilling our relationships will be. I believe I will know and love my wife in the resurrection even more than I do now. Our relationship will be stronger than ever, even if it is not technically called "marriage." Perhaps our relationships will be called something greater.

Jesus then turns the question around on them and makes an argument for the resurrection based on Exodus 3:6 and 15, where God describes Himself to Moses as the God of Abraham, Isaac, and Jacob. That description is significant because it was made long after the death of Abraham, Isaac, and Jacob (and it comes from Exodus, which the Sadducees accept as authoritative). Yet, Yahweh is still (present tense) their God. Death has not dissolved the relationship. This does not mean they have been resurrected yet, but it provides hope for a resurrection in the future. The grammatical argument suggests that God is still their God, and He still has plans for them. God "is not the God of the dead, but of the living" (Mark 12:27).

This argument is deepened when you look beyond the grammar to the narratives about the patriarchs in Genesis. God made promises to the patriarchs about their land that death prevented them from experiencing. At the burnish bush, those promises were yet unfulfilled. If God is their God, He is not done with them. They will experience the full realization of the promises of God and resurrection is how that will happen.

Being the "God of Abraham, Isaac, and Jacob" is a description infused with hope and life and future blessing. It brings resurrection to the table.

This is perfectly in rhythm with God's actions throughout the Torah. God repeatedly gives life in the most dreadful circumstances. Did you ever notice how many barren women give birth in the Bible? If the Bible introduces you to a barren woman, be prepared for a baby. God gives life to the dead, barren wombs of Sarah, Rebekah, and Rachel. In Romans 4:19, Paul describes Abraham's body as "as good as dead," but Abraham maintained faith in the God "who gives life to the dead and calls into existence things that do not exist" (Rom 4:17). Giving life to a barren womb hints at the reality and hope of resurrection. When we read about those barren women in the Bible (especially the wives of the patriarchs), we should see the hope of resurrection through their stories. The God of Abraham, Isaac, and Jacob gives life. God's life-giving power (which the Sadducees fail to see—Mark 12:24) is demonstrated through His experiences with the patriarchs and even in death, there is no reason for that to end. [3]

Reflection Questions

1. Is paying taxes to Rome in Jesus's day similar to paying tribute to Assyria in Isaiah's day? Should Israel make alliances with Rome? Should they pay taxes to pagans? Why is this question so controversial? How does Jesus's answer avoid the trap set by the Pharisees and Herodians?

2. What is the difference between "resurrection" and the "immortality of the soul"? How is this difference significant? How should it impact our view of the world and our bodies? How is God shown to "give

life" to the patriarchs? What do you most look forward to about the resurrection?

Endnotes

1. Joel Marcus, *Mark 8–16: A New Translation with Introduction and Commentary* in *AB* (New Haven: Yale, 2009), 824.

2. Marcus, *Mark 8–16*.

3. A few sources that help flesh out the narratival hermeneutic employed by Jesus in this passage are J. Gerald Janzen, "Resurrection and Hermeneutics: On Exodus 3:6 in Mark 12:26," *JSNT* 23 (1985); 43–58 and Richard B. Hays, "Reading Scripture in Light of the Resurrection" in *Reading with the Grain of Scripture* (Grand Rapids: Eerdmans, 2020), 55–60.

REFLECTION 46
MORE TEMPLE TEACHING

Mark 12:28–44

An Honest Scribe

HEARING ALL THE HUBBUB, a scribe comes to Jesus and asks another question. This question seems more honest than the previous ones. The scribe asks which command is the greatest of all. This is one of the few times that Jesus gives a straightforward answer to a question. Perhaps Jesus responds this way because the question is sincere.

Jesus answers by quoting two passages. Jesus does not say, "You misunderstand the Scriptures. All words of God are equal to all others. No command is more important or less important than any other." Instead, Jesus answers directly and clearly. Let us make sure we all hear Him.

There are two commands that rise above all others. They come from the Law of Moses and Jesus, our Lord, says they are the most important commandments of all. They are still the most important of all. While Jesus does occasionally bump up against parts of the Law of Moses (or at least, traditional interpretations of the Law of Moses), He still sees these Scriptures as authoritative and true.

Jesus's answer comes from two texts: Deuteronomy 6:4–6 and Leviticus 19:18. The answer is to love God without everything you are and love your neighbor as yourself. These are the greatest commands in the Law because they are the essence of the Law. The Law of Moses exists to teach man how to do these two things. If your interpretation of a passage is not promoting love of God or love of man, you are probably misinterpreting a passage.

It's interesting that the greatest commands in the Law do not come from the Ten Commandments, yet if you read the commandments with these two commands in mind, you see how they all fit together. If you truly love God, you will not try to replace Him with other, inferior, gods or insult Him with an image or engraving which can never capture His true glory or essence. If you truly love God and man, you will not take His name for selfish purposes, either in false vows to deceive people, or in a fit of frustration. If you truly love God and man, you will honor the Sabbath in imitation of God, for reflection upon God, and you will give rest and peace to all your family, workers, and even animals. You will enjoy Sabbath and spread that joy to others. Certainly, if you love your neighbor as yourself, you will honor and care for your parents, you will not kill your neighbor, sleep with his wife, steal from him, lie about him, or covet his things (putting your wishes above his). If you truly love God and love your neighbor, you don't need the Ten Commandments because you will already be practicing them. The Law helps you practice love.

The scribe approves of Jesus's answer (wasn't that nice of him?). After telling Jesus that He answered correctly, the scribe goes on to say that loving God and loving neighbor "is much more than all burnt offerings and sacrifices" (Mark 12:33). Remember that this whole series of confrontations and questions started with Jesus cleansing the temple and halting the temple service. Jesus, through the fig tree, predicted the temple's destruction. He authenticated John's baptism, which competed with sacrifices at the temple, as having come from God. He told a parable about the destruction of the vine-growers. In the next chapter, Jesus will explicitly discuss the destruction of the temple by the Romans. When the scribe says that loving God and neighbor are much more than burnt offerings and sacrifices, it is again a challenge to the temple's role in Israel.

Jesus sees standing before Him a sincere and honest scribe. Jesus declares, "You are not far from the kingdom of God" (Mark 12:34). We do not know what came of this man, but I like to think he committed his life to Jesus and accepted the reign of God. A major point we would all do well to remember is that love is how you draw near to the kingdom of God.

Jesus Teaches in the Temple

Jesus now begins teaching in the temple (Mark 12:35). The structure here is similar to the conflict stories in Mark 2:1–3:6. In that section, Jesus's opponents asked four questions in a row (Mark 2:7, 16, 18, 24) and Jesus asked the fifth and final question (Mark 3:4). In this section, Jesus has been asked four questions in a row by the chief priests, scribes, and elders (Mark 11:28), the Herodians and Pharisees (Mark 12:14–15), the Sadducees (Mark 12:18–23), and a scribe (Mark 12:28), but Jesus asks the fifth and final question (Mark 12:35–37).

The final question Jesus asks is how the scribes call the Christ the "Son of David"? We've already discussed that "Son of David" is a Messianic title used by Bartimaeus in Mark 10:47–48, but David Himself, in the Holy Spirit, calls Christ, "Lord." Father's do not usually call their children "Lord." That is a term a child may call a father, but not the reverse.

Jesus's point here is that the Messiah, while He may be a literal descendant of David, is also the Lord of David. Those who are expecting a Christ like David to emerge will be disappointed. The Messiah is greater even than David and will act in greater ways. His kingdom will far exceed the kingdom of David. David's kingdom, forged through bloodshed, reigned in one geographical location, was rife with conflict, and only united one group of people. The Messiah will bring about the kingdom of God which will reign supreme in "all the nations" (Mark 11:17) and unite all tribes, tongues, and peoples, without boasting, borders, or bloodshed (save the blood of the Messiah).

Hypocrisy and Sincerity

The parable of the vineyard, which began chapter 12, condemned the leaders of Israel for hijacking the fruit which belonged to God. There were many good, faithful, fruit-bearing Jews in Israel, but among the leadership, Jesus saw pride, hypocrisy, and violence. As Mark 12 concludes, Jesus compares the prideful scribes and the wealthy elite of Israel to a poor, humble, widow.

Jesus describes how the scribes love to wear long robes, rub elbows with the upper echelon of society, take the chief seats in synagogues and banquets, and offer long prayers to impress all who hear them, yet they devour widows' houses (Mark 12:38–40). Imagine evicting a widow who is mourning her husband and struggling to make the payments and sending her out to the streets just to have a little extra pocket change as you go to luxurious, high-society, parties and then enter the synagogue to offer long prayers about justice, righteousness, and generosity. The scribes would be fine trampling over the widow provided they looked good doing it. Every society has those who live this way, and it is detestable to Jesus.

If we're not careful, we can care so much about the opinions of men, looking good in society, protecting our important friends, that we neglect our call to justice and devalue generosity. This is another example of the leaders of Israel caring more about men's opinions than what is right (Mark 11:32, see Mark 12:14). The scribes only care about their reputations and important places in society; they care only about how people see them.

Some of the wealthiest then go to the temple and make their donations. They gave large sums of money, but it came from their excess. It made them look good, but there was no sacrifice involved. They could give the big dollars without even noticing because they had so much more wealth than they needed. There was also an old widow who showed up that day to give. She gave two copper coins which are worth practically nothing. No temple gets renovated with two copper coins. No names get placed on important buildings with a two-copper coin donation. Universities don't name libraries after poor widows who gave two copper coins.

But Jesus saw it. He saw her love and sacrifice. He saw her sincerity. He saw that she was bearing fruit for the kingdom even when she had so little to offer. This widow who made her trip up to the temple that day donated what could have easily been forgotten and ignored. Instead, that donation is remembered two thousand years later because it illustrates what the kingdom of God is all about. While the poor and widowed are often neglected in this life, and while their houses are devoured by the greedy, God sees and loves them.

Reflection Questions

1. In what practical ways can you love God with all of your heart, soul, mind, and strength? How do you

love God with your heart? Soul? Mind? Strength?
Why would this be the most important command?

2. In what practical ways can you love your neighbor
as yourself? Who is your neighbor? Why would this
be the second most important command?

REFLECTION 47
PROPHET OF DOOM

Mark 13:1–37

The Temple's Disastrous Fate

JESUS IS OFTEN COMPARED to great leaders and prophets in the Old Testament. Some, with signs and wonders, overthrew world powers and the enemies of Israel (i.e. Moses). Some established kingdoms of glory, power, wealth, and renowned (i.e. David). Some, on the other hand, suffered immeasurably as they prophesied against Israel and predicted Jerusalem's doom (i.e. Jeremiah). Who is Jesus going to be?

If you haven't been catching the references so far, it's about to become obvious that the temple is doomed. As Jesus leaves the temple, His disciples point out the beauty of the stones and the architecture. This temple was renovated by the Romans and wealth and beauty were poured into it. It was one of the most impressive construction projects in the ancient world. It became known as Herod's Temple, and it was his pride and legacy. That's one of the many reasons the Jews paid so much in taxes.

When Jesus sees the temple, He does not care about the

wealth and gold and beautiful stones (Jesus isn't impressed by riches), instead Jesus sees a den of robbers (Mark 11:17) and a fruitless fig tree. Jesus sees doom and destruction instead of a house of prayer for all the nations. The Romans who built that temple will soon come and destroy it and the surrounding city.

The destruction of Jerusalem is a surprising message from the Messiah. His job, many believed, was to prevent that from happening. This message of destruction was supposed to be for Rome, not the temple. Jesus is about to prophecy the exact opposite of what Israel wants to hear. Instead of Israel overthrowing the Romans, Rome will instead destroy Jerusalem and her temple. This won't help Jesus with the popular vote.

Jesus warns, "Do you see these great buildings? Not one stone will be left upon another which will not be torn down" (Mark 13:2). Mark 13 must be read as a description of these events. It's extremely easy, if we forget the context, to start making predictions about the end of time from Mark 13, but that's not what Jesus is talking about (at least for the first 32 verses. We'll discuss verses 33–37 below).

Peter, Andrew, James, and John (the first four called, Mark 1:14–20) approach Jesus privately for more info. Jesus just said something massive. He's been alluding to it for several chapters, but now He stated the matter with shocking bluntness. This is what cleansing the temple back in Mark 11 was all about.

The disciples ask when it will happen and what signs they should expect. While Jesus gives them several signs, He does not tell them exactly when it will happen, "But of that day or hour no one knows, not even the angels in heaven, nor the Son, but the Father alone" (Mark 13:32). In Matthew's parallel account, the disciples ask three questions:

1. When will these things happen?
2. What will be the sign of the Your coming
3. And of the end of the age? (Matt 24:3).

I think (and opinions vary) in Matthew, Jesus addresses the destruction of the temple, but then shifts to the end of the age (final second coming) around Matthew 24:36. While the destruction of the temple is also the end of an age, Matthew distinguishes it from the final day of the Lord's coming. Matthew gives several parables through the end of chapter 25 about the final second coming of Jesus. In those parables, Jesus prepares His disciples for a delayed parousia, meaning, the final second coming might not happen for a while. Prepare for the long haul.

In Mark's parallel, there is no discussion of a long, delayed parousia and the disciples do not ask about "the end of the age." There is no obvious sudden shift in topic from the destruction of Jerusalem to the final second coming. A natural reading of Mark 13 would suggest the entire chapter is about the destruction of Jerusalem. I do think verses 32–37 could be applicable in both settings, however. There is a lot of overlap and shared language in the New Testament between the destruction of Jerusalem and the final coming of Jesus, because they are both cataclysmic, apocalyptic, eschatological events. They are days of the Lord and days of judgment and can be described as a "coming of the Lord." They shake the foundations of everything we think we know about reality.

Signs of the Temple's Doom

The key word throughout Mark 13 is "Be on your guard" or literally, "See!" It's the Greek word βλέπετε (blepete) and it is used in Mark 13:5 to begin the whole discussion: "Be on your guard that no one misleads you." It is repeated in verses 9, 23, 33, usually translated as "be on your guard" or "take heed." In verse 33 it is coupled with the word ἀγρυπνεῖτε which is translated "keep on the alert." Another similar word is used in Mark 13:34, 35, and 37, γρηγορέω (grēgoreō), which means "Stay awake" or "stay alert." These words all convey the idea of being watchful, ready, alert, awake, on guard, and prepared for the doom and destruction that is coming.

Jesus warns His disciples not to be duped by false signs and false Messiahs (Mark 13:6, 21–22). There will be "wars and rumors of wars" and "nation will rise up against nation, and kingdom against kingdom." There will also be earthquakes and famines, but these are not reasons for fear. These things always happen, and they are merely the beginning of the "birth pangs" (Mark 13:8).

There will be persecution and suffering and suspicion and betrayal and family strife (Mark 13:9–13) and the gospel will first be preached to "all the Gentiles/nations" (remember what the temple was supposed to be? Mark 11:17). But again, these are to be expected and do not represent the end quite yet.

The sign of the end of the temple is "when you see the abomination of desolation standing where it should not be (let the reader understand), then those who are in Judea must flee to the mountains" (Mark 13:14). Rather than explaining the sign, Mark leaves a cryptic note "let the reader understand." Matthew keeps that same cryptic parenthetical statement in his Gospel but adds more clarity. The "abomination of desolation" is a reference to the prophet Daniel (see 9:2, 26, 27; 11:31; 12:11) and "where it should not be" is "the holy place" (Matthew 24:15). Some unclean abomination, spoken by Daniel, is coming to the temple and will leave it desolate. Luke is the clearest when he writes, "when you see Jerusalem surrounded by armies, then recognize that her desolation is near" (Luke 21:20).

When you see this sign, then run for the hills. Do not go back and pack, just run. Pregnant women and nursing mothers are in a woeful state because it is hard to run and keep your children safe in times of war and violence. Pray that these things don't happen when travel is impeded by winter (Mark 13:15-18). By the way, none of these words or warnings make sense if the final second coming of Jesus is the topic, but they make a ton of sense if Rome is coming to destroy your city.

In Mark 13:19–27 the language becomes increasingly apocalyptic and cosmic. We need to remember the context is the destruction of Jerusalem. This language can be used for judgment days in time or at the end of time or any day of the coming of the Lord with wrath. This section is illuminated with language and allusions to Old Testament texts. The cosmic language of the "sun being darkened" and the "moon will not give its light" comes from Isaiah 13 about the fall of Babylon (which is also not a text about the end of time). The Lord's judgment against Babylon will now be meted out against Jerusalem. The "Son of Man coming in clouds" is from Daniel 7:13 when the beasts (world empires) fall, and the Son of Man receives glory and a kingdom.

I remember a professor describing a helpful way to think of this type of apocalyptic language. He said it's like God is sitting on His throne and watching injustice and evil take over His world. He can only watch for so long before He needs to stand up and do something about it. When the Lord arises to visit His creation with judgment and punishment, His presence is so awesome and terrifying that creation itself cannot handle it. Stars fall, the sun dies out, the moon turns to blood, the mountains shake and crumble, light hides, etc. The world "uncreates" itself in the terrifying divine presence of God. This is what will happen when the temple falls.

When Will This Happen?

Remember when Jesus cursed the fig tree and it withered and died? That was symbolic of what was going to happen to the temple. Now, when Jesus discusses the destruction of the temple, He reminds us, "learn the parable from the fig tree; when its branch has already become tender and puts forth its leaves, you know that summer is near" (Mark 13:28). The leaves are a sign of the end. Likewise, when they see the signs of the coming of the Lord and the temple's destruction, be warned the Lord is near.

All these things will happen before the generation of Jesus's contemporaries passes away (Mark 13:30) and His words are even more certain than the continuation of heaven and earth (Mark 13:31). As for the exact day and hour of these events, only the Father knows (Mark 13:32). No one will know until they see it (Mark 13:14). This is a rare text that presents Jesus, during His incarnation, as lacking an attribute of the divine. This is not ordinarily how Mark has been presenting Jesus throughout this Gospel, but it is a reminder of the humanity and limitations of the incarnate Jesus.

This discussion concludes with a parable stressing the importance of being alert and prepared. A doorman is charged with staying awake all night until the master's return. He may return at any point during the night: evening, midnight, rooster crow, or morning. Jesus is calling His disciples, Peter, Andrew, James, and John, to stay awake and alert all night and be ready. They had to stay ready and alert for the coming of the Lord, can we?

Reflection Questions

1. Why does the destruction of Jerusalem sound so much like the end of the world? What are some of the signs for the destruction of Jerusalem? Are there any signs for the end of the world?
2. What is the abomination of desolation? Why is Daniel a relevant text for the destruction of Jerusalem? What should the disciples do to prepare for the destruction of Jerusalem and the temple?

REFLECTION 48
THE PLOT THICKENS

Mark 14:1–31

Judas Makes a Deal

ANOTHER ONE of Mark's sandwiches appears in Mark 14:1–11. Mark 14:1–2 and 10–11 bookend the story in the middle about the anointing of Jesus. In verses 1 and 2 we are reintroduced to the chief priests and the scribes. This is the same group that confronted Jesus after He cleansed the temple (Mark 11:27–28) and began conceiving ways to kill Him (Mark 12:12). They are terrified of the people, the crowds, that have surrounded Jesus all throughout Mark (Mark 11:18, 32; 12:12; 14:2). As this sandwich concludes, they find a way to arrest Jesus while He is alone, away from the crowds.

Judas Iscariot, one of the twelve, reaches out to the chief priests and offers to betray Jesus. He can provide access to Jesus at night when He is all alone, and they can provide money for the information. They strike an agreement and from that time forward, Judas searches for an opportunity to betray Jesus.

Why would Judas want to betray the Lord? There are a good number of reasonable speculations one could offer. As I read through Mark, I'm continually struck by how difficult the teaching and challenge of Jesus is. Imagine being a faithful Jew who loves Israel, Torah, Jerusalem, the temple, and you are longing for the great kingdom of God and the Son of David to restore Israel's former glory. Then you meet Jesus. He casts out demons, heals the sick, calms storms, walks on water, feeds thousands, and even raises the dead. He is the Messiah (Mark 8:29–30).

This should all be wonderful, hopeful, life-giving news! This is gospel! Jesus is bringing the kingdom of God to earth and finally, freedom from Rome is within grasp, justice will be restored, and peace and happiness are on the horizon.

Then Jesus opens His mouth.

Instead of gaining the world, He calls you to deny yourself and carry a cross (Mark 8:34–37). He calls you to martyrdom, which isn't exactly what you signed up for. He calls you to be "last of all," "servant of all," and "slave of all" (Mark 9:35; 10:43–44). He says you will not have political authority like the kingdoms of men (Mark 10:42–43). He doesn't honor the temple but flips its tables (Mark 11:15–17). He doesn't fawn over Jerusalem but proclaims her destruction and says the temple will become a rubbish heap (Mark 13:2). He criticizes the leaders of Israel (Mark 12:12, 38–40), commends poverty, and condemns the wealthy (Mark 12:41–44).

This has all been extremely hard on the disciples who have failed to understand nearly every step of the way: Mark 4:40–41; 6:37, 52; 8:4, 14-21, 32, 9:5–6, 10, 28, 31–32, 38–39; 10:13, 24–26; 37–38; 13:1–2. Apparently, Judas could not take it anymore. This is not the life, kingdom, or Messiah that he wanted. His exit strategy is to offer up Jesus to the chief priests, take his money, and go live out the rest of his days in the Bahamas. Or something like that.

Mark says less about Judas than any other Gospel. Mark doesn't call him a thief (John 12:6), says virtually nothing about him during the ministry of Jesus, and never mentions his suicide or remorse (Matthew 27:1–10; Acts 1:15–20). Judas quietly vanishes from the story after betraying Jesus and we never see him again.

Jesus Is Anointed

In Mark 14:3, in the middle of the sandwich about His betrayal, Jesus is in the home of a leper. Jesus touches lepers (Mark 1:41), stays in their homes, and reclines at their tables. It's possible that this made Judas (and the disciples) uncomfortable also.

A woman enters the scene and in an act of generosity, reverence, and devotion, breaks open a costly jar of alabaster perfume of pure nard. This jar was worth over 300 denarii. A denarius is a day's labor. Three hundred work days would provide about one year's salary. She could have sold it and spent it on herself. The disciples rebuke her for not selling it and giving it to the poor. Jesus defends her "good deed" (Mark 14:6).

The disciples struggle knowing who to rebuke and shun. They rebuke Jesus (Mark 8:32). They shun the unnamed exorcist (Mark 9:38–39). They rebuke people for bringing children to Jesus (Mark 10:13). They rebuke the blind man for calling out to Jesus (Mark 10:47). They condemn this woman who gave her most prized possession to Jesus (Mark 14:4–5). Interestingly, I don't recall them rebuking the chief priests, scribes, elders, Pharisees, Sadducees, or wealthy. Jesus and the disciples are still on different wavelengths when it comes to authority, service, and others.

When Jesus says, "you always have the poor with you," this is in no way an admonition to care less about poverty or to ignore the poor. As bizarre as it sounds, some have used this phrase to mean fighting poverty is helpless because we will always have the poor. Some have used it to suggest that helping the poor is less important than serving Jesus. We need to remember that helping the poor is a way to serve Jesus and that Jesus Himself was poor!

If you've paid attention to Mark (or any of the Gospels) it's obvious that Jesus cares immeasurably about the poor and wants us to be generous and proactive in alleviating their struggle (Mark 10:21). That is a mission He leaves with us. Caring for the poor is a mission the church will always have while the opportunities to give to Jesus during His lifetime were limited. Never rebuke someone for acting in kindness, especially towards Jesus.

This act of devotion and generosity emphasizes the importance of what Jesus is about to endure. She anointed His body for burial before He even died. This act of faith and love should be remembered by each of us. Jesus says, "Wherever the gospel is preached in the whole world, what this woman has done will also be spoken of in memory of her" (Mark 14:9). This is yet another reference to the wider Gentile mission to which Jesus has been alluding (Mark 13:10; 11:17). It is also a reminder that perhaps we should spend more time talking about this act of service and remembering the example of this woman.

In this sandwich, this woman's actions should be contrasted with Judas. She gave her money to honor Jesus while Judas received money to betray Him. She put Jesus above all earthly riches, while Judas traded Jesus for a little bit of cash. She modeled the self-sacrifice and generosity that Jesus has been challenging His disciples to develop. Judas rejected Jesus, the kingdom, and the goodness of God in a selfish act of rebellion.

This unnamed woman (in Mark's Gospel) outshines the rest of the disciples. In fact, it is women who anoint His body for burial (Mark 14:3–9), remain during His crucifixion (Mark 15:40–41), and follow to the empty tomb (Mark 16:1). It is His male disciples, in Mark 14 alone, who rebuke this woman

(Mark 14:4), betray Jesus (Mark 14:10, 44-46), abandon Him (Mark 14:50), and deny Him (Mark 14:66-72).

Passover and the Lord's Supper

On the first day of Passover, while the lamb was being sacrificed, Jesus sent His disciples to Jerusalem to prepare a room for them to eat (Mark 14:12-16). This scene is quite similar to Mark 11:1-6. The disciples do exactly as Jesus instructed, and at evening they all reclined around a table.

During this meal, Jesus informs the disciples that one of them will betray Him (Mark 14:18-21). He also radically redefines essential elements of the Passover meal. Jesus takes a piece of bread, prays, breaks the bread, and distributes it to His disciples, saying this bread is His body. Taking a cup, He does the same thing. He gives thanks, distributes it to them, and they all drink. He says, "This is My blood of the covenant, which is poured out for many." (Mark 14:24).

The Passover meal is an annual reminder of God's powerful, gracious, saving acts towards Israel when He overthrew the Egyptians and rescued His people. The language and imagery of the Passover come directly from the tenth and final plague over Egypt. After leaving Egypt, being delivered through the Red Sea, and receiving miraculous provisions of food and water, God brings Israel to Sinai. He delivers His Law and offers a covenant to them.

Before offering this covenant, God already saved, rescued, provided, and cared for Israel. He demonstrated His love. He gave them the Law and the opportunity to be a kingdom of priests. After all these blessings, the children of Israel responded that they wanted to enter this covenant. They did not receive the Law until after God's grace and salvation were poured upon them. Then they responded to His grace with obedience.

Exodus 24 describes the ceremony by which they entered God's covenant. Moses read the "book of the covenant" (Exod 24:7) to the people which they agreed to obey. Then Moses took the "blood of the covenant" and sprinkled it on the people (Exod 24:8).

Jesus reaches back to the Passover and this covenant celebration and offers a new interpretation. The "blood of our covenant" was spilled on the cross and our bread is the body of the Messiah. In the kingdom of God, we drink this cup anew with Jesus. Every time we enjoy this meal as a community of believers, we remember God's saving grace through Jesus. We reaffirm our covenant loyalty and rejoice in God's love, grace, and salvation. We look back on Jesus's life, death, and resurrection, and anxiously await our reunion with Him. We give thanks. Currently we acknowledge His presence with us at the table, while at the same time noticing His absence. We long for the ultimate day when we enjoy this meal, reclined at the table, in the very presence of Jesus, in the fully realized kingdom of God.

Reflection Questions

1. How is the Lord's Supper meaningful to you? How does it connect with the book of Exodus? How does it redefine Passover? How is Jesus our Passover (1 Cor 5:7)? Why would Jesus choose Passover for the time of His death?

2. Why would Judas want to betray Jesus? Why did Judas trade the kingdom for money? How is this contrasted from the woman who anointed Jesus?

REFLECTION 49
BETRAYED, ARRESTED, AND TRIED

Mark 14:32–65

Praying or Sleeping

LOOKING BACK TO CHAPTER 13, while discussing the destruction of Jerusalem, Jesus privately discloses signs and warnings to Peter, Andrew, James, and John (Mark 13:3). That lengthy conversation ended with several calls to "Be on the alert!" (Mark 13:34, 35, and 37): "Be on the alert ... in case he should come suddenly and find you asleep" (Mark 13:35–36).

After the meal was over, Jesus walked with His disciples to Gethsemane, and taking Peter, James, and John (sorry Andrew), He told them to "remain here and keep watch" (Mark 14:34). The word translated "Keep watch" or "stay awake" in verse 34 (also 37 and 38), is the same word translated "be on the alert" in Mark 13:34, 35, and 37. The disciples are challenged to stay awake, keep watching, and praying (Mark 14:38), but they cannot even do it for one hour (Mark 14:37). Like so many of us, their spirit is willing, but the flesh is weak (see Romans 7:14–25).

Jesus wants them praying "that you may not come into temptation" (Mark 14:38). Temptation was coming for each of the disciples and Jesus knew prayer was their greatest tool in preparation. He wanted them talking to God and staying alert for the night ahead of them. Instead, they slept. It's no wonder they fail when temptation arrives.

Instead of watching and praying, the disciples repeatedly sleep while Jesus prays. Then the hour finally arrives where, "the Son of Man is being betrayed into the hands of sinners" (Mark 14:41). The words of Jesus in Mark 8:31, 9:31, and 10:33–34 are now coming to pass.

An extremely important discussion point emerges from this scene in Gethsemane during Jesus's prayer. Jesus keeps praying, "Abba! Father! All things are possible for You; remove this cup from Me; yet not what I will, but what You will" (Mark 14:36). The wording in this prayer is slightly different than how Matthew and Luke record it (Matt 26:39; Luke 22:42). Matthew writes, "if it is possible, let this cup pass from Me" and Luke records, "if You are willing, remove this cup from Me."

Mark, however, does not question whether or not God "can" remove this cup. Jesus explicitly says, "All things are possible for You." This is the third time πάντα δυνατὰ, "all things are possible" is used in Mark (Mark 9:23; 10:27; 14:36). This seems to imply that in Jesus's mind, it was possible for God to find a way other than the cross, and Jesus is pleading for it. Jesus is saying, "You can do this. You can do anything, so find another way." Yet at the same time, Jesus is submitting His will to the will of the Father.

There are times in our own prayer lives when we will beg and plead with an omnipotent God to act on our behalf, to forge a new way forward, or to remove some devastation in our lives. And we know He can do it. In the blink of an eye, He could chart a new path for us. In an instant He could heal, save, rescue, and redeem. Often, He does not, and it's one of the biggest stumbling blocks we face. If you have ever struggled with "unanswered prayers," remember Jesus in Gethsemane.

He is "very distressed and troubled" and "deeply grieved to the point of death" (Mark 14:33–34), and He is repeatedly pleading with God in prayer for something He knows God can do, but God does not do it.

I'll never be able to answer why God responds positively to some prayers while others feel ignored. I'll never fully grasp the will of God. What I believe is that, even as God did not remove the cup from Jesus, He still heard, cared, and had compassion. Jesus still considered God to be worthy of obedience and faithfulness. Jesus's prayer was not an ultimatum: "either give me what I ask for or I'll never trust you again." Instead, it was a prayer of immeasurable trust: "give me what I ask for, but either way, I'll trust and follow." Jesus in all things understands our struggles and provides a pattern for how to face them.

Betrayed and Abandoned

This is not the disciples' finest hour. The disciples have repeatedly been confused, blind, deaf, and hard-hearted (Mark 6:52; 8:17–21; 8:32; 9:10, 32, etc.), but this scene is the culmination of their failures. They sleep during Jesus's anguish, Judas betrays Him with a kiss, one resorts to violence, and everyone else abandons the Son of God. What a tragic and disgusting display of irony that Judas betrays Jesus with a kiss, a supposed act of loyalty, love, and friendship. This fraud and betrayal must have hurt Jesus immensely.

This tragic series of events concludes with an odd account of a young naked man fleeing from the authorities (Mark 14:51–52). We know little about this man or why he was following Jesus wearing only a linen sheet. This is one of the rare stories that is only in Mark. Perhaps he had been sleeping in the house when Jesus went to Gethsemane and he woke up, hurriedly covered himself with a sheet and followed to see what was happening. Some speculate this is John Mark, the author of this Gospel. After all, it seems Mark lived in the area (Acts 12:12) and this story was not witnessed by anyone other than those involved. Whoever this naked man was, he must have told this story to others. Perhaps Mark makes a cameo appearance to briefly tell his own story of abandoning Jesus on that fateful night.

Mark 14:43–52 records four shameful displays: Judas betrays Jesus, a disciple responds with violence, everyone abandons Jesus in fear, and one man ends up naked and alone, hiding in a dark garden. N. T. Wright points out a connection between that final scene in the Garden of Gethsemane with the final scene in the Garden of Eden: "Like Adam and Eve, the disciples are metaphorically, and in this case literally, hiding their naked shame in the garden. Their disgrace is complete."[1]

A Sham of a Trial

The chief priests (Mark 8:31; 10:33; 11:18, 27; 14:1, 10, 43, 53, 55; 15:1, 3, 10, 11, 31) were now together with the whole Council (Sanhedrin) to obtain testimony against Jesus. Like Mark 2:1–3:6, try as they might, they cannot obtain any credible accusations against Him. Many even give false testimony. They take His prophetic announcement against the temple and turn it into a violent threat against the temple. They misquote Jesus as saying, "I will destroy this temple made with hands, and in three days I will build another made without hands" (Mark 14:58).

This accusation is fascinating because Mark has recorded nothing like it so far. On the cross, people mock Jesus for saying this (Mark 15:29–30). While He did predict the destruction of the temple, He did not say, "I will destroy this temple." In John (not Mark), Jesus predicts He will raise up the temple in three days (John 2:19-21), and He is speaking of a temple made without hands, "the temple of His body." They take parts of what Jesus said and twist them into something more nefarious, but these false witnesses are not honest or consistent in their accusations (Mark 15:56, 59).

When the high priest addresses Jesus directly, He made no answer (Mark 15:60). Jesus chooses silence. Mark 15:61–62 is the key point in this trial where Jesus commits "blasphemy." Jesus subtly alludes to four key passages from the Old Testament that are fulfilled in His identity.

- By keeping silent and not answering the high priest, Jesus is acting out the descriptions of Isaiah 53:7, "He did not open His mouth; Like a lamb that is led to the slaughter, And like a sheep that is silent before its shearers, So He did not open His mouth." Jesus is the Suffering Servant who gives His life a ransom for many (see Mark 10:45).

- When the high priest asks Jesus if He is "the Christ, the Son of the Blessed?" Jesus gives the most direct statement about His identity in the entire Gospel of Mark. Jesus says, "I Am." This blunt answer echoes back to Exodus 3:14 where God reveals Himself to Moses as the "I Am." As God led an Exodus in the days of Moses, so Jesus is leading a new Exodus.

- Jesus says, "you will see the Son of Man sitting at the right hand of Power, and coming with the clouds of heaven" (Mark 14:62). The phrase "sitting at the right hand" describes what the "LORD says to my Lord" in Psalm 110:1: "Sit at my right hand until I make Your enemies a footstool for Your feet." Jesus already quoted this as a Messianic passage in Mark 12:36 and now alludes to it again about Himself. Jesus shares the throne room with God and exercises the authority of God. He is even David's Lord.

- The phrase, "The Son of Man ... coming with the clouds of heaven" is directly taken from Daniel 7:13–14. This is the passage Jesus referenced in Mark 13:26 and lies behind all of his "Son of Man" teachings. Jesus is the Son of Man who comes with the clouds of heaven and receives "dominion, glory and a kingdom, that all peoples, nations, and men of every language might serve Him. His dominion is an everlasting dominion which will not pass away; And His kingdom is one which will not be destroyed" (Dan 7:14).

This is what Jesus's answer looks like in Greek:

-ἐγώ εἰμι, καὶ ὄψεσθε τὸν υἱὸν τοῦ **ἀνθρώπου ἐκ δεξιῶν καθήμενον** τῆς **δυνάμεως** καὶ **ἐρχόμενον μετὰ τῶν νεφελῶν τοῦ οὐρανοῦ.**

All of the words in bold come directly from these three Old Testament passages: Exodus 3:14; Psalm 110:1; Daniel 7:14. Nearly every word in His answer has an Old Testament referent.

The climactic answer to this question summarizes almost everything said about Jesus's identity in Mark's Gospel. He is the Christ (Mark 8:29). He is the Son of God/Son of the Blessed (Mark 1:1, 11). He is the Lord, the "I Am" (Mark 1:3; 6:50). He is the "Son of Man" (Mark 8:31; 9:31; 10:33–34). He sits "at the right hand of power."

When the high priest hears this answer, there is no need for any more testimony. The trial is over. Jesus is accused of blasphemy (see Mark 2:7). His answer is beyond what any mere mortal can say. They condemn Him to death, spit on Him, blindfold Him, beat Him, mock Him, and slap Him in the face.

Reflection Questions

1. Could God have removed this cup from Jesus? Could there have been any other way? Why is it significant that Jesus prayed while the disciples slept?
2. Why was Jesus accused of blasphemy? How is this passage similar to Mark 2:5–12? Why did they bring forth false witnesses? Why was this trial held at night?

Endnotes

1. N. T. Wright, *Mark for Everyone* (Louisville: John Knox Press, 2004), 200.

REFLECTION 50

DENIED AND SENTENCED

Mark 14:66–15:15

Denied by Peter

AS THE TRIAL before the Sanhedrin concludes, a disheartened Peter warms himself by a fire in the courtyard. A servant-girl of the high priest recognizes him and says, "You also were with Jesus the Nazarene" (Mark 14:67). Peter denies knowing Jesus. Then he denies Him again (Mark 14:70). Then he curses and swears and denies Him a third time (Mark 14:71). Then a rooster crows.

Earlier that very night Peter was so certain that He would never deny or abandon Jesus (Mark 14:27–31). Peter argued with Jesus on this exact point. Jesus predicted Peter would deny Him three times before the rooster crowed twice, yet Peter insisted, "Even if I have to die with You, I will not deny You!" (Mark 14:31).

There appears to be another sandwich structure in this account. The beginning of the sandwich is Mark 14:54 when Peter enters the courtyard of the high priest and sits by the fire.

The end is when Peter denies and the rooster crows (Mark 14:66–72). Reading the passage from Mark 14:54 and skipping ahead to verses 66–72 makes one complete story.

Sandwiched in between Peter's denial is Jesus's trial before the high priest and the Sanhedrin court. During this trial Jesus is explicitly asked about His identity and, for the first time, He declares openly exactly who He is (Mark 14:61-62). These two linked stories intentionally contrast each other in insightful but tragic ways. Jesus openly and clearly confesses His identity while Peter in fear and confusion denies. Jesus is condemned to death for speaking truth while Peter walks away freely because of his lies. Early Christians and readers of Mark will be faced with these same choices. Either confess Jesus and face the consequences or deny Him and walk away.

During Jesus's arrest and trial, when Peter's world began to crumble, so did his loyalty and allegiance. Jesus was Peter's Messiah so long as He was the Messiah Peter wanted. As soon as Jesus left Peter's preferred path, Peter stopped following. Jesus's world is also crumbling around Him, but He continues to faithfully walk the Father's path set before Him. Perhaps this is why Jesus told Peter to "keep watching and praying that you may not come into temptation" (Mark 14:37).

Facing Pilate

When the Sanhedrin court, with the chief priests, scribes, and elders, found Jesus guilty, they led Him away to Pilate early the next morning. By the way, the four stages of the night mentioned in Mark 13:35 have been seen through the night of Jesus's arrest, including specifically the rooster crowing (Mark 14:72) and the morning coming (Mark 15:1). The disciples did not stay alert through the night.

Pilate has some simple questions for Jesus. As a Roman official, he needs to know if there is an insurrection being planned and if there is a self-proclaimed "new king" in town. When Pilate asks, "Are You the King of the Jews?" Jesus gives an ambiguous and confusing answer: σὺ λέγεις. This is translated in different ways in different Bibles. Some read, "It is as you say," or "Yes, it is as you say," or "You have said so." Literally, σὺ λέγεις would mean "you say" or "you yourself say." Pilate could take that as either a "Yes" or a "No." And that's kind of the point.

Some Bibles take that to mean, "Yes, just what you said." Some read more like, "Well, that's what YOU say." Notice how less clear this answer is than Mark 14:62. The lack of clarity in Jesus's answer may stem from the lack of clarity in the question. Yes, in a sense Jesus is the King of the Jews, but probably not the sense Pilate is asking, or the chief priests are hearing (see John 18:33–38). The chief priests take it as a reason to accuse Him harshly (Mark 15:3). Pilate hears it as a complete nonanswer. He says to Jesus, "Do You not answer? See how many charges they bring against You!" Jesus goes back into the silent lamb mode of Isaiah 53:7 and does not give any more answers (Mark 15:5). Pilate is astonished.

Barabbas

A custom of the feast of Passover is introduced in Mark 15:6, in which Pilate would pardon and release an agreed upon prisoner. One man who was considered for pardon was named Barabbas. He was arrested with a group of "insurrectionists who had committed murder in the insurrection" (Mark 15:7).

Several important ideas converge in this scene. Barabbas' name literally means "son of the father" in Aramaic. The word "Bar" means "son" and "Abba" is means "father" (see Mark 14:36). In this scene Jesus, the Son of the Father, is placed next to Barabbas, a son of the father. One of them will be freed and the other will be killed. They both are on trial for similar crimes. Jesus has proclaimed a new kingdom. Barabbas was part of an insurrection to overthrow the kingdom. Jesus overthrows kingdoms through justice, mercy, and love. Barabbas overthrows kingdoms through violence and murder.

The question the crowds faced that day is the same question we face today. Are you willing to choose God's difficult way, through Jesus, of self-sacrificial love? Or will you put more trust in the world's strategy of violence, force, and death? Jesus calls us to a different kind of kingdom and influence (Mark 10:42–43). Barabbas represented the type of revolution many wanted; Jesus represented everything they despised.

Pilate understands envy and impure motives are what brought Jesus before him that day (Mark 15:10). He suspects that a legitimate criminal, like Barabbas, will be an obvious choice for crucifixion. Instead, the crowds are whipped into a frenzy against Jesus (Mark 15:11), and they ask for Barabbas. Jesus stands abandoned, denied, betrayed, and forsaken as the masses shout with one thunderous voice: "Crucify Him! Crucify Him!"

Sentencing

Pilate calls out to the crowds, "Why, what evil has He done?" (Mark 15:14). Instead of giving an answer, the crowds cry out all the more, "Crucify Him!" Pilate must control the people, keep peace in the land, and protect his own neck. If you don't really care about justice and you only want to shut the crowd up and send everyone home, you throw them a bone occasionally. That bone is Jesus. Pilate released Barabbas, had Jesus beaten and scourged, and then delivered to be crucified.

The Roman soldiers, leading Jesus from the Praetorium,

begin mocking Him. This is where the coronation ceremony begins. They dress Him in a royal purple robe, place a crown upon His head, and hail, "King of the Jews!" (Mark 15:16–18). The robe is soaked in blood, the crown of thorns pierces His head, and with laughter and jeering they hail Him. I wonder who it was who placed that crown on Jesus's head? He had no idea that He just crowned the true King of the ages. Irony drips from the page as Jesus, in a scene of mockery and blasphemy, is finally given His robes, crown, and even the Gentiles, Roman soldiers, fall before Him as King.

Instead of giving Him reverence, they beat His head with a stick, spit on Him, and mock Him. When they finish having their fun, they strip Him and lead Him away to an agonizing death. As Jesus continues to live out the destiny of the Suffering Servant who gives His life a ransom for many (Mark 10:45), keep these words in mind:

> He was despised and rejected by men, a man of sorrows and acquainted with grief; and as one from whom men hide their faces he was despised, and we esteemed him not. Surely he has borne our griefs and carried our sorrows; yet we esteemed him stricken, smitten by God, and afflicted. But he was pierced for our transgressions; he was crushed for our iniquities; upon him was the chastisement that brought us peace, and with his wounds we are healed. All we like sheep have gone astray; we have turned—every one—to his own way; and the LORD has laid on him the iniquity of us all (Isa 53:3–6).

Reflection Questions

1. Why did Peter deny Jesus? How did fear and

confusion work against Peter's faith? Was Peter really willing to die for Jesus (Mark 14:31)?

2. Why did Pilate condemn Jesus to death? How did fear and confusion work against Pilate's integrity? Compare and contrast Jesus and Barabbas. Why did the crowd turn against Jesus?

REFLECTION 51
CRUCIFIED

Mark 15:21–39

Simon of Cyrene

AS JESUS IS LED AWAY for His crucifixion, the Romans force a passer-by named Simon to carry the cross. Simon was from Cyrene, a Greek city in northern Africa with a large Jewish population. He was in Jerusalem, possibly for Passover, and was entering the city from the countryside when the cross was placed upon his shoulders to bear.

Mark adds an interesting parenthetical description of Simon of Cyrene, noting that he was "the father of Alexander and Rufus" (Mark 15:21). Mark doesn't usually mention the children of the characters who pop up in his story. In fact, especially in the Passion Narrative, Mark often doesn't even name the character. Think of all the anonymous characters recently introduced in Mark: the woman who anointed Jesus (Mark 14:3–9), the disciple(s) who complained that the oil could have been given to the poor, the two disciples Jesus sent to prepare the upper room for Passover and the man who provided the room (Mark 14:13–15), the man who pulled a sword and struck the high priest's servant's ear and that servant (Mark 14:47), the young man who followed Jesus in a linen sheet and ran away naked (Mark 14:51–52), etc.

Interestingly, several of these characters, while anonymous in Mark, are identified in John's Gospel: Mary (John 12:3), Judas (John 12:4–6), Peter, and Malchus (John 18:10). One theory for this is that Mark's Gospel was written earlier than John's (and possibly using an even earlier source) and there could have been legal consequences for supporting Jesus (and there certainly were for striking a man with a sword). Mark, therefore, protected the identities of the people in his story. By the time John's Gospel was written, most of these characters would already have died, so there was no longer any need to protect them.[1]

Simon of Cyrene is not only named, but Mark gives his city and the names of his two children: Rufus and Alexander. This has, I think correctly, led many to believe that Simon's life was changed that day. Simon likely became a follower of Jesus, and the reason Mark names his two sons is because they were known to Mark's audience. Mark would only mention them by name if those names meant something, otherwise it's a useless description. They must have been known.

Side Note: Most scholars believe the Gospel of Mark was written to the church in Rome. There are several good reasons for this that we won't explore now. If Rufus was known to Mark's audience, and that audience was in Rome, that means Rufus was known to the church in Rome. Romans 16:13 says, "Greet Rufus, a choice man in the Lord, also his mother and mine." Paul mentions a "Rufus" as a well-known Christian in Rome whose mother was like a second mother to Paul. Usually, these types of unprovable connections between names in the Bible feel like a stretch, but this one makes a lot of sense. The time, name, and location all check out. Paul may have known

Simon of Cyrene's sons (whom Mark mentions) and viewed Simon's wife as a mother figure.

Whether that connection works out or not, the account of Simon bearing Jesus's cross provides two helpful reflection points. First, it grounds the gospel story in the history of real people. Simon had two sons and they were real, known people. This did not happen long ago in a galaxy far, far away, but to Rufus and Alexander's dad. Simon probably told people this story throughout his life. It can be connected back to eyewitness testimony.

Secondly, and more importantly for Mark, Simon provides an example cross bearing we are all called to engage. Jesus challenges His disciples to "take up his cross and follow Me" (Mark 8:34). Simon, a foreigner from Africa, will literally carry the cross of Christ. This is a beautiful image of discipleship and is significant for glimpsing the worldwide mission of Jesus.

On the Cross

Arriving at Golgotha (Place of the Skull), Jesus is offered wine mixed with myrrh (possibly as a sedative) which He refuses. Then they crucify Him. They nail His hands to a wooden crossbeam, which was carried by Simon, and His feet to an upright beam. The crossbeam is attached to the upright post and Jesus is raised to hang until exhaustion, asphyxiation, and death take over. They divide up His garments by casting lots (Ps 22:18) and this took place about the third hour of the day (about 9:00 AM).

After an exhausting and agonizing night, Jesus is crucified. Crucifixion is among the most painful, dehumanizing, and disgraceful deaths ever conceived by humans. In fact, Roman citizens were not allowed to be crucified. It was far too disgraceful. On the Roman repulsion to public crucifixion, historian Tom Holland writes,

Exposed to public view like slabs of meat hung from a market stall, troublesome slaves were nailed to crosses ... Naturally, if it were to serve as a deterrent it needed to be public. Nothing spoke more eloquently of a failed revolt than the sight of hundreds upon hundreds of corpse-hung crosses, whether lining a highway or else massed before a rebellious city ... So foul was the carrion-reek of their disgrace that many felt tainted even by viewing a crucifixion.[2]

Among the fools publicly hailed as a failure was the miserable wretch Christians call the Son of God. This is a paradox the world can hardly stomach. Paul calls it a stumbling block to Jews and complete foolishness to Gentiles, "but to those who are called, both Jews and Greeks, Christ the power of God and the wisdom of God" (1 Cor 1:22–23). To worship a crucified man was a great scandal and the most senseless and ridiculous practice of Christianity. Yet it is central to Christianity. It is how the world is turned upside down in God's kingdom.

As if the cross isn't enough, the mockery continues. An inscription is placed above Jesus's head which read, "The King of the Jews" (Mark 15:26). This is the charge for which He is being crucified. Jesus was not crucified because He said, "Love your neighbor," "Regularly find a quiet place to pray," or "Go to church on Sunday." Jesus was crucified because He was the King of the Jews.

The Roman soldiers mocked Him. The plaque above His head mocked Him. The criminals to His right and left mocked Him. Those passing by mocked Him. The chief priests and scribes mocked Him, "He saved others; He cannot save Himself. Let this Christ, the King of Israel, now come down from the cross so that we may see and believe!" (Mark 15:31–32). Jesus has become a laughingstock to all who see Him (Ps 69:9–12).

From noon until 3:00 PM, darkness fell over the whole land. This darkness symbolizes the spiritual condition of the world in these moments. Spiritual forces of darkness and the powers that lead to corruption, violence, depravity, and sin have reached their climax. They rejoice in the ecstasy of victory as the Light of the world is snuffed out. This is the darkest moment in human history and creation cannot help but show it (see Mark 13:24). It's like the world is uncreating itself (Gen 1:2–3).

In these final moments, Jesus utters His only words recorded by Mark on the cross. In fact, Jesus speaks only to the high priest (Mark 14:62) and two quick words (σὺ λέγεις) to Pilate (Mark 15:2) in Mark's entire Passion Narrative until this moment. Jesus has been abandoned by His disciples, denied by Peter, betrayed by Judas, rejected by His countrymen, condemned by the Romans, hated by the crowds, mocked by the soldiers, ridiculed by those who saw Him dying, jeered by the priests, and belittled by the other crucified criminals, and looking up to the heavens, He cries out in anguish to the One who has always been there: "My God, My God, Why have Your forsaken Me?" (Mark 15:34).

This final cry, taken from Psalm 22:1, pictures complete and total abandonment in this dark, apocalyptic moment. Jesus feels the sting of sin and death. Jesus's final words are misunderstood, like so much of what He said and did, and people think He is calling for "Elijah." Someone offers Him sour wine (Ps 69:21–23) as He lowers His head, slumps over, and with a final gurgled cry, breaths His last.

The Centurion's Declaration

The temple, which was at the center of the controversy leading to Jesus's crucifixion, feels the pang of death as the veil is torn in two from top to bottom. The word "torn" directly echoes back to what occurred in the heavens at the baptism of Jesus (Mark 1:10). In that scene a voice from the heavens proclaimed that Jesus is the beloved Son of God. Here on the cross, it is a centurion who declares, "Truly this man was the Son of God" (Mark 15:39).

This is the first time a human character has called Jesus the Son of God, and, of all people, it is a Roman centurion. Like Simon of Cyrene who carried the cross, this moment points forward to the Sonship of Jesus over the whole world, both Jew and Gentile. The death of Jesus was so cataclysmic that the sun stopped shining, the temple's veil was torn in two, and a Roman military man saw the divine glory of a crucified Jew. The Son of God is not Caesar; He is the cruciform Christ.

Reflection Questions

1. Why did Simon of Cyrene carry Jesus's cross? Why were his sons mentioned? How is he a picture of our call to discipleship?
2. What does the death of Jesus mean to you? Why was the world in darkness? Was Jesus truly abandoned by God in His darkest hour? How did the death of Jesus show the centurion that He was the Son of God?

Endnotes

1. Richard Bauckham has a fabulous chapter on a lot of these details in his book, *Jesus and the Eyewitnesses: The Gospels as Eyewitness Testimony* (Grand Rapids: Eerdmans, 2017).

2. Tom Holland, *Dominion: How the Christian Revolution Remade the World* (New York: Basic Books, 2019), 2.

REFLECTION 52
A WHOLE NEW WORLD

Mark 15:40–16:20

The Women and Joseph

AT THE DEATH OF JESUS, Mark introduces us to several new characters: Mary Magdalene, Mary the mother of James and Joses, and Salmone (Mark 15:40). These women, who had been followers and ministers to Jesus, were among a large number of women who came with Jesus to Jerusalem. While the twelve disciples abandoned Jesus, these women watched His crucifixion from a distance. These women are the only hint in Mark's Gospel that Jesus wasn't entirely abandoned on the cross.

The paragraph in Mark 15:40–41 introduces the final "sandwich" in the Gospel of Mark. These women appear again at the end of the sandwich on the first day of the week when they arrive at Jesus' tomb to anoint His body (Mark 16:1). They loved and remained devoted to Jesus during the crucifixion and burial and are the first to see the empty tomb following His resurrection.

In the middle of this sandwich is the story of Joseph of

Arimathea laying the body of Jesus in his tomb. Joseph is from "Arimathea," a Jewish city (Luke 23:51) and a prominent member of the Sanhedrin Council. This is the Council Jesus was condemned by in Mark 14:55, 64. Reading this is a little confusing. Mark says the Council "all" condemned Jesus to death (Mark 14:64), but for some reason a prominent member, who is waiting for the kingdom of God, wants to honor Jesus's body.

This is another example of Mark's ambiguity. He does not answer all our questions. Luke clarifies it by calling Joseph, "a good and righteous man (he had not consented to their plan and action), a man from Arimathea ..." (Luke 23:50–51). Matthew writes that Joseph "had himself also become a disciple" (Matthew 27:57). And John calls him, "a disciple of Jesus, but a secret one for fear of the Jews" (John 19:38). He arrives on the scene in surprising fashion in each of these stories.

All the Gospel writers mention that Joseph of Arimathea requested, honored, and buried the body of Jesus. They all mention that he was part of the Sanhedrin Council and was either a disciple or was waiting for God's kingdom. This is another one of those details that gives historical authenticity to the story of Jesus. The only reason the text would say a prominent member of the Council, which had just condemned Jesus, came to honor and bury His body is if it were true. There would be no reason to make this up and the writers need to give some explanation of how this happened, either he was a secret disciple (John), or he did not consent to the condemnation (Luke). It is a shocking development that a member of the Sanhedrin is a good, righteous, kingdom loving, follower of Jesus.

Joseph is sandwiched between the story of these women. In some ways, he is easily contrasted from them. He is a prominent male figure in Jewish society, while these women are not. He gathers courage to ask Pilate for the body of Jesus (Mark

15:43), while the women at the empty tomb experience trembling, astonishment, and fear (Mark 16:8). Joseph "rolled the stone against the entrance of the tomb" (Mark 15:46), while the women wondered, "who will roll away the stone for us from the entrance of the tomb?" (Mark 16:3).

What Joseph and these women share, however, is their devotion to Jesus. While Mark portrayed the death of Jesus as lonely and forsaken, in the distance there were still people who cared. The women stood at a distance, probably because of fear, but they did not betray, deny, or entirely abandon Him. Joseph seems to have been distant in his discipleship, but the death of Jesus drew him nearer. He asked for the body of Jesus knowing his peers on the Sanhedrin would not approve. He asked Pilate, who just condemned Jesus to death as an enemy of the empire, for the body. This was a socially and politically dangerous move that took tremendous courage.

The Resurrection

When Pilate was asked for the body, he checked with the centurion to see if Jesus had already died. After confirmation was made, Pilate, somewhat surprisingly, granted Joseph the body. Jesus's lifeless corpse was pulled from the cross, wrapped in a linen cloth, and laid in a tomb cut out of a rock. This was the day before the Sabbath (Mark 15:42).

The day after Sabbath, the first day of the week (Mark 16:1), the women appear again, with spices, to anoint the body of Jesus. It was very early in the morning, and they hoped someone might be there to help open the tomb, but there was no need. The tomb had already been opened.

Notice the contrast of the cross and the empty tomb. At the cross the sun was darkened, but at the empty tomb, "the sun had risen" (Mark 16:3). It's like God looked at the darkness of the world and said, "Let there be light." This is a day of new creation. The world is being remade anew through Jesus with new hope and new life. The powers of darkness are losing their stranglehold as the power of death is stripped away.

In amazement, these women looked inside the tomb to see a "young man" wearing a "white robe." In Mark's Gospel, this mysterious nameless young man is alone. He's not called an angel; He is called a "young man" in white clothes. Some scholars believe that the word "young man" is used, instead of angel, to recall the only other time Mark uses that word "young man." It is that mysterious nameless young man in the garden who was following Jesus, had his linen sheet stripped from him, and ran away naked. This isn't to say it is the same individual but comparing the stories can be illuminating.

Leading up to the crucifixion, a young man is in linen, but leaves naked in fear and confusion. The word translated "linen cloth" or "linen sheet" in Mark 14:51–52, by the way, is used elsewhere in the entire New Testament only to describe the burial clothes of Jesus. It's the same word used in Mark 15:46. Comparing Mark 14:51–52 to Mark 15:46, we see that one young man started in a linen cloth but ended up naked, while Jesus started naked but ended in a linen cloth. Then after the resurrection, a mysterious young man appears again, not naked, or in a linen cloth, but in a white robe (the same word used for Jesus's clothing during the transfiguration—Mark 9:2–3).

It is difficult to be certain exactly what Mark is doing here, but there is probably a reason he is using these words and spending so much time describing clothing. Mark talks a lot about clothing and it usually significantly impacts the story or the character (Mark 1:6; 5:28; 9:2–3; 14:51–52; 15:17, 24, 46; 16:5). Perhaps this clothing signifies the transformation from death to life. The linen sheets and naked bodies described during the arrest (Mark 14:51–52), crucifixion (Mark 15:24), and burial (Mark 15:46) represent shame and death, but after the resurrection (and during the transfiguration), the "white" clothes represent glory and life.

This young man in white clothes is the first to declare the resurrection in Mark's Gospel: "you are looking for Jesus the Nazarene, who has been crucified. He has risen; He is not here" (Mark 16:6). Those words dramatically demonstrate the power of the kingdom over the forces of darkness, sin, and death. The disgrace and decay of death is turned into the glory of new life in Christ. In a world of resurrection, there is always hope.

The young man orders the women to go and tell the disciples and Peter that Jesus is raised and is in Galilee and they should see Him there. Instead of hope and joy and faith, it says the women respond with fear and trembling and silence. Mark writes, "they said nothing to anyone, for they were afraid" (Mark 16:8). Fear is the most common response to Jesus in Mark's gospel.

That unsatisfying conclusion is where our earliest copies of the Gospel of Mark end. Mark ends with fear, silence, ambiguity, and more questions. Did the women eventually tell anyone? Did they overcome their fear? By the time Mark was written, the message of Jesus has clearly spread, and the readers believe in the resurrection, so how did the news get out?

If we remember that this ending also concludes a sandwich structure, we may see that this abrupt conclusion lays a challenge before the reader: will you take courage like Joseph of Arimathea (Mark 15:43) or respond with fear and silence like the women at the empty tomb (Mark 16:8)? Ending Mark on this cliff hanger may be a challenge to the reader to finish the narrative in your own life. Don't just passively read the message of Jesus, enter the story, and spread the message yourself! Jesus had been telling people to be silent about Him throughout the Gospel of Mark, now is the time to be vocal! The secret is now revealed! Go public.

The kingdom has come. New life is offered in Christ. By the

resurrection of the dead, Jesus has demonstrated that He is the Son of God with glory. There is a new kingdom, a new hope, and a whole new world. God reigns and you are called to be a part of it! This is the gospel.

The Long Ending

If you don't find that ending satisfying, you are not alone. Many in the early church didn't quite like that ending either. Numerous other endings to Mark were added in early Christian communities. Our English Bibles usually contain at least one or two of the additional endings. Some Bibles contain verse 9-20. Some contain an extra paragraph after verse 20 (which in several manuscripts was placed directly after verse 8). Probably all your Bibles will have a footnote with some additional information about the ending of Mark.

We basically have one of four options for the ending of Mark.

1. Mark intentionally ended abruptly and ambiguously with verse 8. This means Mark concludes with a sandwich and with a final reference to his "fear" and "silence" motifs. It also means that Mark, as he did not include the virgin birth, also did not include any resurrection appearances of Jesus. The reader is challenged to finish the story in faith and tell others about Jesus.
2. Mark continued writing after verse 8, and we lost the original ending, so other endings were written to try to complete the story. The details of those endings were taken by combining details from Matthew, Luke, and John.
3. One of those later endings is original and for some

reasons (intentionally or accidentally) was not included in some early manuscripts.

4. Maybe Mark originally finished at verse 8 and then later decided to write a little more and add some of the resurrection appearances. That way there were two early and original versions of Mark, which are both present in our manuscripts, which were written by Mark.

The language and style of verses 9–20 is a bit different than the rest of Mark. I remember the first time I translated Mark from Greek to English, things immediately slowed down once I got to verse 9. It felt like a switch in language and style and overall "feel" had taken place. You can notice that switch by carefully reading in English too. Not to be overstated, there is still some linguistic and thematic continuity with earlier parts in Mark's Gospel.

There are many similarities in these verses to the other Gospels. If Mark did end at verse 8, nothing significant about our understanding of the resurrection changes or is lost. Mary is reintroduced as the first witness to the resurrection (like John 20:1–18), she reports this to the other disciples who refuse to believe it. Then Jesus appeared to two men (like Luke 24:13–35) who told the other disciples and they still refused to believe it. Then Jesus appeared to the twelve and rebuked them for their hard hearts (see earlier theme in Mark 6:52; 8:17). Jesus sent them out to "all the world" to preach the gospel (see earlier theme in Mark 1:1, 14–15; 13:10; 14:9; 15:39). He says those who believe and are baptized will be saved, but unbelievers will be condemned (like Matthew 28:18–20). Jesus also promised amazing powers and signs would accompany the disciples. Mark 16:19–20 ends with the ascension and the gospel being proclaimed and confirmed (like Luke 24:45–53).

Reflection Questions

1. Why is it significant that women were the first witnesses of the empty tomb? Why is the messenger called a "young man" instead of an angel? Which ending of Mark's Gospel do you think is the best?

2. What does the resurrection of Jesus mean for how you now live? What does it tell you about His ministry? What does it reveal about His identity? How is the resurrection the culmination of the gospel? What does the resurrection mean about the powers of darkness? Why do you love our risen Savior?

BIBLIOGRAPHY

Bates, Matthew W. *Gospel Allegiance: What Faith in Jesus Misses for Salvation in Christ*. Grand Rapids: Brazos Press, 2019.

―――. *Salvation by Allegiance Alone: Rethinking Faith, Works, and the Gospel of Jesus the King*. Grand Rapids: Baker Academic, 2017.

Bauckham, Richard. *Jesus and the Eyewitnesses: The Gospels as Eyewitness Testimony*. Grand Rapids: Eerdmans, 2017.

Bonhoeffer, Dietrich. *The Cost of Discipleship*. United Kingdom: Touchstone, 1995.

Carson, D.A. and Douglass J. Moo. *An Introduction to the New Testament*. Grand Rapids: Zondervan, 2005.

Edwards, James R. "Markan Sandwiches: the significance of interpolation in Markan narratives." *Novum Testamentum* 31 (1989): 193–216.

Evans, Craig. "Mark's Incipit and the Priene Calendar Inscription: from Jewish Gospel to Greco-Roman Gospel" *Journal of Greco-Roman Christianity and Judaism* 1 (2000), 67–81.

Evans, Rachel Held. *Inspired: Slaying Giants, Walking on Water, and Loving the Bible Again.* Nashville: Nelson Books, 2018.

Frankl, Viktor E. *Man's Search for Meaning.* Translated by Ilse Lasch. Boston: Beacon Press, 2006.

Hays, Richard B. *Echoes of Scripture in the Gospels.* Waco: Baylor University, 2016.

———. The *Moral Vision of the New Testament: Community, Cross, New Creation.* San Francisco: HarperSanFrancisco, 1996.

———. *Reading Backwards: Figural Christology and the Fourfold Gospel Witness.* Waco: Baylor University Press, 2014.

———. *Reading with the Grain of Scripture.* Grand Rapids: Eerdmans, 2020.

Holland, Tom. *Dominion: How the Christian Revolution Remade the World.* New York: Basic Books, 2019.

Janzen, Gerald J. "Resurrection and Hermeneutics: On Exodus 3:6 in Mark 12:26," *Journal for the Study of the New Testament* 23 (1985); 43–58.

Lane, William L. *The Gospel according to Mark: The English Text with Introduction, Exposition, and Notes.* Grand Rapids: Eerdmans, 1974.

Marcus, Joel. *Mark 8–16: A New Translation with Introduction and Commentary*. Anchor Bible. New Haven: Yale University Press, 2009.

Powell, Mark Allan. *Introducing the New Testament: A Historical, Literary, and Theological Survey*. Grand Rapids: Baker Academic, 2009.

Rhoads, David, Joanna Dewey, and Donald Michie. *Mark as Story: An Introduction to the Narrative of a Gospel*. 2nd ed. Minneapolis: Fortress, 1999.

Schowalter, Daniel N. "Churches in Context: The Jesus Movement in the Roman World." Pages 517–559 in *The Oxford History of the Biblical World*. Edited by Michael D. Coogan. Oxford: Oxford University Press, 1998.

Walton, John H. *Ancient Near Eastern Thought and the Old Testament: Introducing the Conceptual World of the Hebrew Bible*. Grand Rapids: Baker Academic, 2006.

Witherington, Ben, III. *What Have They Done with Jesus? Beyond Strange Theories and Bad History—Why We Can Trust the Bible*. San Francisco: HarperSanFrancisco, 2006.

Wright, N.T. *Mark for Everyone*. Louisville: John Knox Press, 2004.

———. *Simply Jesus: A New Vision of Who He Was, What He Did, and Why He Matters*. New York: HarperCollins, 2011.

Scripture Index

CREDITS

Select Scripture quotations are taken from the NEW AMERICAN STANDARD BIBLE®, copyright© 1960, 1962, 1963, 1968, 1971, 1972, 1973, 1975, 1977, 1995 by The Lockman Foundation. Used by permission.

Select Scripture quotations are taken from the NEW KING JAMES VERSION®. Copyright© 1982 by Thomas Nelson, Inc. Used by permission. All rights reserved.

Select Scripture quotations are taken from the NEW REVISED STANDARD VERSION BIBLE, copyright © 1989 National Council of the Churches of Christ in the United States of America. Used by permission. All rights reserved worldwide.

Select Scriptures quotations are taken from the Holy Bible, New International Version®, NIV®. Copyright © 1973, 1978, 1984, 2011 by Biblica, Inc.™ Used by permission of Zondervan. All rights reserved worldwide. www.zondervan.com The "NIV" and "New International Version" are trademarks registered in the United States Patent and Trademark Office by Biblica, Inc.®

ALSO BY TRAVIS J. BOOKOUT

King of Glory: 52 Reflections on the Gospel of John

(Cypress Publications 2021)

www.hcu.edu/publications

To see full catalog of Heritage Christian University Press and its imprint Cypress Publications, visit
www.hcu.edu/publications